PLAIN OF OROOMIAH, FROM THE SEMINARY AT SEIR. (See page 34.)

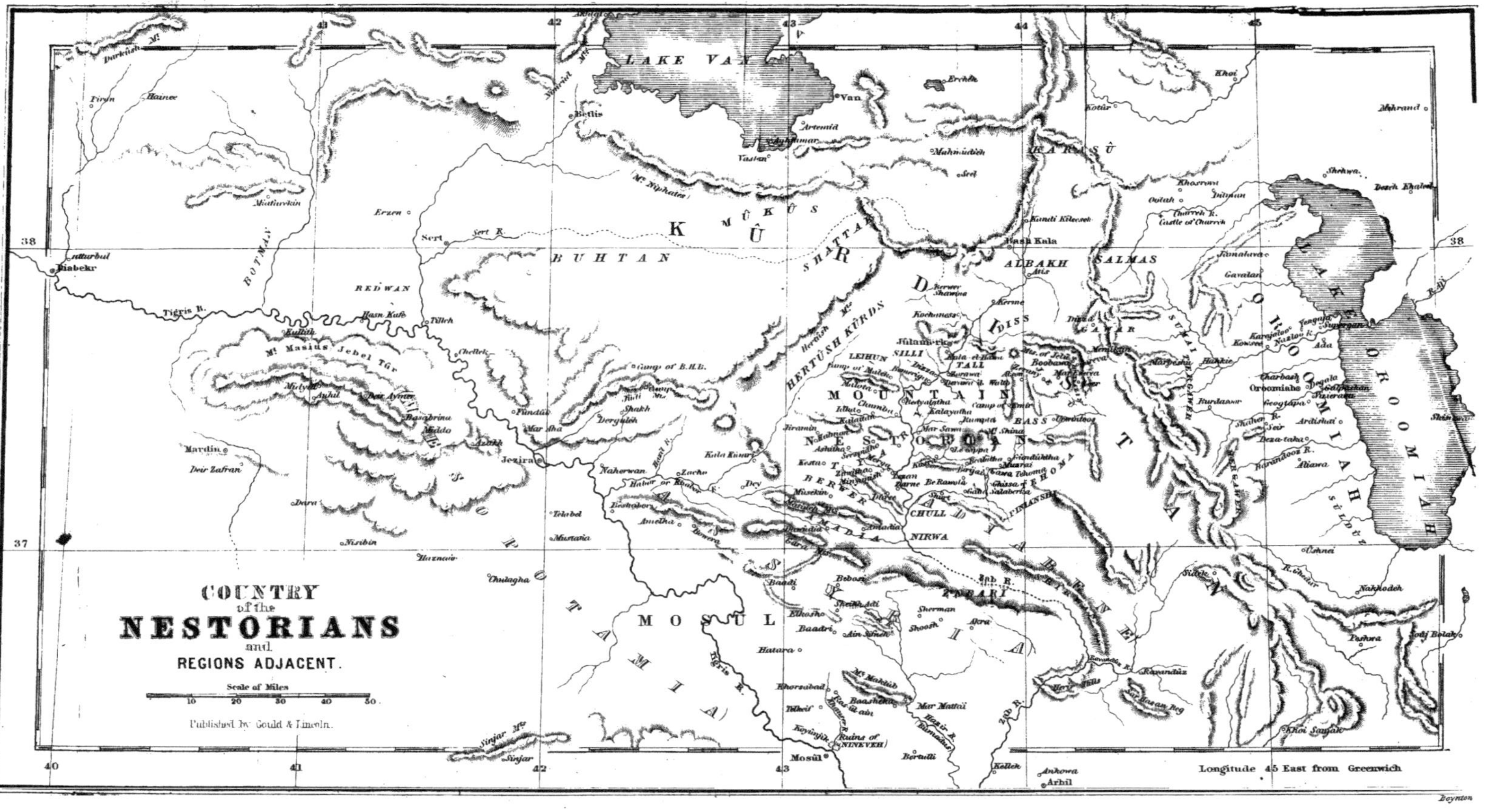
COUNTRY of the NESTORIANS and REGIONS ADJACENT.
Scale of Miles
10 20 30 40 50
Published by Gould & Lincoln.
Longitude 45 East from Greenwich
Boynton
LAKE VAN
LAKE OROOMIAH
OROOMIAH
KURDISTAN
BUHTAN
MESOPOTAMIA
MOSUL
NESTORIANS
MOUNTAIN
HERTÛSH KÛRDS
SALMAS
ALBAKH
REDWAN
Tigris R.
Diabekr
Mardin
Deir Zafran
Nisibin
Jezira
Sert
Erzen
Betlis
Van
Mosûl
Ruins of NINEVEH
Arbil
Oroomiah
Mt. Masius Jebel Tûr

WOMAN AND HER SAVIOUR

IN PERSIA.

BY

A RETURNED MISSIONARY.

WITH

Fine Illustrations, and a Map of Nestorian Country.

BOSTON:
GOULD AND LINCOLN,
59 WASHINGTON STREET.
NEW YORK: SHELDON AND COMPANY.
CINCINNATI: GEO. S. BLANCHARD.
1865.

ELECTROTYPED AT THE
BOSTON STEREOTYPE FOUNDRY.

PREFACE.

Our Saviour bade his disciples gather up the fragments, that nothing be lost; and many who have known of Miss Fiske's fifteen years of labor for woman in Persia, have desired her to prepare for publication the facts now presented to the reader. The writer was one of these; and it was only when he found that she could not do it, that he attempted it, in accordance with her wishes, simply that these interesting records of divine grace might not be lost.

The materials have been drawn from the letters and conversations of those familiar with the scenes described, and especially from Miss Fiske. In all cases, the language of others has been condensed, as much as is consistent with the truthful expression of their ideas; and, in the translation of the letters of Nestorians, it has not been deemed essential to follow slavishly every Syriac idiom, for, instead of these letters owing their interest, as some have supposed, to their translators, they may have sometimes rather suffered from renderings needlessly idiomatic.

It was at one time proposed to embrace the history of both the Male and Female Seminaries, but the proposition came too late, and the memoir of the lamented Stoddard gives so full an account of the former, that now we need to hear only the story of its less known companion; but let the reader bear in mind that as much might have been said of the one as of the other, had the design been to give an account of both.

A strict adherence to the order of events in the following pages would have produced a series of disjointed annals. To avoid such a breaking up of the narrative, each subject has been treated in full whenever introduced, though that has involved a freedom somewhat independent of chronological order.

The notices of the revivals are mere incidental sketches. Their complete history remains to be written.

The beautiful Illustrations introduced are all new, copied from sketches taken on the spot by the skilful pencil of a dear missionary brother, whose modesty, though it will not consent to the mention of his name, yet cannot prevent a grateful sense of his kindness. The Map is an improvement on others previously published, and, besides adding to our geographical knowledge, will be found valuable to the friends of missions.

If the readers of these pages enjoy but a small part of the delight found in their preparation, the writer will not regret his undertaking. May the day be hastened when heaven shall repeat the hosannas of a regenerated world, even as now the abundant grace bestowed upon the Nestorians redounds, through the thanksgiving of many, to the glory of God.

CONTENTS.

CHAPTER I.

WOMAN WITHOUT THE GOSPEL.

CHAPTER II.

MARBEESHOO.

CHAPTER III.

THE SCENE OF THE NARRATIVE.

CHAPTER IV.

MISSIONARY EDUCATION.

CHAPTER V.

BEGINNINGS.

CHAPTER VI.

THE SEMINARY.

CHAPTER VII.

VACATION SCENES.

CHAPTER VIII.

EARLY LABORS FOR WOMEN.

CHAPTER IX.

FRUITS OF LABOR IN NESTORIAN HOMES.

CHAPTER X.

GEOG TAPA.

CHAPTER XI.

REVIVAL IN 1846.

CHAPTER XII.

FIRST FRUITS.

CHAPTER XIII.

SUBSEQUENT REVIVALS.

CHAPTER XIV.

DARK DAYS.

CHAPTER XV.

TRIALS.

CHAPTER XVI.

PRAYERFULNESS.

CHAPTER XVII.

FORERUNNERS.

CHAPTER XVIII.

LABORERS IN THE MOUNTAINS.

CHAPTER XIX.

EBENEZERS.

CHAPTER XX.

COMPOSITIONS.

CHAPTER XXI.

KIND OFFICES.

CHAPTER XXII.

PROGRESS AND PROMISE.

List of Illustrations.

WOMAN AND HER SAVIOUR.

CHAPTER I.

WOMAN WITHOUT THE GOSPEL.

POLITICAL CONDITION. — NESTORIAN HOUSES. — VERMIN. — SICKNESS. — POSITION AND ESTIMATION OF WOMAN. — NO READERS AMONG THEM. — UNLOVELY SPIRIT. — SINS OF THE TONGUE. — PROFANITY. — LYING. — STEALING. — STORY ABOUT PINS. — IMPURITY. — MOSLEM INTERFERENCE WITH SEMINARY.

WE love to wander over a well-kept estate. Its green meadows and fruitful fields delight the eye. Its ripening harvests make us feel as if we too were wealthy. But while the view of what lies before us is so pleasant, our joy is greater if we can remember when it was all a wilderness, and contrast its present beauty with the roughness of its former state.

So, in viewing the wonders of divine grace, we need to see its results in connection with what has been. We can appreciate the loveliness of the child of God only as we compare him with the child of wrath he was before. Paul not only recounts the great things which God had done for the early disciples, but bids them remember that they were once without Christ; and before he tells them that God had made them "sit together in heavenly places in

Christ Jesus," he reminds them that they had "walked according to the spirit that now worketh in the children of disobedience."

In seeking, then, to set forth the great things which God has done for woman in Persia, let us first look on her as his gospel found her, that we may better appreciate the grace which wrought the change.

We can understand the condition of woman in that empire only as we bear in mind that its government is despotic, and that no constitutional safeguards shield the subjects of a thoroughly selfish and profligate nobility. The Nestorians, too, are marked out alike by religion and nationality as victims of oppression. However great their wrongs, they can hope for little redress, for a distant court shares in the plunder taken from them, and believes its own officials rather than the despised rayahs, whom they oppress. Even when foreign intervention procures some edict in their favor, these same officials, in distant Oroomiah, are at no loss to evade its demands.

The Nestorian is not allowed a place in the bazaar;[1] he cannot engage in commerce. And in the mechanic arts, he cannot aspire higher than the position of a mason or carpenter; which, of course, is not to be compared to the standing of the same trades among us. When our missionaries went to Oroomiah, a decent garment on a Nestorian was safe only as it had an outer covering of rags to hide it.

In their language, as in Arabic, the missionaries found no word for *home;* and there was no need of it, for the thing itself was wanting. The house consisted of one large room, and was generally occupied by several gen-

[1] The bazaar is, literally, the market, but denotes the business part of a city.

erations. In that one room all the work of the family was performed. There they ate, and there they slept. The beds consisted of three articles — a thick comfortable filled with wool or cotton beneath, a pillow, and one heavy quilt for covering. On rising, they "took up their beds," and piled them on a wooden frame, and spread them down again at night. The room was lighted by an opening in the roof, which also served for a chimney; though, of course, in a very imperfect manner, as the inside of every dwelling that has stood for any length of time bears witness. The upper part of the walls and the under surface of the roof — we can hardly call it ceiling — fairly glitter, as though they had been painted black and varnished, and every article of clothing, book, or household utensil, is saturated with the smell of creosote. The floor, like the walls, is of earth, covered in part with coarse straw mats and pieces of carpeting; and the flat roof, of the same material, rests on a layer of sticks, supported by large beams; the mass above, however, often sifts through, and sometimes during a heavy rain assumes the form of a shower of mud. Bad as all this may seem, the houses are still worse in the mountain districts, such as Gawar. There they are half under ground, made of cobble stones laid up against the slanting sides of the excavation, and covered by a conical roof with a hole in the centre. They contain, besides the family, all the implements of husbandry, the cattle, and the flocks. These last occupy "the sides of the house" (1 Sam. xxiv. 3), and stand facing the "decana," or raised place in the centre, which is devoted to the family. As wood is scarce in the mountains, and the climate severe, the animal heat of the cattle is a substitute for fuel, except as sun-baked cakes of manure are used once a day for cooking, as is the practice also on the plain. In such houses the buffaloes sometimes break loose and fight furiously, and instances are not rare when they knock down the posts on which the roof rests, and thus bury all in one common ruin.

The influence of such family arrangements, even in the more favored villages of the plain, on manners and morality, need not be told. It is equally evident that in such circumstances personal tidiness is impossible, though few in our favored land have any idea of the extent of such untidiness. If the truth must be told, vermin abound in most of these houses; the inmates are covered not only with fleas, but from head to foot they are infested with the third plague of Egypt. (Ex. viii. 16–19). This last is a constant annoyance in many parts of Turkey as well as Persia. If one lodges in the native houses, there is no refuge from them, and only an entire change of clothing affords relief when he returns to his own home; even there the divans have to be sedulously examined after the departure of visitors, that the plague do not spread. The writer has known daughters of New England, ready for almost any self-denial, burst into tears when first brought into contact with this.

At first, the teachers of the Female Seminary in Oroomiah had to cleanse their pupils very thoroughly, and were glad thus to purify the outside, while beseeching Christ to cleanse the heart. Each one, on her first arrival, had to be separately cared for, lest the enemy should recover ground from which he had already been driven with much labor. Missionary publications do not usually tell of such trials, but those who drew the lambs from the deep pit, loved them all the more tenderly for having gone down into it themselves, that thence they might bring them to Jesus. Such trials are less common now, for it is generally understood that a degree of personal cleanliness is an indispensable requisite for admission to the Seminary; but such a demand, at that time, would have rendered the commencement of the school impossible.

The pupils became much improved in personal appearance, and some of their simple-hearted mothers really thought their children had grown very pretty under their teachers' care. So, as many of them were strangers to the cleansing properties of water, they would ask again and again, "How do you make them so white?"

But if such houses were comfortless abodes for those in health, what were they for the sick? Think of one in a burning fever, perhaps delirious, lying in such a crowd. In winter, there they must remain, for there is no other place, and in summer, they are often laid under a tree in the day time, and carried up to the flat roof, with the rest of the family, at night.

Dr. Perkins, in the early part of his missionary life, tells us that in a village the family room was given up to him for the night, and in the morning he found a little son had been born in the stable. He supposed that he had been the unwitting cause of such an event occurring there; but longer acquaintance with the people shows that woman almost invariably resorts to that place in her hour of sorrow, and there she often dies. The number who meet death in this form is very large.

In Persia, as in other unevangelized countries, women spend their days in out-door labor. They weed the cotton, and assist in pruning the vines and gathering the grapes. They go forth in the morning, bearing not only their implements of husbandry, but also their babes in the cradle; and returning in the evening, they prepare their husband's supper, and set it before him, but never think of eating themselves till after he is done. One of the early objections the Nestorians made to the Female Seminary was, that it would disqualify their daughters for their accustomed toil. In after years, woman might be seen carrying her spelling-book to the field, along with her Persian hoe, little dreaming that she was thus taking the first step towards the substitution of the new implement for the old.

Nestorian parents used to consider the birth of a daughter a great calamity. When asked the number of their children, they would count up their sons, and make no mention of their daughters. The birth of a son was an occasion for great joy and giving of gifts. Neighbors hastened to congratulate the happy father, but days might elapse before the neighborhood knew of the birth of a daughter. It was deemed highly improper to inquire after the health of a wife, and the nearest approach to it was to ask after the welfare of the house or household. Formerly, a man never called his wife by name, but in speaking of her would say, "the mother of so and so," giving the name of her child; or, "the daughter of so and so," giving the name of her father; or, simply "that woman" did this or that. Nor did the wife presume to call her husband's name, or to address him in the presence of his parents, who, it will be borne in mind, lived in the same apartment. They were married very young, often at the age of fourteen, and without any consultation of their own preference, either as to time or person.

There was hardly a man among the Nestorians who did not beat his wife. The women expected to be beaten, and took it as a matter of course. As the wife lived with the husband's father, it was not uncommon for him to beat both son and daughter-in-law. When the men wished to talk together of any thing important, they usually sent the women out of doors or to the stable, as unable to understand, or unfit to be trusted. In some cases, this might be a necessary precaution; for the absence of true affection, and the frequency of domestic broils, rendered the wife an unsafe depositary of any important family affair. The same causes often led the wife to appropriate to her own foolish gratification any money of her husband she could lay hands on, regardless of family necessities. Women whose tastes led them to load themselves with beads, silver, baser metal, and rude trinkets, would not be likely to expend money very judiciously.

In 1835, the only Nestorian woman that knew how to read was Heleneh, the sister of Mar Shimon; and when others were asked if they would not like to learn, with a significant shrug they would reply, "I am a woman." They had themselves no more desire to learn than the men had to have them taught. Indeed, the very idea of a woman reading was regarded as an infringement of female modesty and propriety.

It is a little curious, and shows how we adapt ourselves to our situation, that the women were as unwilling to receive attention from their husbands as they were to render it. Several years after the arrival of Miss Fiske in Oroomiah, the wife of one of her assistants visited the Seminary, and on leaving to return to her village, the teacher, in the kindness of her heart, proposed to the husband to go and assist her to carry the child. She seemed as if she had been insulted in being thought unable to carry it, and sent her husband back from the door in any thing but a gracious mood, leaving the good teacher half bewildered and half amused at this reception of her intended kindness.

Indeed, until some of them were converted, all that was lovely and of good report in woman was entirely wanting.

They were trodden down, but at the same time exceedingly defiant and imperious. If they were not the "head," it was not because they did not "strive for the mastery." They seemed to have no idea of self-control; their bursts of passion were awful. The number of women who reverenced their husbands was as small as the list of husbands who did not beat their wives. Says Miss Fiske, in writing to a friend, "I felt pity for my poor sisters before going among them, but anguish when, from actual contact with them, I realized how very low they were. I did not want to leave them, but I did ask, Can the image of Christ ever be reflected from such hearts? They would come and tell me their troubles, and fall down at my feet, begging me to deliver them from their husbands. They would say, 'You are sent by our holy mother, Mary, to help us;' and do not think me hard-hearted when I tell you that I often said to them, 'Loose your hold of my feet; I did not come to deliver you from your husbands, but to show you how to be so good that you can be happy with them.' Weeping, they would say, 'Have mercy on us; if not, we must kill ourselves.' I had no fear of their doing that, so I would seat them at my side, and tell them of my own dear father, — how good he was; but he was always *obeyed.* They would say, 'We could obey a good man.' 'But I am very sure you would not have been willing to obey my father.'

"It is one thing to pray for our degraded sisters while in America, but quite another to raise them from their low estate. When I saw their true character, I found that I needed a purer, holier love for them than I had ever possessed. It was good for me to see that *I* could do nothing, and it was comforting to think that Jesus had talked with just such females as composed the mass around me, and that afterwards many believed because of one such woman."

Sometimes the revilings of the women were almost equalled by similar talk among the men, as in a village of Gawar, where they said, "We would not receive a priest or deacon here who could not swear well, and lie too." In the same village, a young man spoke favorably of Mr. Coan's preaching in Jeloo. Instantly a woman called out, "And have you heard those deceivers preach?" "Yes," was the reply, "both last year and this, and hope I shall again." Hearing this, her eyes flashed, and drawing her brawny arms into the form of a dagger, with a vengeful thrust of her imaginary weapon, she cried, "The blood of thy father smite thee, thou Satan!" and dreadful was the volley of oaths and curses that followed. Yet she was only a fair specimen of the village.

We of the calmer West do not know what it is to have a mob of such women come forth in their wrath. In one town was a virago, who often, single-handed, faced down and drove off Moslem tax-gatherers when the men fled in terror. No one who has ever heard the stinging shrillness of their tongues, or looked on their frenzied gestures, can ever forget them, or wonder why the ancients painted the Furies in the form of women. Words cannot portray the excitement of such a scene. The hair of the frantic actors is streaming in the wind; stones and clods seem only embodiments of the unearthly yells and shrieks that fill the air; and yet it was such beings that grace made to be "last at the cross and first at the sepulchre."

The East is notorious for profanity, and among the Nestorians women were as profane as men. The pupils in the Seminary at first used to swear, and use the vilest language on the slightest provocation. Poor, blind Martha, on her death bed, in her own father's house, was constantly cursed and reviled. She was obliged sometimes to cover her head with the quilt, and stop her ears, to secure an opportunity to pray for her profane and abusive brother; and though, in such circumstances, she died before her prayers were answered, yet they were heard, for he afterwards learned to serve his sister's God. "Do you think people will believe me," said a pupil to her teacher, who was reproving her for profanity, "if I do not repeat the name of God very often?"

Lying was almost as common as profanity, and stealing quite as prevalent as either. It was a frequent remark, "We all lie here; do you think we could succeed in business without it?"

In the early days of the Seminary, nothing was safe except under lock and key. Sometimes there seemed to be a dawn of improvement, and next, all the buttons would be missing from the week's washing, and the teacher was pretty sure to find that her own pupils were the thieves. Miss Rice tells of one, amply supplied with every thing by her parents, yet noted for her thefts. Indeed, sons and daughters were alike trained to such practices. In 1843, Miss Fiske could not keep a pin in her pin-cushion; little fingers took them as often as she turned away, and lest she should tempt them to lie, she avoided questioning them, unless her own eye had seen the theft. No wonder she wrote, "I feel very weak, and were it not that Christ has loved these souls, I should be discouraged; but he has loved them, and he loves them still." If the pins were found with the pupils, the answer was ready — "We found them," or, "You gave them to us;" and nothing could be proved. But one summer evening, just before the pupils were to pass through her room to their beds on the flat roof, knowing that none of that color could be obtained elsewhere, the teacher put six black pins in her cushion, and stepped out till they had passed. As soon as they were gone, she found the pins gone too, and at once called them back. She told them of her loss, but none knew any thing about it. She showed them that no one else had been there, and therefore they must know. Six pairs of little hands were lifted up, as they said, "God knows we have not got them;" but this only called forth the reply, "I think that God knows you have got them," and she searched each one carefully, without finding them. She then proposed to kneel down where they stood, and ask God to show where they were, adding, "He may not see it best to show me now, but he will do it some time." She laid the matter before the Lord, and, just as they rose from their knees, remembered that she had not examined their cloth caps. She now proposed to examine them, and one pair of hands went right up to her cap. Of course she was searched first, and there were the six pins, so nicely concealed in its folds that nothing was visible but their heads. This incident did much good. The pupils looked on the discovery as an answer to prayer, and so did their teacher. They began to be afraid to steal when God so exposed their thefts, and she was thankful for an answer so immediate. The offender is now a pious, useful woman.

Yet some were so accustomed to falsehood, that, even after conversion, it cost a struggle to be entirely truthful, and missionaries could see, as Christians in our own land cannot see, why an apostle should write to the regenerate, "Lie not one to another." The teacher labored to impress her charge with the sinfulness of such conduct, but in the revival of 1846, they seemed to learn more in one hour than she had taught them in the two years preceding. Yet that faithful instruction was not lost. It was the fuel which the Spirit of God kindled into a flame. The sower has not labored in vain because the seed lies for days buried in the soil.

In that revival, the awakened hastened to restore what they had stolen. One came to Miss Fiske in great distress, saying, "Do you remember the day, two years ago, when Sawdee's new shoes were taken from the door?"—They leave off their shoes on entering a house.—"Yes, I recollect it." "You thought a Moslem woman stole them, but" — and here her feelings overcame her — "I took them, for I was angry with her, and threw them into a well. What shall I do? I know Christ will not receive me till I have confessed it to her. Can I go and confess it to-night, and pray with her, and then may I go and work for money to replace them?" She paid for the shoes, and became a bright light in her dark home. There were many such cases, and from that time the teachers had little trouble from theft. New pupils would sometimes steal, but the older ones were ready to detect them, and show them a more excellent way. Miss Fiske says of this, "The frequent visits of the Holy Spirit have removed an evil which mocked my efforts. God made me feel my utter helplessness, and then he did the work." That same term there was but one case of theft in the Male Seminary, though formerly it was not infrequent there.

In reference to transgressions of the seventh commandment, much detail is not expedient. It is sufficient to say, that the first impressions of earlier missionaries respecting the purity of Nestorian women were not sustained by subsequent acquaintance. The farther they went beneath the surface of things, the more they found of corruption. One might go to Persia supposing that he knew a good deal of the degradation of the people, and yet really know very little of the pit into which he was descending.

A seminary gathering together such a company of young females, was a new thing in Persia, and it will readily be conceived that amid a Mohammedan community it was an object of peculiar solicitude to its guardians. Many a Moslem eye was on those girls, as the results of a religious education appeared in their manners, their dress, and personal beauty. In one instance, an officer of government attempted to take one of them to his harem, but God thwarted his purpose through the interference of the English consul. Similar dangers threatened from other sources, and eternity alone will reveal the burden of care and watchfulness they involved. If only one pupil had been led astray, what a hopeless loss of confidence would have followed among the people! In the early years of the institution, when parents could hardly be persuaded to trust their daughters out of their sight for a single night, it might have broken up the whole enterprise; but in this matter, also, God showed himself the hearer of prayer, and not one danger of the kind was ever allowed to be more than an occasion for renewed intercession, and more confiding dependence on his gracious care. Sometimes, in vacation, it seemed strange to its guardians that they had no longer a fold to protect, and could retire to rest free from that anxious solicitude that sometimes drove sleep from their eyes.

It is not in the beginning of missionary life that all these things are understood: they are learned gradually. This is wisely ordered, that the missionary be not discouraged at the outset. Strength is given each day to meet new trials as they come, and it would not be leaving a truthful impression on the reader, if, at the close of this description of what has been, it should not be recorded, to the praise of divine grace, that a great change has taken place.

There are many to-day to whom the missionary may say, "Such were some of you; but ye are washed, but ye are sanctified, but ye are justified in the name of the Lord Jesus, and by the Spirit of our God." Not only do some who stole steal no more, but many young husbands now provide separate apartments for the bride whom they bring home, and they need all that the word "home" expresses to describe their mutual joy. The hour of suffering is anticipated by a considerate affection, and that affection is so reciprocated that many hearts safely trust in the daughters of the Female Seminary of Oroomiah.

It is not merely education that has wrought this change, but a Bible education. Paul cared for just such converts, and left divine teachings for the use of those who should come after him in the same work. As a young wife said to her teacher one day, after she had been talking with her about her new duties, "I thank you; you are right. I am glad that you have told me what Paul says, and I think that God has told you the same thing." Many a graduate might say, with another, "I thank you for your instructions, and as I look on the trials of ungodly families, every drop of my blood thanks you."

CHAPTER II.

MARBEESHOO.

VISIT THERE. — NATIVE ACCOMMODATIONS. — HOSPITALITY OF SENUM. — MOHAMMEDAN WOMEN.

THE following account of Miss Fiske's visit to Marbeeshoo, in November, 1847, presents a vivid picture of things as they were, and the Christian thoughtfulness of one who had learned a more excellent way: —

"As we sat at dinner a few days since, Mr. Stocking proposed that I spend the Sabbath with him at Marbeeshoo. I said at once, 'I cannot leave my school.' But he forthwith called Sanum, Sarah, and Moressa, my oldest girls, and asked them if they did not love souls in Marbeeshoo well enough to take good care of school, and let me be absent till Tuesday. They were delighted to think of my going where no missionary lady had ever been, and said, 'We will do all we can for the girls, and we will pray for you, if you will only go and try to do those poor women good.' It was hardly two o'clock before we were on horseback. Marbeeshoo is about fifty miles from us, and in Turkey. Two years ago it was said 'no lady should try to go there,' but brother Stocking thought not so now; and I was willing to follow where he led, especially as a former pupil had recently settled there. We must be out over night, but we thought best not to spend it in a tent, on account of the cold. Near sunset we came to Mawana, a village of mud huts. We went to the house of the head man, who joyfully welcomed us to his house. It consisted of a single low room, inhabited by at least a score of men, women, and children. They came in one by one, but already the hens had found their resting place, evidently no strangers there. Several lambs had been brought into their corner, and three or four calves, each had his couch of grass. Our horses had been arranged for the night on the other side of a partition wall, some three feet high. When all were within, the coarse bread and sour milk were brought out for supper. Then Mr. Stocking read from the Bible, and talked, and prayed with the numerous family, and the women sat around me, while I tried to do them good, till about ten o'clock. At that time, the mother of the family rose, saying, 'Now we will settle it.' I listened to hear the settlement of some family quarrel, but to my surprise her meaning was, 'We will settle where to lie down for the night;' and as I looked over the room I thought, surely some little skill in settling is needed, if we are all to sleep here. But soon she took out three of the children to an empty manger, where she put new hay, and quickly settled them; they were covered with an old rug, and at once fell fast asleep. She then returned, saying, 'Now there is room for our guests,' and brought a piece of cotton cloth, which she said was *all* for me. In a short time, one and another was fast asleep. They lay on mats, without either bed or pillow, and the divers breathing or snoring of men, and calves, and lambs was soon heard, all mingled together.

"I found myself sitting alone with the old lady, and so, putting my carpet bag under my head, and drawing my shawl about me, I lay down too. This was a signal for extinguishing the light; but before that, I had marked a road, where I thought I might possibly pass out between the sleepers should I need fresh air. There was no sleep for me; and the swarms of fleas made me so uncomfortable, that before midnight I found my way out, and remained as long as the cold air of that November night allowed, and so passed out and in several times during the night. I watched long for the morning, and at length it came, and the sleepers, one by one, arose. They all hoped I had slept well, and I could not tell them I had not, for they had given me the best they had, and told me again and again how glad they were that I had come, and hoped their house would always be mine when I came that way. There was a proposal for breakfast, but the morning was so fine that I suggested to Mr. Stocking that a carpet bag sometimes furnished a very good breakfast.

"We did enjoy that ride very much after a sleepless night. The road was often only a narrow path on the edge of a precipice, and such as I had never passed over before; but I thanked my God at every step for the pure, fresh air of those mountains. As we approached the village, hid away among the cliffs, and in such a narrow spot that houses were placed one above another on the terraced hill-side, one of our attendants insisted on riding forward, and we were not greatly surprised to find a crowd ready to welcome us. One and another cried out, 'Senum wants you to go to Zechariah's.' So to Zechariah's we went, and there was my pupil, waiting with open arms to receive me. She took me from my horse, exclaiming, 'Is it true that you have come? I have heard where you staid last night, and I know you did not sleep at all. Come right into my room; there are no fleas here; I have a bed that is clean, that I keep for the missionaries. I will spread it for you, and you shall sleep before any body comes to see you.'

The bed was spread; she gave me milk to drink (Judg. iv. 19), and then said, 'I will guard the door so no one shall disturb you, and I will wake you for dinner.' I was soon asleep, and slept two long hours before she woke me.

"When she did, she came with her tray in her hand, where was the freshly baked bread, the nicely cooked little fish, which, she said, 'my husband caught expressly for you and Mr. Stocking,' honey from their own hives, milk from their flock, and other simple refreshments. All was neatly prepared, and we were so thankful for the dear child's attentions! When dinner was over, she said, 'Now I want you to see the women; but they must not come here, for they will leave fleas, and you will not be able to sleep to-night. There is another large room the other side, and we will have meeting there this afternoon.'

"About three o'clock I met there more than one hundred poor women, who of course must ask many questions before their curiosity would be satisfied. They finally became quiet, however, and I could tell them of the Saviour, who had loved to teach just such needy ones as they were. I enjoyed the afternoon very much; it was all the more precious for the discomforts of the night, and the comforts of Senum's house. The next day was the Sabbath, and most of the time I was in the 'large room,' where the women came freely. In the afternoon about three hundred were present. I was weary at night, but Senum's care, with the thought of the privilege of meeting so many who had never before heard of Christ as the *only* Saviour, made me forget it all."

Painful as is this view of woman as she was among the Nestorians, her condition was still worse among the Mohammedans; not, indeed, in matters of outward comfort, for the wealth of Persia is in Moslem hands, and they occupy every position of rank or authority in the land. But in all that pertains to morality and religion, they stand on a lower level.

The Nestorian woman may not have known what was contained in the Bible, yet she knew that it was the word of God, and was ready to receive all its teachings as of divine authority. To her Moslem sister it is not only an unknown book, but one she is taught to regard as superseded by the Koran.

Although the Nestorian woman knew nothing of spiritual worship, yet she regarded the Lord's day as set apart for his service. The Moslem, on the other hand, regards it like any other day of the week, and exalts her Friday to the place that of right belongs to the Sabbath of the Lord.

In all her degradation, the Nestorian woman reverenced the name of Jesus as her God. True, she had no correct idea of salvation or redeeming love; yet even a blind attachment to that sacred name is not without its reward. She may have fallen very low, but there was a power even in her ignorant adherence to Christ, that kept her from falling to the level of those who renounced him for the Arabian impostor. This was seen especially in the blessings that came to her through the institution of Christian marriage, while others groaned under the debasing influence of a sensual polygamy. The wretchedness this occasioned is a topic too large and too painful to dwell upon here. But the wide gulf that separated the two classes was clearly seen, when on her Sabbath the missionary could speak to the Nestorian of her Saviour out of her Bible, while the Moslem knows nothing beyond her kohl and her henna,[1] her dresses and her follies, and other topics at once belittling, debasing, and corrupting.

[1] Kohl is a black powder used to paint the eyebrows and eyelashes. Henna is a plant employed to stain the nails, and sometimes the entire hand and part of the foot, of a dark orange hue.

CHAPTER III.

THE SCENE OF THE NARRATIVE.

NESTORIANS. — THEIR COUNTRY. — FRONTISPIECE. — LAKE. — PLAIN. — FORDING THE SHAHER. — MISSION PREMISES IN OROOMIAH.

We will now glance at the scene of the events to be narrated, as it may not be familiar to every reader. To write of woman in Persia would embrace the whole empire as the field of inquiry; for the existence of woman is co-extensive with the population. But "Woman and her Saviour in Persia" confines our attention to those who have been taught the truth as it is in Jesus; for when Christ sent forth Paul to preach his gospel to the Gentiles, it was that they might receive forgiveness of sins, and inheritance among them who are sanctified by faith that is in him; and how shall they believe in him of whom they have not heard? Our theme, then, confines us to the Nestorians, who number about one hundred thousand souls. About two thirds of these live in Turkey; but the following pages relate principally to those residing in Persia, and hence the title of the volume.

This people inhabit, along with Koords and other races, the territory extending from the western shore of the Lake of Oroomiah to the eastern bank of the Tigris. It includes the Persian province of Oroomiah, and both the eastern and western slope of Central Koordistan. The most inaccessible recesses of the Koordish Mountains have been their refuge for centuries. The whole region extends across four degrees of longitude, with a varying breadth of from one to two degrees of latitude. Attention will be called especially to the city of Oroomiah and the villages around it. The plain of that name is seventy-five miles long and from twelve to twenty miles in width, containing more than a thousand square miles. It is dotted with perhaps three hundred villages, the population varying, according to the size of the village, from less than one hundred to more than a thousand inhabitants.

The frontispiece gives a view of this plain, from the roof of the mission premises at Seir, one thousand feet above the city. The lofty Wolf mountain appears on the right, and the high range west of the narrowest part of the lake on the left. The lake itself is seen beyond the plain at the foot of the mountains which rise abruptly from its eastern shore. The distance makes it seem much narrower than it is, for while one hundred miles in length, it is not far from thirty miles in breadth. Its surface is forty-one hundred feet above the sea, and four hundred feet below the city of Oroomiah. No living thing exists in its waters, which are both salt and bituminous.

The plain is more crowded with villages than here represented, and each one is made conspicuous by its grove of trees, as well as its houses. The city appears prominent at the foot of the hill, though six miles distant from the spectator. It is in the same latitude with Richmond, Virginia, and contains about thirty-five thousand souls. The plain slopes up very gradually from the lake, and Mount Seir rises, behind our point of view, two thousand eight hundred and thirty-four feet above the city. Farther west, the summits of Central Koordistan rise, range above range, to the height of seventeen thousand feet.

We pass down from Seir to the city by a carriage road, now by the side of vineyards, and now near fields of wheat and clover, diversified by orchards and gardens of cucumbers. All of these, and indeed the whole plain, owes its fertility to canals, led out from the rivers which descend from the mountains. Willow, poplar, and sycamore trees line these watercourses. All kinds of fruit trees abound, while the rich verdure of the plain contrasts strikingly with the bare declivities that overlook it from every side. The villages on either hand are clusters of mud houses crowded together for greater security, and every tree in their groves has to be watered as regularly as the fields and gardens.

Before reaching the city we must ford the Shaher, a river that, though frequently all drained off into the fields in summer, is very deep in early spring, when fatal accidents sometimes occur. It was here that, in May, 1846, Miss Fiske narrowly escaped a watery grave. On her way to Seir, with Mr. and Mrs. Stoddard, the horse lay down in the middle of the river, leaving her to be swept off by the rapid current. Mr. Stoddard hastened to the rescue; but the moment his steed was loose, he rushed to attack the horse of Mrs. Stoddard, and, as Miss Fiske rose to the surface, she caught a glimpse of Mr. Stoddard looking back on the battle, and his wife held between the combatants by her riding habit, which had caught on the saddle; but while she looked the dress gave way, and Mrs. Stoddard was safe. She herself had sufficient presence of mind not to breathe under water, and, on coming up for the fifth time, floated into shallow water near the opposite shore, forty rods below the ford, just as Mr. Stoddard reached the same point.

From the river, beautiful orchards line the road on both

sides to the city gate, of which a representation is given on page 154; and about one eighth of a mile inside of that, where the Nestorian and Moslem sections of the city join each other, stand the mission premises, built of sun-dried bricks, like the houses around them.

They occupy a little more than an acre, in the form of a parallelogram; and if, for the sake of clearness, we compare it to a window, the bottom of the lower sash is represented by a long, earthen-roofed structure, half of it a dwelling house, once the home of Dr. Grant, but now the dwelling of Dr. Wright. It is the building on the left of the engraving at page 131, and the round object occupying the nearest window in the second story is a clock, the gift of a well-known merchant of Boston, brother of one of our deceased missionaries. Let our lower sash be filled by two large panes in modern style, and these are represented by two courts surrounded by pavements, and shaded by large sycamore trees. In the engraving just referred to, the spectator stands in one of these courts, looking over a low wall into the other. For the top of the lower sash, we have another building, extending across the premises. The left half of this appearing on page 131, behind the trees, and on the opposite page represented without them, was the first home of Dr. Perkins, and is now the Female Seminary; but repeated additions and modifications have been required to transform a building, originally erected for a private residence, into a structure suitable for such a school.

Miss Fiske first taught in one room of a building to the right, which does not appear in the engraving, though a part of it is seen on page 131; then, as the school grew larger, another room was added, and when those quarters became too strait, this building was remodelled for its use.

FEMALE SEMINARY AT OROOMIAH.

As we shall have a good deal to do with the Seminary in these pages, let us become familiar with its home. Between the central door and the one on the left, those three windows belong to a large room once used as a chapel, but since then as a guest room for the accommodation of the women whom we shall see coming here to learn of Jesus. In this room, Nestorian converts first partook of the Lord's supper with the missionaries. The left of the three windows directly over these, with the rose-bush in it, belongs to Miss Fiske's private room, and the other two to her sitting room. This the pupils have named "The Bethel," and it is so connected that the teacher can step into recitation room, dining room, or kitchen, as occasion requires. The last named apartment is on the rear of the building. The largest recitation room, by a curious necessity, is in the form of a carpenter's wooden square, with the teacher's desk in the angle between the two compartments. One of these is on the back side of the building, out of sight; the other, extending across the end, is represented in front by the window at the extreme left.

Over the central door is, first, the steward's room, and then closets over that; for one of the results of the successive alterations and additions is, that parts of the building are two, and other parts three, stories high. Miss Rice's room is directly over the door on the left hand, as the steward's is here. The three windows in the second story, to the right of the two central closets, open into the dining room, and one of the girls' rooms occupies the corner beyond. On the lower floor, going from the central door to the right, is first a closet, and then a large guest room for visitors; and underneath the whole is the cellar where the boys' school was first taught, that has since grown into the Male Seminary at Seir.

The rooms of the pupils are mostly in the rear. These are large enough to accommodate six or eight occupants, as the Oriental style of living does not require so much furniture as ours. In each room is a member of the senior class, who exercises a kind supervision over her younger companions. Every room has two or more closets, designed especially, but not exclusively, for devotion; and some sleep in the recitation rooms, as such a use of them at night does not interfere with other uses during the day.

But we had almost forgotten our imaginary window, the upper sash of which remains to be described. In that we have only one pane, representing a large court, with the chapel on one side, and the wash rooms and other outbuildings of the Seminary on the other. This court is more garden-like than the other two, has fewer trees, and a long arbor, covered with grape vines, forms a covered walk in the middle of it. It was in this arbor that the tables were spread for the collation in 1850, to be described hereafter. This court is invaluable as a place for out-door exercise, where the pupils may enjoy the fresh air, free from the annoyances and exposures of the streets in an Oriental city.

A stream is led through all these courts in a channel lined with stone. Its murmuring waters are a pleasant sound at early dawn, when they mingle sweetly with the morning song of birds. Here many Nestorian women come to fill their earthen pitchers, as the water is not carried through the courts of Christian houses. The mission premises belonged to Mohammedans; and here, in the shade of the tall sycamores, Mrs. Grant used to sit, with her children, and talk with the women who came for water. Her successors find time to continue the same practice, and as the natives let down their pitchers (Gen. xxiv. 18), and now and then one is broken (Eccles. xii. 6), realize that they live in a Bible land, and seek to make its daughters feel the power of Bible truth.

The Seminary is outwardly very humble, and would contrast very unfavorably with the stately edifices of similar institutions at home. But we shall see that the Saviour has not disdained to honor it with his presence, and its earthen floors and mud walls[1] have witnessed many a gracious visit of the Holy Spirit. Though the glory of Lebanon has not come unto it, yet has God himself beautified the place and made it glorious..

[1] The pilasters in the engraving are made of brick, and not only support the large timbers of the roof, but, by their greater projection, protect the softer material of the wall from the weather. The whole is plastered outside with a mixture of lime and clay, that requires frequent renewal.

CHAPTER IV.

MISSIONARY EDUCATION.

OBJECT. — MEANS. — STUDY OF BIBLE. — PUPILS KEPT IN SYMPATHY WITH THE PEOPLE. — PEOPLE STIMULATED TO EXERTION AND SELF-DEPENDENCE. — TAHITI. — MADAGASCAR.

LET us now look at some of the principles on which missionary education was here carried on, that we may see what kind of an instrumentality God was pleased to crown with his blessing.

The Seminary was founded, not to polish the manners, refine the taste, or impart accomplishments, but to renovate the character by a permanent inward change. The main dependence for bringing this about was the power of the Holy Ghost—the only power that can impart or maintain spiritual life in man. This dependence was expressed in fervent prayer, offered for years amid discouragement and opposition, and, instead of ceasing when an answer came, only offered by a greater number. It is worthy of note that some of the seasons of greatest revival were preceded by disasters that threatened the very existence of the mission.

The principal text book was the word of God; partly, as we shall see, through a providential necessity, but chiefly because it was God's own chosen instrumentality for the salvation of our race; and it was eminently adapted for the education of such a people. The teachers could say, with a beloved co-laborer on Mount Lebanon, "To the Scriptures we give increased attention; they do more to unfold and expand the intellectual powers, and to create careful and honest thinkers, than all the sciences we teach." It is also most efficient in freeing mind and heart from those erroneous views that are opposed to its teachings; and actual trial developed a richness and fulness of practical adaptation to the work that astonished even those who already knew something of its value. Its precepts and instructions were also clothed with power: requirements and counsels which from the missionary had only awakened opposition, coming from the Bible were received as messages from heaven. Said a Nestorian to a missionary who had been speaking to him the words of God, "His words grew very beautiful while we were talking." In reference to every suspicious novelty or distasteful duty, the Bible was the ultimate appeal. The missionary could say to them as Paul did to an early church, "When ye received the word of God, which ye heard of us, ye received it not as the word of man, but, as it is in truth, the word of God, which effectually worketh also in you that believe." Besides, those thus educated were to teach others, and needed to be thoroughly furnished from the divine oracles with the truths they were to impart. It is not strange, then, that in the Seminary the Bible was studied both doctrinally and historically; that they had a system of theology and tables of Scripture chronology; that biblical biography and geography were regular studies; that different portions of Scripture occupied different years; and that, instead of Butler's Analogy and Wayland's Moral Science, were the Epistles to the Romans and Hebrews studied with all the accurate analysis and thoroughness bestowed elsewhere upon the classics. Such teaching would yield good fruit any where, and the good seed found good ground in Persia.

So much for the instrumentality; but, then, influences are every where at work to check the growth of the plant of grace, and these must be overcome. There is danger that missionary education may be made worse than useless by allowing the sympathies of pupils to become alienated from the masses around them. Children from heathen families may be puffed up with an idea of superiority to their own people. Their taste may be cultivated so as to render disgust with heathen degradation stronger than the Christian desire to do them good. A foreign language, foreign dress, and foreign habits may widen the gulf that separates them from their people, till, what with an undue exaltation on the one hand and a suspicious jealousy on the other, usefulness is well nigh impossible. But here such tendencies have been carefully watched and guarded against. The pupils have been trained with the view of doing good among their own people. No line of separation has been drawn in dress or diet, furniture or household arrangements. While taught to be neat, the goal kept ever in sight has been, a happy usefulness in their own homes, the elevation of the mass just as fast as was consistent with mutual love and sympathy, the people not feeling that their daughters were denationalized, and they not lifted out of sympathy with the homes they were to bless. Hence, even in 1844, we find the mud floor of the small school room covered with straw mats; one window, of oiled paper, admitting the light; and a brick stove, with a few rude benches, its only furniture. In the other room, where the cooking was done, the pupils ate, and spent their time out of school. Here were two windows of like material; and besides the mats, the floor was covered with a thick felt, on which they spread their beds at night. A table was provided, covered with a coarse blue and white check. There were also a set of coarse plates and a few other dishes, but no knives nor forks. They eat their soup with wooden spoons, and their other food with their hands. Their clothing, like their cooking, was mostly in native style; and they were taught to make it for themselves.

Another object in missionary education is, to do enough to stimulate to exertion, and yet not foster inefficiency or undue dependence. The Nestorians are poor, but doing too much for them may make them still poorer. They must be brought to sustain their own institutions at the earliest possible moment, and their training should keep that end in view. Hence Miss Fiske writes, "At first I was inclined to do more for them than afterwards, and at length settled down on this principle,—to give my pupils nothing for common use which they could not secure in their own homes by industry and economy. So I furnished only such articles as they could buy in the city. I preferred that they should make all their own clothing, and may have grieved friends sometimes by declining clothing which they offered to send for them. We chose rather to spend our own strength in training them to provide for themselves. I do not mean that I am not glad to see foreign articles in Oroomiah; but we were in danger of fostering a more expensive taste than they would have the means of gratifying. Our great object is to raise up the most efficient coadjutors from among the people, and they must labor among their neighbors as of them, and not as foreigners, and be prepared to carry forward the work when we leave it.

"At first we clothed as well as boarded our pupils, and then led them to provide one article after another, till they clothed themselves. It was delightful to see the interest parents began to take in clothing their daughters, in order to send them to school after they provided their own garments. They took better care of them, and so learned to take better care of other things. Since I left, Miss Rice has advanced farther in this matter; and last year most of the pupils paid a trifle for tuition, amounting in all to over twenty dollars. It often costs more than the amount to secure these pittances; but it does our pupils good, and we spared no pains to this end."

It is touching to see the spirit manifested by some parents in this connection. One very poor widow, whose little field of grain had been devoured by locusts, brought a large squash and a quantity of raisins which she had earned by laboring for others — a self-denial almost equal to her previous giving up of her only bed for the use of a daughter in the Seminary, which she brought, saying, "I can sleep on the *hasseer* [rush mat], if you will only receive her into school."

It certainly is not benevolence to do for others what they can do as well for themselves, or to do for them in a way to diminish either their ability or disposition to provide for themselves. Missionaries may be in danger of staying too long and doing too much for a people, rather than of leaving them too soon after the gospel has taken root among them.

Native pastors came into being at Tahiti simply because the French drove off the missionaries. They were not ordained before, but at once proved themselves equal to the work that Providence assigned them; and after twenty years of French misrule, in spite of Popery on the one hand and brandy and vice on the other, there are now more church members under these native pastors than ever before.

Twenty years ago the European shepherds were driven from Madagascar, and a few lambs left in the midst of wolves; but God raised up native pastors, and, instead of tens of Christians under Europeans, there are now hundreds, yea, thousands, under these natives.[1] Those missionaries are wise who aim constantly at results like these; and it is in such a spirit that work has been done among the women of Persia.

[1] Rev. Dr. Tidman, secretary of the London Missionary Society, in "Conference of Missions at Liverpool," 1860, p. 225.

CHAPTER V.

BEGINNINGS.

MRS. GRANT. — EARLY LIFE AND LABORS. — GREAT INFLUENCE. — HER SCHOOL. — HER PUPILS. — CHANGED INTO BOARDING SCHOOL. — GETTING PUPILS. — CARE OF THEM. — DIFFICULTIES FROM POVERTY OF PEOPLE. — PAYING FOR FOOD OF SCHOLARS. — POSITION OF UNMARRIED MISSIONARY LADIES. — BOOKS.

We have seen that among the Nestorians it was counted a disgrace for a female to learn to read; and even now, in the districts remote from missionary influence, a woman who reads, and especially one who writes, is an object of public odium, if not of persecution. How, then, could the Nestorians be induced to send their daughters to schools? What overcame this strong national prejudice? These questions open a delightful chapter in divine providence, showing how wonderfully God adapts means to ends, even on opposite sides of the globe.

A Christian gentleman in the State of New York, on the death of his wife's sister, adopted into his own family her infant child. She was trained to the exercise of a practical Christian benevolence, and her superior mind was improved by an education remarkably thorough. In the classics and mathematics she exhibited uncommon aptitude, and made unusual attainments; so that it was truly said of her, "Perhaps no female missionary ever left our country with a mind so well disciplined as Mrs. Judith S. Grant." She sailed for

Persia, July 11, 1835; and there she displayed rare ability in acquiring the language of the people. The Turkish she soon spoke familiarly. In a short time she read the ancient Syriac, and acquired the spoken language with at least equal facility. Previous even to these acquisitions, she taught Mar Yohanan and others English; and as they noticed the ease with which she turned to her Greek Testament, whenever ours seemed to differ from the ancient Syriac, they regarded her with feelings in which it would be hard to say whether wonder, love, or reverence was the strongest. Some might have cried out, when her fine intellect and rare acquirements were devoted to the missionary work, "Why is this waste of the ointment made?" But had her friends searched the round world for a sphere of greatest usefulness, they could not have selected one where her rare gifts would have accomplished so much; and when such a woman manifested deep solicitude for the education of her sex, ancient prejudice fell before her. She taught her own domestics to read. She sedulously cultivated the acquaintance of both Christian and Mohammedan women; nor did she rest till she had opened a school for girls in what is now Mr. Coan's barn. Such was her zeal, that when her health would not allow her to go there, she taught the pupils in her own apartment. She commenced with only four scholars, but at the same time prepared the maps for Parley's Geography in modern Syriac, and the old map of Oroomiah, so familiar to the readers of the Missionary Herald, was her handiwork. Nor was her usefulness confined to her school room. Hers was the privilege of creating such a public sentiment in favor of the education of woman, that her successors have found the gates wide open before them, and often wondered at the extent and permanence of the influence she acquired.

There is no one topic of which Miss Fiske has spoken to the writer so frequently, and with such enthusiasm, as the great work that Mrs. Grant accomplished for woman in Persia, during her short missionary life. She was the laborious and self-denying pioneer in female education, and every year thus far has brought to light new evidence of her extensive usefulness. It was no empty compliment, when the venerable Mar Elias said, "We will bury her in our church, where none but very holy men are laid. As she has done so much for us, we want the privilege of digging her grave with our own hands."

Miss Fiske writes, shortly after her arrival, "The first Syriac word I learned was 'daughter;' and as I can now use the verb 'to give,' I often ask parents to give me their daughters. Some think that I cannot secure boarding scholars, but Mrs. Grant got day scholars; and when I hear men, women, and children say, 'How she loved us!' I want to love them too. I mean to devote at least five years to the work of trying to gather girls into a boarding school, as Mrs. Grant desired to do. She has gone to her rest. I wonder that I am allowed to take her place." And again: "I am usually in school till three P. M., and then I go out among the poor mothers till tea time. They often say to me, 'Mrs. Grant did just as you do.' Her short life was a precious offering. I feel each day more and more that I have entered into the labors of a faithful servant of Christ."

Among the pupils of Mrs. Grant was Selby, of Oroomiah, who was hopefully converted while teaching some day scholars connected with the Seminary, in 1845. Raheel, (Rachel,) the wife of Siyad, the tailor mentioned in the Memoir of Mr. Stoddard, was another. So were Sanum, the wife of Joseph; Moressa, the wife of Yakob; and

Sarah, the daughter of Priest Abraham, and wife of Oshana, of whom we shall hear more hereafter.

After the death of Mrs. Grant, January 14, 1839, the school was continued under the charge of Mr. Holladay, who employed native teachers to assist him, the ladies of the mission coöperating as they could. It then passed into the hands of Dr. Wright, who had the care of it when Miss Fiske arrived in Oroomiah, June 14, 1843. During all this time it was only a day school, and contact with vice in the homes of the pupils greatly hindered its usefulness. It was for this reason that Miss Fiske was exceedingly anxious to make it a boarding school, so as to retain the pupils continuously under good influences. But would they be allowed to spend the night on the mission premises? This was doubted by many, and all had their fears; yet in August an appropriation was made for the support of six boarding pupils, who were to be entirely under the control of the mission for three years. Some said they could not be obtained for even one year, and not one of them would remain to complete the three. Even Priest Abraham said, "I cannot bear the reproach of having my daughter live with you." At that time, scarcely a girl twelve years old could be found who was not betrothed; and years were devoted to the preparation of a coarse kind of embroidery, a certain amount of which must be ready for the wedding.

One day in August, Mar Yohanan said to Miss Fiske, "You get ready, and I find girls." She devoted that month and the next to preparation for her expected charge. But the day came for opening the school, and not one pupil had been obtained. The teacher was feeling somewhat anxious, when, from her window in the second story, she saw Mar Yohanan crossing the court, with a girl in either hand. One of them was his own niece, Selby, of

Gavalan, seven years of age; the other, Hanee, of Geog Tapa, about three years older. They were not very inviting in outward appearance; but it did not take Miss Fiske long to reach the door, where the bishop met her, and placing their little hands in hers, said, in his broken English, "They be your daughters; no man take them from your hand." She wrote to a friend an account of her success, adding, "I shall be glad to give them to the Lord Jesus, and love to look on them as the beginning of my dear school." These two pupils were supported by ladies in Malden, Massachusetts, and the number soon increased to six; but fifteen days after, two of them, finding the gate open, suddenly left for home. Their teacher did not think it advisable to follow them; nor did she see them again till, ten years after, an invitation for a reunion of all her scholars brought two whom she did not recognize. She said, "Perhaps you were here under Mrs. Grant?" "No, we were your own scholars for fifteen days, and we are very sorry we ran away." They are now both useful Christians, and the places they left in 1843 were speedily filled by others.

The care of the school was much more exhausting than its instruction. When the teacher went out, and when she came in, she must take her pupils with her, for she dared not leave them to themselves. Indeed, so strong were the feelings of their friends, that they allowed them to remain only on condition that they should lodge with or near their teacher, and never go out except in her company. A native teacher rendered such help as he could, needing much teaching himself; and every thing combined to make the principal feel that hers was to be a work of faith and prayer. As the first of January approached, she thought how sweet it would be to be remembered by dear friends at Mount Holyoke; and when it came, she wrote to Miss

Whitman, "In looking over Miss Lyon's suggestions for the observance of the day, last year, I cannot tell you how I felt as I read the words, 'Perhaps next new year's day will find some of you on a foreign shore. If so, we pledge you a remembrance within these consecrated walls.' I thought not then that privilege would be mine; but since it is, I count your prayers the greatest favor you can confer."

At Oroomiah, the missionaries met together for prayer at one o'clock, and after that Dr. Perkins and Mr. Holladay preached to the assembled Seminaries, while the ladies of the mission met separately for prayer; then united intercession again closed the day. And they needed to wait on God, for many difficulties combined to prevent success.

One was the poverty of the people. To say merely that they were poor gives no true idea of their situation to an American reader. They were extremely poor, and grinding oppression still keeps them so. In 1837, Mr. Stocking found very few pupils in the schools wearing shoes, even in the snow of midwinter; and one sprightly lad in Sabbath school had nothing on but a coarse cotton shirt, reaching down to his knees, and a skull cap, though the missionary required all his winter clothes, besides a fire, to keep him comfortable.

Another evil growing out of their poverty was, that the missionaries, in order to give the first impulse to education, resorted to some measures which, after an interest was awakened, had to be laid aside in order to increase it. For example, poor parents could not be persuaded to earn bread for their children while they sent them to school; hence, to get scholars at first, the mission furnished their daily bread; and this having been done for the boys, had to be done for the girls also. So, in the winter of 1843–44,

5 *

twenty-five cents a week was paid to the day scholars, the others having their board instead. But the current having once commenced to flow in the new channel, such inducements became more a hinderance than a help, and, in the spring of 1844, Miss Fiske told her scholars that no more money would be paid for their bread; and though some of the mission feared it would be necessary to resume the practice, instead of that it was soon dropped in the other Seminary also.

But the special difficulty growing out of the condition of woman in a Mohammedan country demands our notice. Some may suppose that because Miss Fiske and Miss Rice have succeeded so well, an unmarried lady from this country has nothing to do but to go there and work like any one else. This is not true; such a one cannot live by herself; her home must be in some missionary family. She cannot go out alone, either inside or outside of the city. In many things she needs to be shielded from annoyances here unknown. And God provided all that the teachers of the Seminary needed of such help; first, in the kind family of Mr. Stocking, and, after his death, in the pleasant household of Mr. Breath. Indeed, not one of all the missionary circle ever stood in need of such a hint as Paul gave the church at Rome concerning the deaconess of Cenchrea. As Miss Fiske says, playfully, "Whenever we went with them to visit pupils at a distance, they always made us believe that it was a great privilege to take us along;" and every lady who goes out, in a similar way, to labor in the missionary field, will find just such Christian kindness indispensable to her comfort and usefulness. In such a sphere of action, a lady's dependence is her independence.

Another difficulty was the want of books. Such a thing

as a school book had been unknown among the Nestorians. The only ones to be had in 1843 were the Bible in ancient Syriac, — a language unintelligible to the common people, — and the Gospel of John, with a few chapters of Genesis, in the spoken language, besides a few tracts. Later came the Gospel of Matthew, and, after that, the four Gospels. Mr. Stocking prepared a Spelling Book of fifty-four pages, 8vo, a Mental Arithmetic of twenty-four pages, and afterwards a larger Arithmetic. Mr. Coan, a Scripture Spelling Book of one hundred and sixty pages, 8vo. Mr. Stoddard issued a very full and complete Arithmetic for the older scholars in 1856, but his System of Theology did not appear till after his decease, in 1857. Dr. Wright was the author of a Geography of three hundred and two pages, printed in 1849. Mr. Cochran's Scripture Geography appeared in 1856, and Barth's Church History was published the same year. But the book studied more than all others, and most efficient in enlightening and elevating the people, was the Bible, of which the New Testament appeared in 1846, and the Old in 1852. As many as three hours a day were devoted to that; and no recollections of missionary education in Persia are so pleasant as those of the Bible lessons. The pupils have pleasant memorials of some of them in the form of Bible maps, drawn by themselves, which now form a conspicuous and appropriate ornament of their homes.

It may seem to some as though so much study of the Bible would make the pupils weary of its sacred pages; but precisely the contrary was true. When the New Testament, shortly after it was printed, was offered to those who, during recreation hours, would commit to memory the Scripture Catechism, containing more than one thousand texts, some learned it in three weeks, and others in a longer time; and their joy in receiving the reward could hardly be expressed. It was near the close of the term, and some who had not quite finished when vacation began remained to complete the task; for they said they could not go home unless they carried with them their Testament; and the diligent use they made of it afterwards showed that their desire was more than mere covetousness. Even eighteen months after, writing to a friend in America, they say, "Now we have each of us this blessed book, this priceless blessing; would that in it we might all find salvation for our souls. This book is from the unspeakable mercy of God; nor can we ever repay our dear friends for it." I cannot forbear quoting here the closing sentence of the letter—"Dear friend, the gentle love of the Saviour be with you. Amen."

CHAPTER VI.

THE SEMINARY.

MAR YOHANAN. — STANDARD OF SCHOLARSHIP. — ENGLISH BOOKS READ IN SYRIAC. — EXPENSE. — FEELINGS OF PARENTS. — DOMESTIC DEPARTMENT. — DAILY REPORTS. — PICTURE OF A WEEK DAY AND SABBATH. — "IF YOU LOVE ME, LEAN HARD." — ESLI'S JOURNAL. — LETTER FROM PUPILS TO MOUNT HOLYOKE SEMINARY. — FROM THE SAME TO MRS. C. T. MILLS.

WHEN Mar Yohanan returned to Persia after his visit to the United States, in 1843, Prince Malik Kassim Meerza, who could speak a little English, asked him, "What are the wonders of America?" He replied, "The blind they do see, the deaf they do hear, and the women they do read; they be not beasts." Having visited Mount Holyoke Seminary, he often said, "Of all colleges in America, Mount Holy Oke be the best; and when I see such a school here, I die;" meaning that then he would be ready to die. When he brought her first boarding scholars to Miss Fiske, he said, "Now you begin Mount Holy Oke in Persia."

As she sought to reproduce one of our female seminaries, as far as was possible in such different circumstances, it seems fitting to enter somewhat into the minutiæ of its arrangements.

Resemblance to similar institutions at home is not as yet to be sought in the standard of scholarship, though that is rapidly advancing. In an unevangelized community, the people move on a lower level. Not only social condition, but morality and education, feel the want of the elevating influence of the gospel. A seminary that commences operations by teaching the alphabet must advance far, and climb high, before its graduates will stand on a level with those whose pupils were familiar with elementary algebra when they entered; yet its course of study may be the best to secure the usefulness of its members in their own community. If ragged village girls, untutored and uncombed, studying aloud in school hours, and at recess leaping over the benches like wild goats, now study diligently and in silence, move gently, and are respectful to their teachers and kind to each other, a thorough foundation has been laid; and if, in addition to that, the literary attainments of the lower classes to-day exceed those of the pupils who first left the school, the superstructure rises at once beautifully and securely.

Leaving out the Bible, — which has been already spoken of, — to the original reading, writing, singing, and composition; have been added by degrees, grammar, geography, arithmetic, and theology; with oral instruction in physiology, chemistry, natural philosophy, and astronomy.

But we should neither understand the attainments of the pupils, nor the source of their marked ability as writers, did we not notice that, as a reward for good conduct during the day, their teacher was accustomed to translate orally to them, at its close, at first simple stories, and then such volumes as Paradise Lost, The Course of Time, and Edwards's History of Redemption. To these were added such practical works as Pike's Persuasives to Early Piety, Pastor's Sketches, and Christ a Friend; and the pupils understood books a great deal better in the free translations thus given, than in the more exact renderings issued from the press. Baxter's Saints' Rest, poured thus hot and glowing into a Syriac mould, was more effective, at least for the time, than the same after it had cooled and been laboriously filed into fidelity to the original.

The Seminary was unlike similar schools at home in the matter of expense. In 1853, the cost for each pupil was only about eighteen dollars for the year, including rent, board, fuel, lights, and clothing in part; and as this was paid by the American Board, education to the people was without money and without price. We have already alluded to the efforts of the teachers to train up the people to assume this expense themselves.

Let us now trace the progress made in getting the pupils away from the evil influences of their Persian homes. In 1843, besides her six boarding pupils, Miss Fiske had a few day scholars; next year she had still fewer; and the year after that, they were dropped entirely. Many wished to send their daughters in this way; but she was decided in her refusal to receive them, because thus only could the highest good of the pupils be secured. At first, so great was her dread of home influences, that she sought to retain them even in vacation; but she soon saw that their health and usefulness, their sympathy with the people, and the confidence of the people in them, required them to spend a part of the year at home. This also gave their teachers a good opportunity to become acquainted with their friends and neighbors, and a door was opened for many delightful meetings with women, in which the pupils rendered much assistance. It also secured the influence of the parents in favor of what was for the good of their daughters, and made them interested in the school. During Miss Fiske's entire residence in Persia, fathers rarely disregarded her wishes concerning their daughters in her school.

The only time that the teachers were ever reviled by

a Nestorian father was in the case of a village priest. He came one day to the Seminary to see his daughter, and because she did not appear at once, — she was engaged at the moment, — he cursed and swore, in a great passion, and when she did come, carried her home. No notice was taken of it, and no effort made to get her back; but three years after, the first indications of his interest in religion were deep contrition for his conduct on that occasion, and a letter full of grief for such treatment of those who had come so far to tell him and his of Jesus. He at once sent his daughter back, and three weeks after she too came to the Saviour, and even begged, as a favor, to have the care of the rooms of the teachers her father had reviled. Since then, the priest has written no less than three letters, as he says, to be sure that so great wickedness was really pardoned, it seemed to him so unpardonable.

The circumstances of the Seminary required a domestic department. It was difficult, in Persia, to have girls only ten years old take charge of household affairs; yet a beginning was made; but how much labor of love and patience of hope it involved cannot be told to those who have not tried it. At first, their one hour of work each day was more of a hinderance than a help; but gradually, through watchfulness and much effort, they were brought to do the whole without the least interference with their regular duties in school. They were thus trained to wait upon themselves, and so one deeply rooted evil of Oriental life was corrected. This practice also relieved the school of the bad influence of domestics, while it prepared the pupils for lives of contented usefulness among a people so poor as the Nestorians. Besides, in this way they acquired habits of regularity and punctuality such as they never saw in their own homes.

But while these Western habits were inculcated, such of their own customs as were harmless were left untouched. They were carefully taught to do things in their own way, so as naturally and easily to fall into their proper place at home.

At first, in their daily reports, Miss Fiske dared not ask any question the answer to which she could not ascertain for herself. The earliest she ventured to put was, whether they had combed their hair that day. The pupils all stood up, and those who had attended to this duty were asked to sit down. The faithful ones were delighted to comply. The others, mortified and ashamed, remained standing; but if one of them tried to sit down, a glance of the eye detected her. This simple method laid a foundation for truthfulness and self-respect; and from this the teacher gradually advanced to other questions, as their moral sense became able to bear them, till, when they could answer five satisfactorily, such as, "Have you all your knitting needles?" "Were you at prayers?" "Were you late?" — things that could be ascertained at once, — they thought themselves wonderfully good, little dreaming how much the teacher did not dare to ask, lest she should lead them into temptation. After the first revival, she could ask about things that took place out of her sight; and now this exercise is conducted in the same way as in our best schools at home. There is very little communication now between them in the school room. In 1852, there were only five failures on this point for four months, and those by new scholars. Dr. Perkins wrote, that year, "The exact system in this school, and the order, studiousness, good conduct, and rapid improvement of the pupils, in both this and the other Seminary, are probably unsurpassed in any schools in America."

In reply to a request for the picture of a day in the Seminary, Miss Fiske writes, in 1862,—

"You ask for a day of my life in Persia. Come, then, to my home in 1854. You shall be waked by the noise of a hand-bell at early dawn: twenty minutes after, our girls are ready for their half hour of silent devotion. The bell for this usually finds them waiting for it, and the perfect quiet in the house is almost unbroken. At the close of it, another bell summons us to the school room for family devotion, where, besides reading the Scriptures and prayer, they unite in singing one of our sweet hymns.[1] In a few minutes after this, another bell calls us to breakfast, and, that finished, all attend to their morning work. Tables are cleared, rooms put in order, and preparations made for supper — the principal meal in Persia; then for an hour they study silently in their rooms. At a quarter before nine o'clock I enter the school room, while Miss Rice cares for things without. We open school with prayer, in which we carry to the Master more of our little cares and trials than in the early morning. My first lesson is in Daniel, with the older pupils, while two other classes go out to recite in another room. Yonan stays with me, for I want him to help and be helped in these Bible lessons. The class enjoy it exceedingly, and the forty minutes spent on it always seem too short. The other classes now come in, and all study or recite another forty minutes. After that, a short recess in the yard makes all fresh again. The older classes then study, while one of the younger ones has a Bible lesson with me on the life of Christ. Each time I

[1] At first, only one hymn was printed on a separate sheet; then a little hymn book of five, — as many as Luther commenced with at the Reformation. Now the hymn book contains about two hundred hymns, and some of the pupils can repeat them all.

go over it with them I find things which I wonder I had not perceived before. It is delightful to hear them express their own thoughts of our blessed Saviour. We trace his journeyings on maps prepared by the pupils, and they study the Scripture geography of each place. After this, one class recites ancient Syriac to Yonan, and another, in physiology, goes out to Miss Rice, leaving me to spend forty minutes with the older girls on compositions. At present the topic is, "The Christ of the Old Testament;" and I am thankful that I studied Edwards's History of Redemption under Miss Lyon. This done, fifteen minutes remain for a kind of general exercise, when we talk over many things; and then the noon recess of one and a half hours allows the girls to lunch, see friends, and recreate, till fifteen minutes before its close, when they have a prayer meeting by themselves.

"In the afternoon, Miss Rice takes charge of the school, and I have the time out. At present the first hour is given to writing; soon astronomy will take its place. Recitations in geography follow till recess, and after that singing or spelling. The last hour, I go in and hear a lesson in Hebrews. On this Epistle we have full notes prepared in Syriac, and we study it carefully, in connection with the Old Testament. Miss Rice also has a lesson in Judges, and then all come together for the daily reports, more as a family than a school. There is still an hour before supper for mutual calls, knitting, sewing, and family duties. After supper and work are over, and they have had a little time to themselves, come evening prayers. Then they have a short study hour in their rooms, followed by the half hour for private devotion, which closes the day.

"Of course, at another time, the studies might be somewhat different. The hours that Miss Rice and I are out of school we spend in seeing visitors, holding prayer meetings, going out among the women, and sometimes devote a whole day to a distant village."

Having thus looked in on a day of study, let us, through the same glass, take a view of the Lord's day. The letter is dated December, 1855.

My dear Friend: I have learned here that He who fed five thousand with the portion of five can feed the soul to the full with what I once counted only crumbs. May I give you one of the Master's sermons? A few Sabbaths ago, I went to Geog Tapa with Mr. Stoddard. It was afternoon, and I was seated on a mat in the middle of the earthen floor of the church. I had already attended Sabbath school and a prayer meeting with my pupils, and, weary, I longed for rest. It seemed as if I could not sit without support through the service. Then I remembered that after that came my meeting with the women readers of the village; and O, how desirable seemed rest! But God sent it in an unexpected way; for a woman came and seated herself directly behind me, so that I could lean on her, and invited me to do so. I declined; but she drew me back, saying, "If you love me, lean hard." Very refreshing was that support. And then came the Master's own voice, repeating the words, "If you love *me*, lean hard;" and I leaned on him too, feeling that, through that poor woman, he had preached me a better sermon than I could have heard at home. I was rested long before the services were through; then I spent an hour with the women, and after sunset rode six miles to my own home. I wondered that I was not weary that night nor the next morning; and I have rested ever since on those sweet words, "If you love me, lean hard."

But I intended to tell you of our Sabbaths in school. Saturday is the girls' day for washing and mending, and we are busy all day long. Just before sunset, the bell calls us to the school room, and there we inquire if the last stitch is taken, and the rooms are all in order. If any thing is still undone, the half hour before supper sees it finished. After leaving the table, every thing is arranged for the morning, and then we have a quiet half hour in our rooms. After this, half the pupils come to Miss Rice, and half to me. Each has a prayer meeting, remembering the absent ones, also the Female Seminaries in Constantinople, South Hadley (Mass.), and Oxford (Ohio). All retire from these precious meetings to their "half hour," as they call it, and before nine o'clock all is quiet, unless it be the voice of some one still pleading with her God.

The first bell, Sabbath morning, is at half past five, when all rise and dress for the day. Morning prayers are at half past six; then comes breakfast, and, our few morning duties being done, the girls retire to study their Sabbath school lessons, and sometimes ask to meet together for prayer. At half past nine, we attend Syriac service in the chapel. The Sabbath school follows that, numbering now about two hundred pupils. About two thirds of our scholars are teachers in it, and it is a good preparation for teaching in their homes. Those who do not teach form a class. We then go home to lunch, flavored with pleasant remembrances and familiar explanations of the morning service. The afternoon service commences at two o'clock, and our Bible lessons an hour before supper, though some are called earlier, to help us teach the women who come in for instruction. At supper, all are allowed to ask Bible questions, and before leaving the table we have evening prayers. At seven o'clock, Miss Rice and I go to the

English prayer meeting, while the pupils meet in six or seven family meetings, as they call them, the inmates of each room being by themselves, and the pious among them taking turns in conducting them. If any wish to come to us after this, we are glad to see them; and often this hour witnesses the submission of souls to God.

Besides these there is a weekly prayer meeting on Tuesday evening, a lecture on Friday afternoon, and on Wednesday, as well as Sabbath evening, the school meets in two divisions for prayer.

The following journal, kept during the revival, in 1860, by Esli, an assistant teacher, forms an appropriate continuation of this interior picture of the Seminary:—

"*February* 1*st*. To-day, a part of the girls wrote compositions on 'anger,' and a part on 'the gospel.'

"3*d*, *Friday*. John was here to-day writing to Mount Holyoke Seminary, and attended our noon prayer meeting. In the afternoon, Deacon Joseph of Degala preached from the words "King of kings and Lord of lords." In the evening, Mr. Coan sung with us, and we read the weekly report of our conduct.

"5*th*, *Sabbath*. In the forenoon, Dr. Wright preached from Acts ii. 37. He said that we must know what sin is; that we are sinners; and that we cannot save ourselves. In the afternoon, Priest Eshoo preached from Luke xv. 32. The evening prayer meetings were very pleasant.

"9*th*. A blessed morning. Some of the girls are thoughtful. This was seen in the quiet at table and the silence in the kitchen. The work was done both earlier and better than usual. During the study hour, the voice of prayer sounded very sweetly in every room. When the girls walked in the yard, it was very quiet, and so when they came in. Our noon prayer meeting was very pleasant; Miss Rice said a few words on the shortness of time. While Hanee prayed, some wept. When Miss Rice dismissed us, no one moved; all were bowed on their desks, weeping. She then gave opportunity for prayer, and while I prayed, all were in tears. The girls have kept all the rules well to-day. This evening, the communicants met with Miss Rice, and the rest with Martha. Miss Rice read about Jonah in the ship, and said a few words; after that, Raheel the teacher prayed. Then Hanee spoke a little of her own state, and asked us to pray for Raheel of Ardishai, who is thoughtful. I spoke, and asked them to pray for Hannah and Parangis, who are in my room.

"10*th*. The state of our school is the same. Mr. Cochran preached on the faithfulness of the Jews under Nehemiah, when they rebuilt Jerusalem. After meeting he told us that the members of the Male Seminary spent yesterday as a day of fasting and prayer, and many rose confessing their sins. One very wicked man, also from the village, asked them to pray for him. After work was done in the kitchen this evening, a little time remained, and the girls there asked to have a meeting. With gladness of heart I knelt and mingled my tears with theirs, as though I, too, were commencing the work. Afterwards Mr. Coan came and sung with us, and we read the accounts of the week."

Esli, the writer of the above, is the daughter of Yohanan, a pious man in Geog Tapa, who for a time was steward of the Seminary. She was one of the first fruits of the revival of 1856, and graduated after Miss Fiske's return to America. She has since been a most faithful assistant of Miss Rice, and is very much beloved by the pious Nestorians. But the following letter to Miss Fiske, from her own pen, dated April, 1859, will form her best introduction to the reader:—

"When I recall your love to me, my heart is full. I remember the times when we knelt together before our Father in heaven, in godly anguish for priceless souls. Especially do I remember when God first came near to me, how you shared my sorrow by day and by night, and pointed me to Him who bled for me. After you brought me to Christ, you showed me the helps to a Christian life; that I must pray not only in my closet, but also in my heart, when at work or studying, that God would keep me. O that I had heeded your counsels more!

"This winter the Lord led me to see my cold state. For a time the Saviour's face was hidden; then it seemed to be midnight; but I looked above, and the darkness fled. I saw him standing with open arms, and quickly I threw myself into those arms. Tears of joy fell from my eyes, and by the grace of God I was enabled to go forward day by day. Secret prayer has since been very pleasant to me.

"We have had pleasant seasons of prayer in our school this winter, and we trust that some souls have been born again. I have the care of a circle of girls in the kitchen. They work well, and keep it clean. I think you know that such work is difficult, but if you were to come in you would find every thing in order. Every Wednesday we scour all the shelves and the doors.

"The girls have made the yard very pleasant; but one thing is wanting there: we miss you at the cool of the day, walking in it to see if any evil has grown up in your garden.

"I went to my village in vacation; the prayer meetings there were very pleasant, and I enjoyed much, praying with the women alone. Our seasons of family devotion also were delightful. In the morning we read the Acts in course; and as each read a verse, my father asked its meaning. When he went away to preach, I used to lead, and we then read the portion for the day, in the book called 'Green Pastures for the Lord's Flock.'

"In the school we have studied Ezra, in connection with Haggai and Zechariah, and are now in Nehemiah. In the New Testament we are on Paul's third journey, and have nearly finished Scripture geography and theology."

The Seminary keeps up a Christian intercourse with the institution at South Hadley, as the following letters will show; and the beautiful melodeon in the sitting room is a tuneful testimony to the liberality of Holyoke's daughters.

"Many salutations and much love from the school of Miss Fiske to you, our dear sisters of the school at Mount Holyoke. We rejoice that there is such a great institution full of holy words and the warm love of Christ: we hear that many of you have an inheritance above, and are daily looking forward to it. We want to tell you how glad we are that the Holy Spirit has come among you, and that God has turned so many to himself. Though we are great sinners, we rejoice exceedingly in the success of the work of God in every place; and we beg you to pray that the Holy Spirit may visit us also, and our people, and strike sharp arrows into flinty hearts, that they may melt like wax before the fire. Blessed be God, that though we had become the least of all nations, and adopted many customs worse than the heathen, and our holy books were carefully laid away and never used, yet he put love into the hearts of his servants, that they should come to this dark land. We are greatly obliged to you and to your people for so kindly sending us these missionaries. They have greatly multiplied our books, and, as we trust, brought many souls to Christ. Some of us, formerly, knew not who Christ was, or whether a Redeemer had died for us; but now he has gathered us together in this school of godly instruction; and some of us are awaking to our sins, and to the great love God has shown in sending his Son to die for us. We thank God very much that we know Jesus Christ, the only Saviour.

"Again, we want to thank you for sending Miss Fiske to teach us the way of life; we love her because she greatly loves us, and desires our salvation. Every day she takes much trouble that we may be the daughters of God. But her burdens are so great, that we fear she will not remain long with us, unless some one comes to help her. And now we have a petition to present: we hear that in many of you dwelleth the spirit of our Master, Jesus Christ; and that you are ready to leave home and friends, and go to distant lands, to gather the lost sheep of Christ. Dear sisters, our petition is, that you will send us a teacher.[1] We shall greatly rejoice if one comes, and will love her very much. We ask this, not because we do not love Miss Fiske. No! no! this is not in our hearts; but she is weak, and her work is more than she can do alone. We shall expect one to come, and pray God to bring her to us in safety.

"Please remember us in your closets and in your meetings, and ask your friends to pray for us and for our people. Farewell, beloved sisters."

The following extracts are from a letter written by them, in 1848, to Miss Susan L. Tolman, now Mrs. Cyrus T. Mills of the Sandwich Islands, and formerly of Ceylon:—

"Much love from the members of the Female Seminary of Oroomiah to you, our dear Miss Tolman. We are very

[1] Miss Mary Susan Rice, already mentioned in these pages, went out this same year (1847), from the Seminary in South Hadley.

glad to find one who loves us so much, and prays for us. Our delight in your letter was greater than we can express. Miss Fiske came in joyfully with it in her hand, and while she read, it seemed as if you were present, inviting and drawing us to Christ.

"Give our love to all in your favored school, and ask them to pray for us. We love all those dear ladies, because they have been so kind to us, and have been willing that Miss Fiske and Miss Rice should leave them, and come here for our sakes. Though they were dear to you, we think that now they have come to us, your joy in them is greater. We hope to hear of many of you carrying the leaves of life to the dark corners of the earth.

"Dear Miss Tolman, you said, 'You love Miss Fiske, you must also love Miss Rice.' Did you think that we would not love her? We love them both, not only for leaving their friends to come to us, but also because they are full of the love of our dear Redeemer.

"We have heard that you are going to India. We are glad, and love you more for it, because the love of Christ constrains you to this, and thus in spirit you come very near to our dear teachers. We entreat Almighty God to be with you, and bring you in safety to the place he appoints for you, that you may be a light among a dark people. We hope that when there you will not forget us, but write us about your work, and about the daughters of India, whether they love you much or not. Tell your friends not to sorrow for you, but to rejoice that they have a friend ready to go and teach those who know not Christ. The Saviour guide you in all your labors."

Those who aided Miss Lyon to carry out her large-hearted plans in New England, little dreamed that offshoots from the vine they planted would so soon be carried to the ends of the earth. Who does not admire that grace which, in this missionary age, raised up such a type of piety to be diffused over the globe? Doubtless it will undergo changes in Persia, as it has done already; but the devout student of Providence will watch its growth with interest, and its developments will not disappoint his hopes.

CHAPTER VII.

VACATION SCENES.

IN GAWAR AND ISHTAZIN. — VILLAGES OF MEMIKAN. — OOREYA, DARAWE, AND SANAWAR. — IN GAVALAN. — ACCOMMODATIONS. — SABBATH SCHOOL.

To the interior pictures of the school in the last chapter we add some vacation scenes, though chronologically in advance of other things yet to come.

Towards the close of July, 1851, Mr. Stocking and family, with Misses Fiske and Rice, and several native helpers, spent the vacation in Gawar. Mr. Coan accompanied them on his way to regions beyond. Wandering from

TENTS.

place to place, like the patriarchs of old, they pitched their tents at first near the village of Memikan. A sketch of these tents is here presented. The women there were frequent visitors, and few went away without some idea of the truth as it is in Jesus. The pious natives were unwearied in labor, and sometimes woke the missionaries in the morning with prayer for the people round about them. On the Sabbath, there was preaching in as many as five different villages, and after morning service in Memikan, the women came to the tents to receive more particular instruction from their own sex. In the evening, a mother who had buried her son in February — then a very promising member of the Seminary at Seir[1] — brought her youngest daughter, about six years of age, saying, "We give her to you in the place of Guwergis. He has gone to a blessed place. You led him there. We thank you, and now intrust to you our little daughter." Eshoo, the father, spoke of his departed son with much feeling, but most sweet submission. He said to Miss Fiske, as the big tears glistened in the moonlight, "I shall not be here long. I shall soon rejoin him. My hope in Jesus grows stronger every day." The death of that dear son was not only a great spiritual blessing to him, but the mere mention of his name at once secured the attention of the villagers to any thing the missionaries had to say about his Saviour.

On Monday, they left for a visit to the Alpine district of Ishtazin. Unable to take horses along those frightful paths, they rode on hardy mules. In a subsequent journey over the same road, the fastenings of Miss Fiske's saddle gave way, and she fell, but providentially without injury. Sometimes they climbed, or, more hazardous still, descended, a long, steep stairway of rock, or they were hid in the clouds that hung around the higher peaks of the mountain. Now the path led them under huge, detached rocks,

[1] Nestorian Biography, p. 127.

that seemed asking leave to overwhelm them, and now under the solid cliffs, that suggested the more grateful idea of the shadow of a great rock in a weary land. Down in the valley were pleasant waterfalls, little fields rescued by much labor from the surrounding waste, choice fruits, and such a variety of flowers, that it seemed as if spring, summer, and autumn had combined to supply them. Then, in looking up, the eye rested on silver threads apparently hanging down from far-off summits, but really foaming streams dashing headlong down the rocks, yet so distant that no sound came to the ear from their roaring waters.

The party stopped at Ooreya, on one of its flat roofs, shaded by a magnificent walnut tree. The villagers brought mulberries, apples, and other fruits, till they could prepare something more substantial, and seemed to forget their fears of the patriarch in their zealous hospitality. After supper, all adjourned to the churchyard, and there, in the bright moonlight, a crowd of eager listeners heard of Christ, and redemption through his precious blood. The silence of night was broken only by the voice of the preacher, and the echoes of the surrounding cliffs seemed to repeat joyfully the unwonted sounds. Yonan preached from the words "Jesus went about all Galilee, teaching in their synagogues, and preaching the gospel of the kingdom." He commenced by asking whether Christ was right in so doing. They replied, "Certainly he did right." "Yes," said the preacher, "and as he did, so must his followers do; and you must expect to see them in Ishtazin. When we cease to climb over these precipices to come to you, fear lest we have become Mussulmans, for Christians cannot but go from village to village to preach the gospel." The reader will see the force of such an appeal, when he remembers that Mar Shimon had forbidden these people to receive the missionaries because they preached. This was followed by a statement of the doctrines that Jesus preached, in which he did not fail to bring out the essence of the gospel. When he sat down, Khamis, the brother of Deacon Tamo, followed with a most impassioned exhortation. The missionaries had thought him a good preacher before, but the place and the circumstances — he was among his own native mountains — seemed to carry him beyond himself. All through this region, the people appeared to render as much honor to him as they would have done to Mar Shimon. The assembly dispersed, and the travellers lay down where they were, to battle with the sand-flies till the welcome dawn lit up the conspicuous summits high above them.

Almost every moment of the next forenoon was filled by personal religious conversation with many who never heard such truths before. In the evening, even more fixed attention was given to another service in the open air, at the village of Boobawa, for the pious Mar Ogen[1] was then living there, and the bright light of his piety had not shone in vain. Several were earnestly inquiring how to be saved.

On Thursday, the day after their return to Memikan, Mr. Coan, Priest Dunkha, Khamis, and Deacon John left for Central Koordistan, and Deacon Isaac went to Kochannes. But though the laborers were fewer, the number of visitors continued the same. Next Sabbath, besides two services, and two meetings with the women in Memikan, there was preaching in three other villages. In Chardewar, the home of Priest Dunkha, Miss Fiske found his daughter, who had come with them from Oroomiah, already full of work. She had just dismissed her Sabbath school, and was read-

[1] Nestorian Biography, p. 267.

ing the Bible with her cousin, the village priest, who did all in his power to help her, both in her school through the week, and her meetings with the women. One Sabbath, almost every woman in the place had been present, as was the case also when she was visited by Misses Fiske and Rice, and Sanum said that she could not ask for a better place in which to work for Christ. There was more of real hunger for the truth here than any where else in the mountains.

Leaving Memikan, the travellers removed to Darawe, the village described on page 21. Here they could scarcely get permission to pitch their tent, or procure provision for themselves and horses; yet even in such a place, the manifestation of Christian love was not without fruit, though many bitterly opposed them to the last. The neighboring villages wondered at the missionaries going there at all, and still more at their being able to remain.

At Keyat, the kindness of the people, and pleasant intercourse with them, were all the more grateful for the contrast with what had gone before. Here Miss Fiske met with that kind reception from Mar Shimon, then passing through the place, described on page 159, while the tent literally flowed with milk and honey furnished by the villagers, whom he had charged to take good care of their visitors.

On the following Sabbath, Yonan preached to a congregation of about two hundred, at Sanawar, where forty families of refugees from Saat were spending the summer. When Miss Fiske and Miss Rice visited their camp, they found a number of temporary huts enclosing a circle, where the domestic labors of spinning, weaving, and cooking were actively going on. All the women at once left their work, and welcomed their visitors with every mark of confidence and gladness. Some of them had heard the gospel from the missionaries in Mosul, as they had often spent the winter near there. So they drank in every word with eagerness.

The ladies were delighted with their visit, especially with a widow, who, though unable to read, showed unusual familiarity with the Bible, and, as they hoped, a spiritual acquaintance with its doctrines. When the topic of our fallen nature was mentioned, "Yes," said she, "we were all shapen in iniquity, as David testifies." When asked if she had any hope of being saved from sin, she replied, "I am very far from God, yet my only hope is in the wounded side of Jesus Christ. If penitently I stand beneath the blood dropping from his cross, I hope that my sins, though red like scarlet, may become as white as snow." Her views of the way of salvation were not only clear, but beautifully expressed. It was exceedingly refreshing, in that region where they had expected only darkness, thus to find the rays of light struggling through from their associates in another mission; and it gave a delightful foretaste of the time when the voice of one watchman upon those mountain tops should reach to another, and on all sides the eye behold the trophies of Immanuel. It was with feelings of peculiar interest that they heard, some years after, that this stranger in Sanawar, but, as they fondly hoped, their sister in Christ, held fast her confidence in his grace to the end, and so fell asleep in Jesus.

For a companion picture to the preceding, we turn to the summer of 1852. Mr. Stocking moved out to Gavalan, the native place of Mar Yohanan, early in the season, and both teachers followed, with thirteen of their pupils, about the middle of June. The village lies near the base of a range of mountains, at the northern end of the plain of Oroomiah, forty miles distant from the city. On the east, the blue waters of the lake seem to touch the sky, and stretch away to the south in quiet loveliness. Sometimes, when reposing in the gorgeous light of sunset, or reflecting the red rays of the full moon, they remind the beholder of the "sea of glass mingled with fire" revealed to the beloved disciple. The breeze from the lake, in the long summer days, is very grateful, and the evening air from the mountains makes sleep refreshing.

Mar Yohanan gave the school free use of two rooms as long as it remained. In the court yard before them a large tent was pitched, that served for dining room, dormitory, and reception room, or diwan khaneh. An adjoining house afforded a comfortable recitation room. Here the regular routine of the school went on, and while men from the village found their way to Mr. Stocking's at the hour of evening prayer, women also came to the school room at the same hour. At the last meeting of this kind before Miss Fiske returned to the city, nearly forty were present, listening with quiet attention to the words of life. On the Sabbath, the sides of the tent were lifted outward from the bottom, and fastened in a horizontal position, so as to admit the air and exclude the sun. The ground beneath was covered with mats, and formed quite a pleasant chapel. In the forenoon, this was thronged with attentive hearers. The children of the boys' school in the village sat close to their teacher. The members of the girls' school could be distinguished from their playmates by the greater smoothness of their hair, the whiteness of their faces, and general tidiness. Among the old men, the venerable father of the bishop was very conspicuous. The members of the Seminary crowded round their teachers so as to leave more room for others, and still all could not get under the shadow of the wings of the tabernacle. Mr. Stocking preached in the forenoon, and in the afternoon the people came together again as a Sabbath school. Each of the pupils of the Seminary had a class of women or girls, and seemed to learn how to do good faster than ever before. They visited them at their houses during the week; they sought out the absentees; and it was delightful to go round the school and note the interest of both scholar and teacher. If these were zealous in teaching, those were no less so in learning. The classes, after the introductory services, filled every available corner in the rooms, the tent, the front of the house, and even sat on the low mud wall of the court. With the same variety of character, there was greater diversity of lessons than in schools at home. Some studied the Old Testament, and some the New; others were just learning to read, and those who could not read at all were taught the Scriptures orally. One class of Armenians was taught in Turkish.

Matters went on very well for two Sabbaths, but on the third, women and children had vanished. What was the matter? It had been reported that all this labor was only a preparation to transport them to America, and the simple-minded mothers staid away with their children in great trepidation; but visits from house to house, during the week, dispelled their fears, and next Sabbath all were again in their places, and this pleasant labor in Gavalan continued till September.

CHAPTER VIII.

EARLY LABORS FOR WOMEN.

FIRST MEETINGS WITH THEM. — FIRST CONVERT. — FIRST LESSONS. — WILD WOMEN OF ARDISHAI.

THE teachers of the Seminary did not confine their labors to its inmates; they expended both time and toil for adult women as well as for their daughters, and never felt that they gave them too large a proportion of their labors. At first there was a strong feeling among most of the women that they might not worship God along with deacons and readers; and so they could not be persuaded to attend public preaching. But Miss Fiske found that a few would come to her room at the same hour; so, encouraged by her missionary sisters whose hearts were in the work, but whose family cares prevented their doing it themselves, she visited the women at their houses, to urge them to come in. Then, as her own knowledge of the language was as yet imperfect (this was in 1844), and she wisely judged that listening to a gentleman would sooner prepare them to come in to the regular service, she secured one of the missionary brethren to conduct the meeting. The first day only five attended; but soon she enjoyed the sight of about forty mothers listening to the truth as it is in Jesus. On the third Sabbath, she was struck with the fixed attention of one of them, and, on talking with her alone, found her deeply convinced of sin. She had not before seen one who did not feel perfectly prepared to die; but this one groaned, being burdened, and seemed bowed to the dust with the sense of her unworthiness. When Miss Fiske prayed with her, she repeated each petition in a whisper after her, and rose from her knees covered with perspiration, so intensely was she moved: her life, she said, had been one of rebellion against God; and she knew that no prayers, fasts, or other outward observances, had benefited her, or could procure forgiveness. In this state of mind she was directed to Christ and his righteousness as her only hope; and though for some time little progress was apparent, at length, as she herself expressed it, "I was praying, and the Lord poured peace into my soul." The change in her character was noticed by her neighbors. From being one of the most turbulent and disagreeable of the women in her vicinity, she became noted for her gentleness and general consistency. She has since died, and her last days were full of a sweet trust in her Saviour. She was the first inquirer among Nestorian women.

This meeting was given up as soon as the women found their way to the regular service; but ever since there have been separate meetings for them at other hours.

Until the revival in 1846, those who conducted these meetings had to labor alone, for there were none of the Nestorians to help them. Indeed, Miss Fiske had been in Oroomiah more than two years, before women came much to her for strictly religious conversation, or could be induced to sit down to the study of the Scriptures.

Some of her first efforts to interest them in the Bible were almost amusing in the difficulties encountered, and the manner in which they were overcome.

She would seat herself among them on the earthen floor, and read a verse, then ask questions to see if they understood it. For example: after reading the history of the creation (for she began at the beginning), she asked, "Who was the first man?" *Answer.* "What do we know? we are women;" which was about equivalent in English to "we are donkeys." The passage was read again, and the question repeated with no better success. Then she told them, Adam was the first man, and made them repeat the name Adam over and over till they remembered it. The next question was, "What does it mean?" Here, too, they could give no answer; not because they did not know, for the word was in common use among them; but they had no idea that they could answer, and so they did not, and were perfectly delighted to find that the first man was called *red earth*, because he was made of it. This was enough for one lesson. It set them to thinking. It woke up faculties previously dormant. The machinery was there, perfect in all its parts, but so rusted from disuse, that it required no little skill and patience to make it move at all; but the least movement was a great gain; more was sure to follow. Another lesson would take up Eve (Syriac, *Hawa*, meaning *Life*). Miss Fiske would begin by saying, "Is not that a pretty name? and would you not like to know that you had a great-great-grandmother called *Life?* Now, that was the name of our first mother — both yours and mine." It was interesting to notice how faces previously stolid would light up with animation after that, if the preacher happened to repeat the name of our first parents, and how one would touch another, whispering with childish joy, "Didn't you hear? He said Adam."

Such were the women who came to the Seminary for instruction; but the teachers also went forth to search out the no less besotted females in the villages; and, as a counterpart to the above, we present an account of labors among the wild women of Ardishai, a village twelve miles south-east from Oroomiah.

When Miss Fiske had been in Oroomiah about one year, Mr. Stocking proposed a visit to Ardishai. So the horses were brought to the gate, one bearing the tent, another the baskets containing Mr. Stocking's children, and a third miscellaneous baggage; besides the saddle horses. The first night, the tent was pitched on one of the threshing floors of Geog Tapa; but as American ladies were a novelty in Ardishai, the party there, in order to secure a little quiet, had to pitch their tent on the flat roof of a house. It was Miss Fiske's first day in a large village, and she became so exhausted by talking with the women, that she can never think of that weary Saturday without a feeling of fatigue. As the village is near the lake, the swarms of mosquitoes allowed them no rest at night; and morning again brought the crowd with its idle curiosity as unsatisfied as the appetite of more diminutive assailants. About nine o'clock, all went to the church, where Mr. Stocking preached, while the women sat in most loving proximity to their strange sisters, handling and commenting on their dresses during the discourse. Mr. Stocking could preach though others talked, and readily raised his voice so as to be heard above the rest. At the close, Priest Abraham, without consulting any one, rose and announced two meetings for the afternoon; one in another church for men, and a second in this for women, who must all come, because the lady from the new world was to preach. So the news flew through the neighboring villages. The good lady called the priest to account for his doings; but he replied, "I knew that they would come if I said that, and you can preach very well, for your girls told me so." He was greatly disappointed, however, when he found that his notice left him alone to preach to the men, while Mr. Stocking preached to some six hundred women, with half as many children. They were a rude, noisy company, not one of them all caring for the truth; and there was no moment when at least half a dozen voices could not be heard besides the preacher's. When he closed, as many as twenty cried out, "Now let Miss Fiske preach." So he withdrew, and left her to their tender mercies. Her preaching was soon finished. She simply told them, that when she knew their language better, she would come and talk with them, but she could not talk at the same time that they did, for God had given her a very small voice, and her words would no more mingle with theirs than oil and water. They said, "Oil and water never mix; but we will be silent if you will come and preach." Months passed on, and she again visited the village. The women remembered her promise, and hundreds came together; but they did not remember to be silent. As soon as she began, they began; and if she asked them to be quiet, each exhorted her neighbor, at the top of her voice, to be still; and the louder the uproar, of course the louder the reproofs. At length Miss Fiske said, "I cannot say any more, unless you all put your fingers on your mouths." All the fingers went up, and she proceeded: "I have a good story to tell you; but if one takes her finger from her mouth, I cannot tell it." Instantly muzzled voices, all round the church, cried, "Be still, be still, so that we can hear the story!" Some minutes elapsed, and the four hundred women were silent. "Once there was an old woman—I did not know her, nor did my father, and I think my grandfather did not; but he told me—" Here commenced many inquiries about said grandfather; but again the fingers were ordered to their places, and their owners told that they should hear no more about the woman if they talked about the grandfather. "Now, this woman talked in meeting, — I should think she must have been a relative of yours, for ours do not talk in meeting, — and after many reproofs she was forbidden to go to church any more if she continued to do so. She promised very faithfully; but, poor woman, she could not be still; then, as soon as she heard her own voice, she cried out, 'O, I have spoken in meeting. What shall I do? Why, I keep speaking, and I cannot stop.' Now, you are very much like this woman, and as I think you cannot stop, I must." By this time their fingers were pressed closely on their lips, and no one made a reply. Having thus secured silence, Miss Fiske took the New Testament, and read to them of Mary, who, she was sure, never talked in meeting; for if she had, Jesus would not have loved her so much. She talked to them about fifteen minutes more, and prayed with them, and they went away very still and thoughtful.

Miss Fiske gave this account to the writer, with no idea that he would print it. But he thinks — and the reader will doubtless agree with him — that in no other way could he convey so vivid an idea of woman as she was in Persia, or the tact needed to secure a first hearing for the truth. Miss Fiske was often called to deal with just such rude assemblages, and by varied methods she generally succeeded in securing attention. In subsequent visits to Ardishai the number of hearers was never again so large; but they came together from better motives, and, as we shall see, not without the blessing of the Lord. In March, 1850, Miss Rice met nearly three hundred women in the same church, some of them awakened, and a few already hopefully pious.

CHAPTER IX.

FRUITS OF LABOR IN NESTORIAN HOMES.

USEFULNESS AMONG RELATIVES OF PUPILS. — DEACON GUWERGIS. — REFORMED DRUNKARD AND HIS DAUGHTER. — MATERNAL MEETINGS. — EARLY INQUIRERS FROM GEOG TAPA. — PARTING ADDRESS OF MR. HOLLADAY. — VISIT TO GEOG TAPA. — SELBY AND HER CLOSET.

Having thus glanced at early labors for women in the Seminary and in the villages, let us now turn to another field of usefulness among the relatives of the pupils, who came to visit them in school; and here we are at no loss for a notable illustration.

In the autumn of 1845, Deacon Guwergis, of Tergawer, — and almost every reader was either priest or deacon, — brought his oldest daughter, then about twelve years of age, and begged for her admission to the Seminary. He was known as one of the vilest and most defiantly dissolute of the Nestorians, and Miss Fiske shrunk from receiving the daughter of such a man into her flock. Yet, on the ground that, like her Master, she was sent not to the righteous, but to the lost, she concluded to receive her. Still the father, during his short stay, showed such a spirit of avarice and shameless selfishness, — he even asked for the clothes his daughter had on when she came, — that she rejoiced when he went away.

His home was twenty-five miles off, in the mountains, and she hoped that winter snows would soon shield her from his dreaded visits. Little did she think that his next coming would result in his salvation. In February he again presented himself at her door in his Koordish costume, gun, dagger, and belt of ammunition all complete. He came on Saturday, when many of the pupils were weeping over their sins; and the teacher could not but feel that the wolf had too truly entered the fold. He ridiculed their anxiety for salvation, and opposed the work of grace, in his own reckless way. She tried to guard her charge from his attacks as best she could; but they were too divinely convinced of sin to be much affected by what he said. His own daughter, at length, distressed at his conduct, begged him to go alone with her to pray. (The window on the right of the central door of the Seminary points out the place.) He mocked and jeered, but went, confident in his power to cure her superstition. "Do you not think that I too can pray?" And he repeated over his form in ancient Syriac, as a wizard would mutter his incantation. His child then implored mercy for her own soul, and for her perishing father, as a daughter might be expected to do, just awakened to her own guilt and the preciousness of redemption. As he heard the words "Save, O, save my father, going down to destruction," he raised his clinched hand to strike; but, as he said afterwards, "God held me back from it." No entreaties of his daughter could prevail on him to enter the place of prayer again that day.

The native teacher, Murad Khan, then recently converted, took him to his own room, and reasoned with him till late at night. Sabbath morning found him not only fixed in his rebellion, but toiling to prevent others coming to Christ. At noon Miss Fiske went to the room where he was. (The two lower windows on the right of the engraving of the Seminary mark the place.) He sat in the only chair there, and never offered her a seat; so she stood by him, and tried to talk; but he sternly repelled every attempt to speak of Jesus. She then took his hand, and said, "Deacon Guwergis, I see you do not wish me to speak with you, and I promise you that I will never do it again unless you wish it; but pledge me one thing: when we stand together in judgment, and you are on the left hand, as you must be if you go on in your present course, promise me that you will then testify, that on this twenty-second day of February, 1846, you were warned of your danger." He gave no pledge, but a weeping voice said, "Let me pray." The hand was withdrawn, and he passed into the adjoining room, whence soon issued a low voice, that Miss Fiske could hardly yet believe was prayer. The bell rung for meeting, and she sent her precious charge alone, while she staid to watch the man whose previous character and conduct led her to fear that he was only feigning penitence in order to plunder the premises undisturbed. She staid till a voice seemed to say, What doest thou here, Elijah? then went and took her place in the chapel; soon the door opened again very gently, and Deacon Guwergis entered; but how changed! His gun and dagger were laid aside; the folds of his turban had fallen over his forehead; his hands were raised to his face; and the big tears fell in silence; he sank into the nearest seat, and laid his head upon the desk. After Mr. Stoddard had pronounced the blessing, Miss Fiske requested Mr. Stocking to see Deacon Guwergis.

He took him to his study, and there, in bitterness of soul, the recent blasphemer cried out, "O my sins! my sins! they are higher than the mountains of Jeloo." "Yes," said Mr. Stocking, "but if the fires of hell could be put out, you would not be troubled — would you?" The strong man now bowed down in his agony, exclaiming, "Sir, even if there were no hell, I could not bear this load of sin. I could not live as I have lived."

That night he could not sleep. In the morning, Miss Fiske begged Mr. Stoddard to see him, and after a short interview he returned, telling her that the dreaded Guwergis was sitting at the feet of Jesus. "My great sins," and "My great Saviour," was all that he could say. He was subdued and humble, and before noon left for his mountain home, saying, as he left, "I must tell my friends and neighbors of sin and of Jesus." Yet he trembled in view of his own weakness, and the temptations that might befall him. Nothing was heard from him for two weeks, when Priest Eshoo was sent to his village, and found him in his own house, telling his friends "of sin and of Jesus." He had erected the family altar, and at that moment was surrounded by a company weeping for their sins. So changed was his whole character, and so earnest were his exhortations, that for a time some looked on him as insane; but the sight of his meekness and forgiving love under despiteful usage amazed them, and gave them an idea of vital piety they never had before. He returned to Oroomiah, bringing with him his wife, another child, and brother, and soon found his way to Miss Fiske's room. As he opened the door, she stood on the opposite side; but the tears were in his eyes, and extending his hand as he approached, he said, "I know you did not believe me; but you will love me — will you not?" And she did love him, and wondered at her own want of faith. In a few days, he was able to tell Mr. Stocking, with holy joy, that two of his brothers were anxiously seeking the way of life. His own growth in grace surprised every one, and his views of salvation by grace were remarkably clear and accurate.

When his daughter returned to school, on the 30th of March, she was accompanied by one of her father's brothers, who seemed to have cast away his own righteousness, and to rely on Christ alone for pardon. As no missionary had conversed with him, Mr. Stocking felt desirous to know how he had been led into the kingdom, and learned that he had promised Deacon Guwergis to spend the Sabbath with one of the native teachers of the Female Seminary. This teacher and others prayed with him, till he threw away his dagger, saying, "I have no more use for this," and in tears cried out, "What shall I do to be saved?" He gave no evidence then of having submitted to Christ, but in his mountain home he seemed to make a full surrender, and became well acquainted with the mercy seat. The native helpers felt that he was moving heavenward faster than themselves. In April, it was found that as many as nine persons in Hakkie, the village of Deacon Guwergis, gave evidence of regeneration, five of them members of his own family; and the whole village listened to the truth which the zealous deacon constantly taught.

He always remembered the school as his spiritual birthplace, and ever loved to pray for it. Once, when rising from his knees in the Male Seminary, where he had been leading in evening devotion, he exclaimed, "O God, forgive me. I forgot to pray for Miss Fiske's school." So he knelt again and prayed for it. And Mr. Stoddard said he did not think there was a smile on a single face, it was done with such manifest simplicity and godly sincerity.

In June, 1846, Miss Fiske visited Hakkie with Mr. and Mrs. Stocking. It was the first time ladies had been in the mountains, and the good deacon was greatly delighted.

Labors were then commenced for females there that have been continued ever since. The annexed sketch will give

MISSIONARY SCENE IN TERGAWER.

a more vivid idea of the nature of such labors than the most accurate description. One day the party was toiling up a rough ascent, and the deacon, as much at home among the rocks as the wild goats, offered his assistance. The reply was, "We get on very well." At once his eyes filled, and he said, "You once helped me in a worse road; may I not now help you?" And his aid was at once gratefully accepted. At the top of the hill, while the party rested, they heard his voice far off among the clefts of the rocks, pleading for them and their relatives in distant America.

After his conversion, the deacon devoted himself to labors for souls, especially in the mountains. One might always see a tear and a smile on his face, and he was ever ready, as at first, to speak "of sin and of Jesus." He traversed the mountains many times on foot, with his Testament and hymn book in his knapsack. In the rugged passes, he would sing, "Rock of Ages, cleft for me," and at the spring by the wayside, "There is a fountain filled with blood" flowed spontaneously from his lips. He warned every man, night and day, with tears, and pointed them to Jesus as their only hope. He rested from his labors March 12th, 1856, and, as his mind wandered in the delirium of that brain fever, he dwelt much on those days when he first learned the way to Christ. He would say, "O, Miss Fiske was right when she pointed out that way;" and then he would shout, "Free grace! free grace!" till he sunk away unconscious. Again he would say, "That blessed Mr. Stocking! O, it was free grace." These were almost his last words. The daughter who prayed with him that first Saturday was by his dying bed, and her voice in prayer was the last earthly sound that fell upon his ear.

It may strike the reader as strange that a man so notorious for wickedness as Deacon Guwergis was, should be allowed in the Seminary; but Oriental notions of hospitality are widely different from ours; and in order to do good to a people, however rude, they must feel that you are their friend. No protection from government can take the place of this feeling of affectionate confidence from the people; and while sufficient help was at hand to repel any overt wickedness, the highest usefulness required that patient love should have its perfect work, and in this case, at least, its labor was not unrewarded.

The usefulness of the Seminary among the relatives of its pupils was illustrated in another case that occurred about the same time. March 2d, 1846, the father of one of the girls called and inquired, with tears, if his daughter was troubled for her sins. Surprised at such an inquiry from a notorious drunkard, he was exhorted to seek his own salvation. He then told how he had been taught the plague of his own heart, and, as a ruined sinner, was clinging to Christ alone. His prayers showed that he was no stranger at the throne of grace. Father and daughter spent the evening mingling their supplications and tears before the mercy seat. The daughter had given more trouble than any in school, and several times had almost been sent away. Four days later, her mother came, and remained several days, almost the whole time in tears, and hardly speaking, except to pray. Her daughter and the pious members of the school were unwilling to let her go till she came to Christ, and she seemed to take him for her Saviour before she left. She was a sister of Priest Abraham, and had been so exceedingly clamorous and profane in her opposition to religion, that her brother had for years dreaded to see her. How did he rejoice, when, instead of the customary oath, he found her uttering the praises of her Saviour! The sister of her husband had been one of the vainest of the vain, wearing an amount of ornament unusual even for a Nestorian; but she no sooner put on the righteousness of Christ than she sold her ornaments, and, giving the proceeds to the poor, clothed herself with that modest apparel which becometh women professing godliness. The husband himself, though an illiterate laborer, preached the gospel while at work in the field, and often took two or three of his associates aside to pray with them, and to tell them of Christ and his salvation.

But these cases must suffice: we can only indicate the ways in which the school became a centre of holy influence, especially for woman; but it is impossible to narrate all the facts.

After the revival, the Seminary was thronged with

visitors, who desired the time to be filled up with religious instruction. That year witnessed a rich ingathering of wives and mothers, brought by their converted husbands and children to be taught the way of salvation. The teacher who received visitors always found enough to do both by day and by night. As soon as there were two praying women in a village, Miss Fiske and Miss Rice sought to establish female prayer meetings; and when they visited a village, the women expected to be called together for prayer; and when the women returned the visit, they each sought to be prayed and conversed with alone. This was done also with the communicants generally three times a year. The prayers and remarks of the pious members of the school often gave a high spiritual tone to the weekly prayer meeting. Occasionally there were maternal meetings; and on such occasions one teacher met with the mothers, and the other with the children in a separate room.

These took the place of the early meetings with women mentioned in the beginning of the chapter, and were very useful.

Nestorian families have been already described in part, but the absence of the religious element in them can hardly be realized by Christians here. They did not believe that a child was possessed of a soul until it was forty days old. This belief affected all their feelings towards children, and their custom of burying unbaptized infants outside of their cemeteries did not serve to correct such impressions.

Family registers were unknown. In 1835, probably not five Nestorians could tell their birthday, and but few knew in what year they were born. Miss Fiske kept a list of all the children, which was read at every meeting; but at first she could record the birth of only the very youngest. The deceased children were written down in a separate page, and it was sad to see how much they exceeded the number of the living. One childless mother, who had buried eleven, was always present; for she said she wanted to pray for the children of others, though her own were not. They assembled in Miss Fiske's room, sometimes to the number of thirty, with such of their little ones as were too small to attend the other meeting, and, seated on the floor around her, were never more happy than when telling their troubles, asking questions, and receiving instructions about family duties, much more specific than could be given on other occasions. Now and then she read to them, from English books, facts and truths adapted to their needs. One good man in Fairhaven, Connecticut, who had heard of this, sent a complete set of the Mother's Magazine, to be used in that way. So interested were they, that many of them walked regularly three miles and back again, under a burning sun, to enjoy these gatherings; and from a monthly, it had to be changed to a weekly meeting. It sometimes lasted three hours, but never seemed to them too long; and, commenced in 1850, it is still kept up with as much regularity as Miss Rice's many other duties will allow. It would be interesting to dwell on its results; but a single incident may suffice. One mother, whose husband was not a Christian, was very regular in private devotion, but thought she could not offer prayer in the family, till her husband became dangerously sick, when, in the agony of her intercession for him, she vowed that, if God would spare him, she would establish family prayer. So, as soon as he was able to bear it, she gathered her children around his bed, and after they had read the first chapter of Matthew, verse about, she led in prayer, and so went on reading the New Testament in the morning and the Old Testament in the evening, till she got through with the whole of the former, before any one of the missionaries knew that she had commenced.

The teachers of the Seminary enjoyed very much the visits of the early inquirers from Geog Tapa, in the summer of 1845, most of whom became hopefully pious the following winter. Let us look in on one visit made towards the end of May. A pupil announces that two women below, wish to see Miss Fiske; and a middle-aged stranger is shown into her room. In answer to the usual inquiry, "From whence do you come?" she replies, "I have come from Geog Tapa, for I have heard that you have repented, and I want to know about it." She has walked six miles on purpose to make the inquiry. "I wish that you, too, had repented," calls forth the reply, "Alas, I have not! I am on my way to destruction." Feeling that the Bible was the safest guide for such an inquirer, Miss Fiske reads appropriate portions, explaining as she reads. The visitor shows a great deal of Bible knowledge for one who cannot read, indicating that she had not been inattentive to the faithful instructions of Priest Abraham and Deacon John, and her questions are numerous and intensely practical. Among other things, she asked, "Is it true, that for one sin Adam and Eve were cast out of Eden?" and on being told that it was so, "There," said she, turning to the unconcerned neighbor, who had come with her, "do you hear that? What will become of you and me, who have sinned so often?" At length prayer was proposed, to which she eagerly and tearfully assented; and though the tongue that commended her to Jesus, in that strange language, might have faltered, the heart did not share in the embarrassment. The woman, like the first inquirer, repeated every word of the prayer in a low whisper, as though unwilling to lose a single syllable. The conversation was then resumed till it was interrupted by the entrance of some of the pupils on business. "Have you finished?" was the woman's eager inquiry. "I wish very much to hear more of these things." Her companion now begged her to go home. "No," was the kind reply; "you may go, but I must stay here to prayers." Evening prayers were earlier than usual that evening for her sake, but still she lingered. She had not yet found rest. Selby, one of Mrs. Grant's pupils, then in the Seminary, now conversed with her; and as there seemed to be a sympathy between them (Selby had recently found peace in believing), they were left by themselves. After supper, Selby remained with her an hour or more, that they might pray together, till it was quite dark, and her friends had sent for her repeatedly. She left, having first begged permission to come in to morning prayers. Morning came, and before sunrise she was again listening intently to the reading of the Word, and, after devotions, left for home, earnestly begging Miss Fiske to come and spend a week in Geog Tapa.

The Seminary was dismissed June 5th. On that day, several hundreds of the parents and friends of the pupils, in both Seminaries, were invited to a simple entertainment, got up in native style. The gentlemen of the mission ate in one room, with the men and boys, and the ladies in another, with their own sex. The confidence and kind feeling manifested by all towards the school was very gratifying. After dinner, the whole company, seated in the court, listened to an address from Mr. Holladay, then about to return home. He spoke to parents and children on their duties, privileges, and responsibilities: towards the close, he spoke of the almost certainty of never meeting them again till the judgment, and bade them an affectionate farewell. His utterance was often choked, and his hearers wept; and well they might, for in him they parted with a faithful friend. During the exercises, the members of the two schools sang twice, to the great gratification of their friends.

That evening most of the pupils went home, all but a few of the girls carrying with them a copy of the four Gospels, in modern Syriac, which they had paid for with their needles.

Miss Fiske left for Geog Tapa on the 14th of June with Mr. Stocking, reaching that place as the people were coming out from evening prayers in the church. The first to welcome them were six pupils, residents in the village, who greeted their teacher with a hearty good will. Next to them came Pareza, the inquirer, changed somewhat in her feelings, but with no loss of religious interest. John, too, was there (the native pastor): he had been busy, day and night, instructing the people, and had taken special care of the pupils, that they might both improve themselves and exert a good influence on others. When Mr. Stocking asked him about matters in the village, "O sir," said he, "it is a very good time here now; very many love to hear the truth; their hearts are very open. O sir, I have very much hope!" After supper, the villagers poured into the room for a meeting, to the number of one hundred, while some thirty or forty more were unable to get in. This was all the more welcome, as no notice whatever had been given. It was a clear moonlight evening, and the groups outside were distinctly visible, through the latticed side of the room. John commenced with an earnest prayer for a blessing on the evening; asking, in his simplicity, that "the people might run after the word like sheep after salt"— a strange expression to us, but most appropriate and striking there. Fixed attention was given to Mr.

Stocking's discourse: then John, who feared that those around the door had not been fed, spoke to them of Zaccheus. "The crowd about him," said he, "did not know his feelings; but Jesus knew them, and loved him; and so, mothers and sisters"—they, as an inferior class, had to take the lowest places while the men were within—"if you have come here to-night with a broken heart, though we have not seen you, Jesus has." He then, with Miss Fiske's pupils, sung a hymn, and the meeting closed. Still, many women lingered; some sitting down by Miss Fiske, and others in little groups, talking over what they had heard; very different from previous visits, when dress and such things were the most interesting themes of conversation. This was the first meeting in the village in which the missionaries noticed much religious interest.

Early in the morning, Miss Fiske's pupils were gathered together for a Bible class. The women soon filled the room. The exercise continued all the forenoon, simply because it could not be closed. It was impossible to send away unfed those who hungered for the word. Among the women were a few men, one of them the husband of the inquirer. He was asked, "Have you and your wife chosen the good part?" He covered his face for a moment; the tears rolled down his cheeks; and then he said, "By the grace of God, I hope we have." His heart was too full to say more.

Soon after noon, Mr. Stocking preached in the church, on the barren fig tree, to a crowded assembly. The heat and the multitude made the place very uncomfortable, but the interest deepened till the close. As soon as they were out of the church, many women crowded around Miss Fiske, some of whom she could look on as truly pious, and more as thoughtful. One, who was the first to be awakened about a year before, seemed now a growing Christian.

On leaving, she said, "Perhaps I shall not see you again till I meet you in heaven." She seemed to be looking forward with humble hope to a sinless home. With others, she had encountered much opposition from her family and friends. She has since entered into rest.

On the 19th, Selby visited Miss Fiske, and in answer to a question about a place for private devotion, "O, yes," said she, "there is a deep hole under our house, like a cellar, and there I go every day to pray."

A brief account of her may not here be out of place. In 1830, when she was an infant in her mother's arms, the cholera in five days carried her father and five of his household to the grave. In 1838, she was one of the first pupils of Mrs. Grant. She learned more rapidly than the rest, and yet was so amiable that she was loved by those whom she excelled. Still, she was a stranger to God, and she felt it. When thirteen years of age, her brother took her out of school, replying to her earnest pleadings, to be allowed to remain, "You have been there already too long." At the same time she was forced to marry a boy twelve years of age, with whom she had never spoken. For days previously, tears were her meat and drink; nor was she the only one that wept. After this, the missionaries seldom saw her, till, one cold Sabbath in the winter of 1844–45, a girl entered the chapel, wrapped, as brides usually are, in a large, white sheet. She was not recognized, of course, till her mother led her forward, saying, "I have brought Selby here to-day to listen to the words of God; she loves them and you very much." She was feeble and much depressed, and expressed a strong desire to return to school. Her father-in-law consented to her teaching in the primary department, on condition that her husband was received into the Boys' Seminary, which was done.

9*

She now manifested much interest in religion, and one day wept much, and inclined to be alone. The next evening, she went to Miss Fiske, distressed with a sense of sin. Said she, "I have lied, and stolen, and sworn; nor that only, but have lived so long without once loving my kind, heavenly Father! When I felt sadly about dying at home, I thought then only of hell; but now my sins — O, how many they are! I never knew before that I was such a sinner." The next day, at her father-in-law's request, she was to spend the Sabbath at home. She was very loath to go, but it was not thought best to try to retain her, and she went. There she found neither closet nor Christian friend, and the house was full of guests from morning till night, whom she was required to entertain. Yet in the morning she returned with even increased interest in spiritual things. Said she, "Two or three times I was left alone for a moment, and then I tried to commit my soul to my Saviour." Those few moments she seemed to value above all price. Not long after, she found peace in Jesus, who became her chosen theme. No wonder she loved to point others also to the Lamb of God, and lead them to the mercy seat.

CHAPTER X.

GEOG TAPA.

DEACON MURAD KHAN IN 1846. — PENTECOSTAL SABBATH IN 1849. — MEETINGS IN 1850 AND 1854. — EXTRACTS FROM JOURNAL OF YONAN IN 1858.

THE village of Geog Tapa is so prominent, and has been so largely blessed, that, though there is not room for a continuous account of the work in that place, we here give a glimpse of its progress in different years.

Deacon Murad Khan, one of the assistants in the Seminary, and a native of the place, spent some Sabbaths there in May, 1846. He took turns with the other native teacher in this, going Saturday, and returning on Monday. He tells us that, after morning prayers in the church, pious men met together to pray for a blessing on the day; twelve of their number then went to labor in other villages, the rest remaining to work at home. Passing through a vineyard, he found hidden among the vines a youth setting home gospel truth to a group of others about his own age. At their request, he expounded the parable of the ten virgins to them till it was time for forenoon service; then they separated, to spend a few moments in private devotion before entering the church.

In 1849, the pious men of the village divided it into districts, and visited from house to house for religious conversation and prayer. Meetings were held daily, and well attended. The most abandoned persons were hopefully converted. Crimes committed twenty-five years before were confessed, and restitution made. One Sabbath in February, Mr. Stocking and Mar Yohanan found a large assembly in the house of Mar Elias, listening to an exhortation from Priest Abraham. Mar Yohanan, who had not been there since his conversion a little while before, was then called on, and spoke of himself as the chief of sinners, having led more souls to destruction than any other of his people, and being all covered with their blood. In regard to his flock he said, the fattest he had eaten, the poorest he had cast away, the lame and the sick he had neglected. He begged them no longer to look to their bishops for salvation, but to repent at once and turn to God. Priest Abraham, then recently awakened, also made a humble confession of his sins as their priest, and besought them, one and all, to attend to the salvation of their souls.

In the afternoon, the church was crowded, and a number, unable to gain admission, retired to a school room, where a meeting was conducted by a member of the Male Seminary. In the church, they sung the hymn, "Come, Holy Spirit, heavenly Dove." Mar Yohanan offered prayer, and Mr. Stocking preached from the text, "Now, then, we are ambassadors for Christ," and produced a very deep impression, which was increased by short addresses from the bishop and others. This was known afterwards by the name of the Pentecostal Sabbath.

In 1850, those previously renewed gained new light, and those whose piety was doubtful — to use Deacon John's broken English, — were "very much firmed." Miss Fiske and Miss Rice spent a day in the village, after the close of their spring term, and had delightful intercourse with about twenty women hopefully pious, and many more inquirers. In the evening, supper was hurried through, and men, women, and children hastened to the house of the pastor. Mr. Stocking preached there to a crowded assembly of men, while the teachers adjourned to a neighboring house, to meet with the women. Their hearts were full at meeting so many for whom they had alternately hoped and feared, now sitting in heavenly places in Christ Jesus; they remembered seeing their first penitential tears, and could hardly restrain their own for joy. The house was full, and in a silence interrupted only by stifled sobs, they communed together concerning Jesus and his grace. It seemed as though God perfected praise that night out of the mouths of babes, by keeping them perfectly still in their mothers' arms; and as the pupils of the Seminary belonging to the village, in their prayers, laid mothers, sisters, and friends at the feet of Jesus, the place seemed near to heaven. Next day, about one hundred and fifty attended another meeting, and it was with difficulty the teachers could tear themselves away. One of the pious mothers could not bear to have her daughter, recently converted in the Seminary, leave her sight; and more than once a day they bowed together at the throne of grace. When this mother met Miss Fiske her feelings were so intense she could only say, "Thank God," over and over, and weep. Her husband was moved by his child's anxiety for his salvation. Once, when she urged him to pray, he replied, "I cannot; but you may pray for me." She at once knelt and interceded for him, with many tears. The gray-headed man knelt also, deeply moved, and tears flowed from eyes not used to weep. When she ceased praying, she rose; but his strength was gone; he could not rise. Yet the love of the world was strong within him, and it is to be feared that he resisted the Holy Ghost.

In 1854, Miss Fiske found about sixty families maintaining family prayer, and hardly a family in which there was not some one that seemed to be a true disciple. John held a prayer meeting Sabbath morning with those whom he sent out, two and two, to preach in the neighboring villages, and in the evening they reported what they had done. Sabbath school commenced about nine o'clock, and before it opened, almost all were reading or listening to those that read; and then the school continued in session two hours, without a sign of weariness. The number wishing to learn to read was so large that it was difficult to provide for them. Men came begging good teachers for their wives, and women came pleading for spelling books for their husbands. After school, at their own request, Miss Fiske met twenty-one girls, who had been members of her school (twenty of them now teachers in the Sabbath school), and gave them a word of counsel and encouragement in their work. At the close of afternoon service, the women who could read staid with her till near sunset, they never so thankful before, and she never more thankful to be with them.

The next glimpse we take of Geog Tapa shall be from a native standpoint. A young man of the village, possessed of more than ordinary abilities, was early taken into the Male Seminary. His influence over the rest was so great, and so decidedly opposed to religion, that he was about to be sent away, when grace made him the first fruit of the revival in 1846. Yonan (for that is his name) was a teacher in the Female Seminary from 1848 till 1858, and, as he was generally accustomed to spend his Sabbaths in his native village, on Monday morning he handed in to Miss Fiske a written report of the labors of the previous day; and from these we now give some extracts:—

"*January 17th*, 1858. I had a pleasant time in morning

family prayer, at which several young persons were present. The Sabbath school was followed by a meeting, at the close of which I returned to my room with four young men. I talked with them about two hours, first about coming to church, — for they attend only occasionally, — and in this they promised to do better. I then questioned until I reached their inmost souls. I asked one, 'What is the distance between you and God?' 'My teacher, there is a very great distance between us.' 'Is it God's fault, or yours?' 'It is mine.' I then looked on another, noted for his wickedness, and said, 'Beloved, did not Christ come for you? His stripes, his anguish, his crucifixion, — were they not for you? Why, then, treat him so ill? Has he left the least thing undone for you?' He admitted the truth, but seemed like a rock. At length I said to them, 'Now, Satan has provided something or somebody outside the door, to drive these thoughts from your hearts.' One replied, 'True, Satan has let down all the nets of the Sea of Ardishai[1] for us.' I prayed for them, and they left me, serious. Then I prayed for them alone. Soon my little sister Raheel came in, who is under Papal influence. I talked with her about prayer to the saints, and opened to the ten commandments, and began to read; but she did not want to hear. My heart yearned over my poor sister, and I prayed with her.

"Moses preached in the afternoon about Achan, and after that I had my usual meeting with the pious women. Guly returned with me for conversation. I think she is a blessed Christian. She labors and prays with two of her companions. She told how her cousin ridiculed her, and I encouraged her to go forward, but said, 'If all the world think you a Christian, don't rest till you can say, "I know

[1] Lake of Oroomiah.

in whom I have believed."' We prayed together, and O, what a prayer she offered! Deacon Siyad led the evening meeting.

"*January 24th.* After morning service, I took Baba Khan and Guwergis to my room. The first I had labored with last year, and thought him interested. His wife fears God, and has often asked me to talk with him. He is seldom absent from church or prayer meeting, and often goes out with our young men when they preach. This was my thought in talking with him: 'Near the kingdom, but not in it.' I earnestly pressed these questions: What do you think of yourself? What is your dependence for salvation? Have you repented? In short, on which side are you? He was troubled; tears ran down his cheeks, and for a time he made no reply. At last he said, 'I cannot tell.' A companion began to answer for him, with the confidence of ignorance, judging Christians and finding holes in the coats of the righteous: 'Who knows whether a man is a Christian? God alone.' I said, 'Are there any Christians in our village?' 'Yes.' 'Then you know some as Christians?' His words were many, while Baba Khan's were few. My father here came in, but I prayed with them all, and then went to church, where I preached from the words, 'And thou mourn at the last.'

"To-day I conversed with Sadee. I found her in the habit of praying with her sisters in Christ one by one. I advised her to try and lead some of her unconverted neighbors to Christ by her labors and prayers. She promised to do so. We spent more than an hour speaking the language of Canaan, and then knelt at the feet of the Saviour whom we love. She prayed, spreading out her hands to heaven, as I think the early saints used to do; and it seemed as though God would fill us with blessing in answer to that prayer. She left me alone, and thanking God for these blessed opportunities to labor.

"*January* 31*st.* After meeting, conversed with Munny, daughter of Mukdesseh. It was profitable to talk with her. She said that her sainted mother used to say, "When my heart is cold, I go to Christ, and never rise from my knees till he warms it." She has some hope for her husband, and also fear, since he does not forsake wine. She told of a woman for whom she had prayed and labored five or six years, and promised to do so with others. O, what a sweet savor of piety did I receive from her! If we had many such mothers in Geog Tapa how changed it would be! I cannot write all our pleasant words; they remain for eternity.

"*February* 7*th.* I took home from Sabbath school two young men, for whom I have fears because they drink too much wine. I talked long with them, not as though I would take a pledge from them, or that it is a sin ever to drink at all, for I thought this would not be profitable; but I asked them questions, that they might themselves distinguish what is right; as, 'Does wine make you to sin?' They owned that it did. Their hearts seemed won to the right, but the work is the Lord's. May he save them from this temptation.

"In the afternoon, I began to talk with Sanum without feeling, but ended in tears. I did not ask questions, but carefully explained the difficulties and the fight of faith, also the special grace of God to his people. When I said to her, 'I want you to enlarge your heart, and take in one more besides the two women whom you now labor with,' she selected a very ignorant one. I am afraid that I do differently, seeking rather an easy work.

"*February* 22*d.* This afternoon I sent for Nargis. I

10

had never thought of her as a Christian, but I found that I was greatly mistaken. It is all my own fault. I had seldom met her, and never prayed with her. I commenced: 'Do you think yourself a Christian?' 'I do.' 'How long have you thought so?' 'About eight years.' 'How is it that I have not known it?' 'Yakob was my pastor, and since he left I have had none.' Then she told of her awakening, and sufferings for Christ's sake, between her betrothal and her marriage. 'I used to go to evening meetings with Yakob, and on my return my uncle would take me by the braids of my hair and throw me on the ground, saying, "You go because there are young men there." Sometimes I found the door barred against me; then I went to a neighbor's to lodge, or oftener to the stable, and slept in a manger; but I was never afraid, for Christ was with me: for a time my betrothed wished to put me away. It was then I found Christ, and I have never forsaken him since.' She is now poor and in distress. She attends church and Sabbath school, but cannot go to evening meeting, as her two little children keep her at home. She lamented this, not thinking that she could serve Christ in the care of these little ones. I told her, 'I preach that prayer and the care of children are equally a duty.' She was greatly comforted: these words seemed like oil poured into the flickering lamp. I gave her the 'Green Pastures,' and prayed with her. I have great confidence in her piety.

"On Friday forenoon, I saw Martha, the wife of Eshoo. I trust she has grace in her heart; and her husband hopes that he is a Christian, but looks after her more than himself. She sees him not doing right, and tells him in love; he is not pleased. Still, she thinks him a Christian. She wished I would talk to them together, that their path might be one. I told her I did not think it best that she should talk much to him, but be very quiet, pray for him, be obedient to him, and hope to win him by her chaste conversation coupled with fear. She received my words well.

"*February* 28*th*. I talked with Moressa. We hoped, seven or eight years ago, that she was a Christian; but her husband soon prevented her attending meeting, and so she remained, till lately she came to church again. I did not know that one of the sisters in Christ had prayed regularly with her all this while, but supposed that she had gone back to her dead forms, and that God moved me to call her to repentance. But I found her trusting that she had been set in Christ's breastplate, the light of which can never go out. I said, 'Do you think you love the Saviour?' 'Yes, as the apple of my eye.' 'Are you sure that you have not forsaken him in all these years?' 'I have been very sinful all the time, but do not think I have taken my hand from Christ.' My heart was now drawn towards her. I said, 'Moressa, forgive me. I have been an unfaithful shepherd. I have not once searched for you. I confess my faults.' 'I have faults. I have been a wandering sheep, forsaking the fold.' 'Have you kept up secret prayer during all these years?' 'I have.' I found that she had learned to read at home, and I gave her a Testament. I have a good hope for her; but how negligent I have been! There may be many Christians unknown."

These extracts might be extended; but enough have been given to illustrate the inner workings of Nestorian piety, and the labors of those so appropriately called "native helpers." It was such men that Paul called his helpers in Christ Jesus.

The women of Geog Tapa, in a letter to Miss Fiske,

written Feb. 1861, thanking her for her labors among them, say, "We often think, What are we more than the women of other nations, that we should have such heavenly blessings? and are ready to cry, Blessed is the dust of the land that sends forth such good news, and makes known the way of life to the world." They add, that at their last communion more than eighty souls sat down at the Lord's table; and it seemed as if He who sitteth between the cherubim was present in the church.

CHAPTER XI.

REVIVAL IN 1846.

PREPARATORY WORK. — SANCTIFIED AFFLICTIONS. — NAME FOR REVIVAL. — SCENES IN THE SEMINARIES IN JANUARY. — DEACON JOHN, SANUM, AND SARAH. — MR. STODDARD. — YAKOB. — YONAN. — MEETING IN THE BETHEL. — PRIEST ESHOO. — DEACON TAMO. — PHYSICAL EXCITEMENT AND ITS CURE. — ARTLESS SIMPLICITY OF CONVERTS. — MISSIONARY BOX. — MEETINGS BEFORE VACATION. — MR. STODDARD'S LABORS. — FEMALE PRAYER MEETING. — REVIVAL IN THE AUTUMN.

THE first revival in Oroomiah seemed to burst forth like a fountain in the desert. Yet, as such a fountain, though springing full grown from the earth, is connected with unseen arrangements working out that visible result, so was this revival connected with an extended process of preparation. For years there had been a laborious inculcation of divine truth, especially in the Seminary. True, there had been few conversions; but those few were an essential part of the preparatory work. The roots of this revival extended back as far as the conversion of Deacon John, in 1844. Even in those still unconverted, there had been a wonderful preparation of the way of the Lord. No one could compare the condition of the places yet unblessed by missionary labor, with those so favored, and not feel this. Religious education had made a marked improvement in the appearance of the pupils of both Seminaries, in their personal habits, their intelligence, and especially in their knowledge of the doctrines of the gospel. Old superstitions had lost their hold; they could no longer trust in fasts and ceremonies, and they had an intellectual understanding of the way of salvation through a Redeemer. True, all this did not necessarily involve a spiritual work; but God is pleased to have the way thus prepared for that Spirit who sanctifies through the truth. Those who had received the most instruction were the first to come to Christ, and have since lived the more consistent Christian life.

Then, in the good providence of Him who always observes a beautiful order in the manifestations of his grace, other influences tended to the same result. The very delay of the blessing called forth earnest prayer from the husbandmen who were waiting for precious fruit, and had long patience for it, till they received the early and the latter rain. The trials which the missionaries had passed through in 1845 also tended to produce that despair of help from themselves which usually precedes blessing. In 1844 they numbered sixteen souls; but in 1846, from various causes, they were diminished to ten. These were not discouraged, but remained at their post confident that labors in the Lord cannot be in vain. Then the persecution under Mar Shimon shut them up to God as their only hope, while it rid them of some native helpers, who cared chiefly for their own temporal advantage. The army of Gideon, on all sides, was being diminished in order to secure obedience to that precept, "He that glorieth, let him glory in the Lord." The feeling was general, "all our springs are in God." One of the missionaries said, in the autumn of 1845, "God never formed a soul that Christ cannot redeem from the power of sin. I know this people are sunk in sin and degradation; but Jesus died to save them, and we may see them forever stars in his crown of rejoicing, if we are only humble and faithful enough to lead them to the Saviour."

At the time of the revival, Dr. and Mrs. Perkins resided at Seir, and Dr. and Mrs. Wright were temporarily with them in that village. Mr. Breath was in the city, but using the Turkish mainly, he never ventured to give religious instruction in Syriac; so that Mr. Stocking and Mr. Stoddard were the only laborers in Oroomiah. They lived on the mission premises already described; and at that time the Male Seminary occupied a building in the same enclosure.

One day in the autumn of 1845, Mr. Stocking, Miss Fiske, and Deacon John were riding together, when John asked in English, "If we ever have a revival here, what shall we call it?" Mr. Stocking replied, "Let us get it first; then we will find a name;" and when it did come, the pious Nestorians at once called it "an awakening."

Towards the close of December, Mr. Stocking noticed repeated indications of deep seriousness among the pupils of Mr. Stoddard, and felt that they were on the eve of a revival. About the same time, Deacon John was more active in labor, and earnest in prayer. In the Seminaries, the teachers did not think so much of what their pupils were, as of the power of God to make them like himself. They labored in hope, expecting a blessing; but it came sooner than they looked for, and in larger measure. The first Monday of the new year, January 5th, was spent as a day of fasting and prayer; and the missionaries had just begun to pray, when they found that some were praying for themselves. Miss Fiske went into her school, as usual, at nine o'clock, and, after telling her flock that many prayers were being offered for them that day in a distant land, led their morning devotions, and then sent them into another room to study with a native teacher. Sanum and Sarah lingered behind the rest; and as they drew near, she asked, "Did you not understand me?" They made no reply; and she saw they were weeping. "Have you had bad news?" Still no reply; but when they got near enough, they whispered, "May we have to-day to care for our souls?" and Sarah added, "Perhaps next year I shall not be here." There was no private room to give them, but they made a closet for themselves among the fuel in the wood cellar, and there spent that day looking unto Jesus; nor did they look in vain. Their teacher did not know where they had gone, till, long after one of them had died, the survivor gave her an account of that memorable day.

On Sabbath evening, January 18th, the words at the English prayer meeting were few; but the prayers carried the dear pupils and laid them at the feet of Jesus. At the close of the meeting, Mr. Stoddard was lighting his candle to go home, when Mr. Stocking asked if he saw any indications of interest in his school. There was no reply; but the expressive face, and the candle dropping unnoticed as he held it, showed that thought was busy, and the heart full. At length he said, with deep feeling, "I should expect to see interest if we felt as we ought to feel;" and passed out. All were impressed with his manner, so earnest, yet so humble. He retired to his study, called John, and talked with him on the state of the school. He proposed that they should each day make some one pupil a subject of special prayer and personal effort, and begin that night with Yakob of Sooldooz. They prayed together for him, and then he said, "John, I want to talk with him to-night; we don't know what may be on the morrow; go and call him." Yakob, who had acted badly in meeting that day, came, expecting to be punished; but when Mr. Stoddard kindly asked him to come and sit down by him, and, taking his hand, said, "Have you ever thought that you have a soul to be saved or lost?" he broke down at once. He confessed that the whole school had combined to shut out the subject from their thoughts, but really felt so uneasy, that if one of them should be brought to Christ he thought all would follow. Then the good man, who was so distressed that day because he could see no impression made by the sermon, thanked God and took courage. Not willing to devote Monday to Yakob alone, he conversed with another of the same name, and he too went away weeping to his closet. The two had been in the recitation room but a little while before their feelings became so intense that they had to ask leave to retire. "It is God!" "It is God!" was whispered from seat to seat; and at noon a group collected to discuss what was to be done. One proposed to rise up against the work, and put it down; but at length Yonan of Geog Tapa said, "I don't want to be a Christian; I don't mean to be; but I am afraid to oppose this; we had better let it alone. If it is God's work we cannot put it down, and if it is man's work it will come to nought without our interference." Nothing more was said, but before school commenced that afternoon, some of those boys were on their knees in prayer.

In the evening, Mr. Stoddard sent for two leaders in the opposition, very promising scholars, but of late forward in every thing that was evil — one of them this Yonan, and as he himself told afterwards: "Mr. Stoddard said, 'If you do not wish to be saved yourselves, I beg of you, from my inmost soul, not to hinder others;' and eternity so opened up before me, that I was ready to be swallowed up. I longed for some one to speak to me of the way of escape; but no such word was spoken to me that night. I could not sleep, for I was almost sure there was but a step between me and death." Late on Thursday evening, the other Yonan, of Ada, came to Mr. Stoddard in extreme agitation, who conversed with him a while, and then left him there to pray alone. That night he too could not sleep. The years he had spent in sin rose up before him in the light of God, and filled him with anguish; but next morning, in conversing with Mr. Stoddard, he seemed to find rest in submitting to sovereign mercy.

On Monday evening, the indications of interest in the Female Seminary were such, that the teacher invited those disposed to seek salvation at once, to come to her room at five o'clock. Before that hour, a number had retired to pray for themselves. Just then, Mr. Stoddard came to the door of the teacher, saying, "I cannot stop; but I wanted you to know that four or five of my boys are much distressed for their sins." This was the first intimation she had of what was taking place in the other school; and she turned away from Mr. Stoddard to find five of her pupils in the same condition. Mr. Stoddard came in again, in the course of the evening, to pray and consult; and Mr. Stocking gave up every thing else to labor with the pupils in both schools. Both Dr. Perkins and Dr. Wright came down frequently from Seir. Every day brought out new cases of those who were being taught of God. Wednesday evening, at the conclusion of a sermon from Mr. Stocking, on the words, "Behold, I stand at the door and knock," no member of the Male Seminary seemed willing to leave his seat. After a few words of exhortation, they were dismissed to their rooms; but so intense were their feelings that they came in crowds to the teacher's study, where he preached Jesus Christ, and forgiveness through his blood, till near midnight; then, fatigued and exhausted, he retired to rest. Thursday evening, in the English prayer meeting, Mr. Stoddard said, "God will assuredly carry forward his own work. Let us give ourselves up to labor for him, in pointing these precious souls to Christ." After the meeting, the teachers of both Seminaries left to engage in that blessed work till midnight. Eleven years after, on the same evening, and about the same hour, one was called to see the other pass from earth into the presence of the Saviour whom he then set forth so faithfully. No wonder the survivor recalled it in the hush of that parting scene.

It is difficult to describe the occurrences of this eventful week. The teachers' rooms were in such demand as closets for the pupils, that they could hardly command them long enough for their own devotions. They were ready to write "Immanuel" on every thing around them. The girls were very free to express their feelings, and they had such perfect confidence in their teacher, that often, during the revival, some of them woke her in the morning, standing at her bedside, with some inquiry about the way of life.

The two schools hardly knew any thing of each other till Friday evening, when they met in a room fitted up for the Female Seminary the preceding autumn. The first time Mr. Stoddard entered it after this, he looked round, and said, "May this room be wholly consecrated to the Lord forever;" and this evening Christ seemed to take possession of it. The boys sat on one side, and the girls on the other; and seldom, perhaps, has there been a company more under the influence of things unseen. It seemed as though God himself spoke that evening through his ministering servants, and this and that one was born there and then. It was in the same room that that last prayer meeting of the teacher with her former pupils was held, July 15th, 1858. In the engraving, the two upper windows, immediately to the left of the small ones over the central door, belong to this room.

At the close of the week, ten of the pupils were trusting in Christ; and of the next Lord's day it might truly be said, "That Sabbath was an high day," for the Lord was present, and many strong men bowed before him. Priest Eshoo had watched the boys; he had watched his own praying Sarah; and now he looked within. He had never been known to weep; he scorned such weakness; but when, at the close of the afternoon service, Mr. Stocking took his hand, saying, "Be sure you are on the right foundation," he buried his face in his handkerchief and wept aloud. Nor did he weep alone; Deacon Tamo, too, — whose levity all through the week had been a sore trial to Mr. Stoddard, so that he had asked, "Can it be that God has let him come here to hinder the work?" — now trembled from head to foot. Mr. Stoddard prayed with him, and as they rose from their knees, Tamo looked him in the face, and, with streaming eyes, said, "Thank you, thank you for caring for my soul."

During the following week, most of the inmates of both Seminaries were deeply convinced of sin, and daily some souls seemed to come to the Saviour.

But some things rendered it apparent that the interest was not all from above. One evening, fifteen or twenty boys were found rolling on the floor, groaning and crying for mercy. Measures were taken at once to prevent the repetition of such a scene, and at evening prayers Mr. Stocking commenced his remarks by asking if any of them had ever seen the Nazloo River, at Marbeeshoo, near its source. Startled by what seemed a very untimely question, a few answered, "Yes." "Was there much water in it?" Wondering what he could mean, the answer was, "No; very little." "Did it make much noise?" "Yes; a great deal." The catechist went on: "Have you seen the same river on the plain?" By this time, every ear was listening, and all replied, "Yes." "Was it deep and wide?" "Yes; it was full of water." "And was it more noisy than at Marbeeshoo?" "No; it was very quiet and still." The parable was now applied very faithfully. He said that he had hoped the Holy Spirit had been teaching them the evil of their hearts; but their noise and confusion that evening showed him that there was no depth to their experience. The effect was wonderful; they hung their heads and quietly dispersed, and from many a closet that night might have been heard the petition, "Lord, make me to know my heart, and let me not be like that noisy river." What threatened to be an uncontrollable excitement became at once a quiet but deep sense of guilt. Their desires were not less intense, but more spiritual; their consciences were very tender, and their feelings contrite, but subdued and gentle.

In this revival, the converts had a great deal of feeling, but no knowledge of the mode in which such feelings find expression in Christian lands; and in the freshness and strength of their emotions they yielded to every impulse with an unconscious simplicity that was exceedingly interesting. If they were under conviction of sin, that found immediate and unrestrained utterance. If they thought they were forgiven, that, too, at once found expression. There was a wonderful transparency of spirit that revealed each varying aspect of their feelings, and withal a tendency to undue excitement that needed careful handling. Indeed, it was found necessary to watch their social meetings very closely, and sometimes to direct them to pray alone.

For three weeks, very few visitors came to the Seminary. The time seemed to be given expressly for the benefit of the pupils, and it was like one continual Sabbath. Every corner was consecrated to prayer, and most of the work was direct effort for the salvation of souls. But after that, visitors began to come, and then the young converts became helpers in Christ Jesus, even the sight of their devotion turning the thoughts of others to spiritual things. Often ten or fifteen women spent the night on the premises; and at such times, all the spare bedding was brought into the great room, which was transformed into a dormitory. The teacher often staid with them till midnight, and then, from her own room, could hear them praying the rest of the night. In connection with this, one incident claims our notice. One day in February, a box arrived from America for the Seminary; but so engrossed was the teacher with more important duties, that it was midnight ere she could open it. Next morning, all were invited to her room, to see the contents. She told of the kind friends who had sent it, and the love of Christ, that constrained to such kindness. They were moved to tears, but not one rose to examine the things, and not a word was spoken, till the proposal was made that the quilts should be kept for the use of their friends who came to hear the word of God. All joyfully agreed to that, and then, after looking at the articles, they returned to pray for their benefactors.

The last meetings of the school before the March vacation were called thanksgivings, and fitly, too, for in the two Seminaries as many as fifty souls had begun to love the Saviour. When they left, the universal cry was, "Pray for us." "Pray for us in the temptations that await us at home." One little girl said, "Did you ever see a new-born lamb cast into the snow and live? And can we live?" Thank God, most of the hopeful converts did live, and we trust are to live forever, with the good Shepherd who gave his life for their salvation.

It does not fall in with the design of this volume to give a complete account of the revival, but we cannot leave it without a word more about the instrumentality of Mr. Stoddard in connection with that work of grace. He was abundant in preaching. He did not think that the most ordinary sermons are good enough for the mission field; for he knew that the Nestorians could discriminate as well as others nearer home, and so wrote out his sermons carefully in English, but in the Syriac idiom, noting on a blank page the books consulted in their preparation. He also excelled in labors for individuals. The first inquirer became such while Mr. Stoddard pressed home upon his conscience his guilt as a sinner against God; and the same is true of many others. After conversing with a person, he always led him to the throne of grace, and then had him present his own offering there; and after such a one had left, he seemed unable to turn his thoughts to any thing else, till again in private he had commended him to God. Indeed, he often began to do this before they descended the stairs. He kept a little book, in which he recorded every case, the state in which he found the person, and any subsequent change; and it was noticed that where he began, he continued to labor, not only till there was hope, but even assurance of hope. Such labor is as exhausting as it is delightful; and no wonder his strength proved less than his zeal and love.

It was a great joy to him when his people could take

part in prayer meetings. He divided the thirty converts among them into three circles, and met each of them twice a week: this furnished him a season of refreshment every day, and each of them took part at least once a week. They were thus early initiated into a course of Christian activity, and taught that they would lose much themselves, besides failing to do good to others, if they held back. The converts were so rooted and grounded in this truth, that once, when Miss Fiske was in Geog Tapa, a brother said to her that she must not leave the village till she had induced a woman to pray with her, whom they all regarded as a Christian, but who would not take part in their female prayer meetings; and when she objected to urging her, Deacon John replied, "If she was an ordinary Christian, we might let her pass; but her position is one of such prominence, that the other women will do just as she does; and so she must do right." Miss Fiske talked long with the delinquent, but she insisted that she could not do it. The missionary told of her own trials in the matter, — how she had staid away from meeting lest she should be called on, and remained unblessed till she was willing to do her duty. She prayed with her once and again, even a third time, before she consented, saying, "I will not displease God any more in this." So, drawing very close to her instructor, she offered two petitions for herself, and one that her friend might be rewarded for showing her her duty. Hannah was soon active in the women's meetings, and is to this day a most useful and consistent Christian.

Another marked feature in Mr. Stoddard's labors was his tact in setting others to work for Christ. He taught his pupils that they must toil as well as pray, and soon after the first converts were brought to Christ, definite labor for others was assigned to them, not only among their schoolmates and those who visited the premises, but also in gathering in those not disposed to come to meeting. Once, when three fourths of the pupils were hopefully pious, Mr. Stoddard said, "I must bring in more, just to furnish work for these converts." He himself was happy in his work, because he gave himself wholly to it, without the least reservation; and amid the many trials that marked the years of his residence in Persia, he looked beyond them all, to Him who not only can give joy in suffering, but, by means of it, bring sinners to the Saviour.

The hopeful converts in the Seminary, after spending the summer of 1846 at their own homes, in circumstances of great trial and temptation, returned, all save one, not only retaining their interest in spiritual things, but established in Christian character. Their friends also testified to their thoughtfulness, prayerfulness, and cheerful obedience at home, and the influence of their piety was happy on others.

For a while, in the autumn of 1846, the school was disbanded on account of the cholera. But, contrary to the fears of many, after a separation of two months, all were spared to meet again, though hundreds had fallen on all sides. Three weeks afterwards, the Christians among them seemed more than usually earnest in prayer for the conversion of the impenitent, and at once the answer came. The first one awakened was Moressa, now the wife of Yakob, of Supergan, and then about fourteen years of age. She had been taken into the family of Mrs. Grant nine years before, and that of Mr. Stocking afterwards. She had received much religious instruction, with apparently little effect; but now her convictions were deep, though she did not submit to Christ for nearly a week after she felt she was lost. Her case deeply enlisted the sympathies of her fellow-pupils, and soon several others passed through a season of deep distress, to rest in the grace of Christ.

One of these was Eneya, sister of Oshana, and now the wife of Shlemon, in Amadia. Her widowed mother had fled with her children to Oroomiah before the Koordish invasion of her native Tehoma. Few children have so deep a sense of sin as she had, or exercise such implicit trust in the Saviour. At that time, her teacher wrote, "May she become a messenger of great good to her countrywomen;" and now, that prayer is being answered in her usefulness in that distant and lonely field of labor. Altogether there were seven who seemed at this time to take the Lord Jesus Christ as their God and Saviour.

CHAPTER XII.

FIRST FRUITS.

SARAH, DAUGHTER OF PRIEST ESHOO. — MARTHA. — HANNAH.

LET us now turn aside to take a nearer view of the first fruits of this revival. The first to ask the way to heaven, to find it, and to enter through the gate into the city, was Sarah, or Sarra, as the Nestorians pronounce it. She was born among the rude mountaineers of Gawar, in 1831. Her father, Eshoo, then a deacon, regarded her at first with the aversion Nestorian fathers usually felt towards their daughters; but her strong attachment to him while yet a child, so won his heart, that when the Koords overran Gawar, in 1835, and the family fled from their smouldering village, he was willing to be seen carrying her on his back, in the same way that his wife bore her younger sister. The family stopped for a time at Degala, and subsisted by begging from door to door, lodging at night in a stable. The fine intellect of the self-taught father soon brought him to the notice of the missionaries; and one day Mrs. Grant, then just about securing her long-cherished desire of a school for girls, asked him, in her winning way, "Have you any daughters? and will you not send them to our little school? The inquiry revived a wish that he had felt while yet in Gawar, that his daughter should learn to read; and in the spring of 1841, when he moved from

Degala to the city, he sent her to the mission school. She had just entered her tenth year — a tall, slender, dark-eyed girl, even then giving indications of her early death, and though often a great sufferer, she applied herself so diligently to study, that she soon became, as she ever continued to be, the best scholar in the school.

The ancient Syriac Bible was the principal text book; and she so far mastered that language as to acquire a knowledge of Scripture rarely attained in any land by a child of her years. She was the walking concordance of the school; and her knowledge of the doctrines of the Bible was even more remarkable. Under the teaching of Mrs. Harriet Stoddard, she had also learned to sing sweetly our sacred music. Still, with all her acquirements, she was destitute of grace; and her declining health led her teacher to feel much anxiety for her salvation.

On the first Monday in 1846, she said to Sanum, one of her schoolmates, who, she knew, was thoughtful, "Sister, we ought to turn to God. Shall we ever find a better time than when so many are praying for us?" They together resolved to spend the day in seeking salvation; and the manner in which they made known this purpose to their teacher, and carried it out, has been already related. (See p. 116). From that day, she never seemed to waver. As soon as she found peace for herself, she sought to make others acquainted with her Saviour; not forgetting, however, that prayer of the Psalmist, "Search me, O God, and know my heart; try me, and know my thoughts. See if there be any wicked way in me, and lead me in the way everlasting." Feeble as she was, she never shrank from labor. Hours every day were spent in her closet, and the rest of her time was sacredly used for Christ. She had much to do with the conversion of the twenty schoolmates whom she was permitted to see in Christ before she went home; and she did much for the women who came to the Seminary. Her teacher never knew a young person more anxious to save souls. Both pupils and visitors loved to have Sarah tell them the way. They said, "We can see it when she tells us." No wonder they saw it, for she seemed to look on it all the time. Her teacher depended much on her, and yet often remonstrated with her for such incessant labors. Still she felt that she must be about her Father's business while the day lasted. Her desires for the salvation of her father seemed to commence with her anxiety for herself; and his feelings were soon so tender that he could not answer an inquiry about his own state without tears. Sarah was the first to know that he had found peace. His first religious intercourse with her was to tell her that he had found Jesus. He had known that she was thoughtful, but was not prepared to find her so full of humble hope and holy joy. Next day, when urged by a missionary to labor for the salvation of his family, he replied, "Sarah knows the way to heaven better than I do. She can teach me far better than I could her." Their previous strong attachment now ripened into Christian love. He never felt that his daily bread had been given him, if he had not knelt with her in prayer, and his heart been lifted up by her petitions as well as his own. Her mother at first scoffed; but soon she, too, sought the Saviour; and her younger daughter, whose evil ways for a time tried Sarah sorely, was also afterwards brought into the kingdom.

Mr. Stocking used to call her "the best theologian among the Nestorians," and often said, "If I want to write a good sermon, I like to sit down first and talk with Sarah, and then be sure that she is praying for me."

Her attachment to the means of grace was strong. She went to every meeting, even after she could not reach the chapel without help. Her emaciated form, her hollow cough, her eye bright with unnatural lustre, all told that she was passing away, but, combined with her sweet singing and heavenly spirit, led her companions sometimes to whisper, as she took her seat in the chapel, "Have we not an Elizabeth Wallbridge among us?" — "The Dairyman's Daughter," in Syriac, had just then issued from the press, and was a great favorite with the Nestorians.

As early as March, it was seen that she must die. Still she clung to the school, and not for nought. She had a mission to fulfil, and her Saviour strengthened her for the work to which he called her. As yet, none of the pious Nestorians had finished their course. With the converts, victory over death was something heard of, but never witnessed; and Sarah was chosen to show them "in what peace a Christian can die." Perhaps the last days of no young disciple were ever watched with more eager interest. "Will Christ sustain us to the last? Will he be with us through the dark valley? Will he come for us and receive us to himself, as he promised?" These were to them momentous questions; and they stood ready to answer them according as the Lord supported her. Ever since her death they have looked upon the last change from a new point of view. But we must not anticipate.

The five months between her conversion and her decease were very precious to all who knew her. She sometimes sat with her teacher and talked an hour at a time on the home of the blessed. She seemed to look in upon its glories, and share its gladness; and then her thoughts turned to the perishing around her, saying, "I would labor a little longer for them, if it is my Father's will." The young converts whom she had taught could not bear the thought of her leaving them; but they sought to stay an angel in his course. The dross had been consumed, and the spirit was made meet for the inheritance of the saints in light.

About the middle of May, it was felt that she must go home to her father, whose house was near the Seminary. It was a beautiful day in a Persian summer. The morning

COURT YARD OF THE FEMALE SEMINARY.

exercises were closed. When her teacher told her what they thought, she replied in a whisper, "I think I had better go, but I want to be alone a little before I leave not to return." With weary step she sought the closet where first she found her Saviour: it was occupied. Perhaps He saw she might think more of the place than was meet; so she spent an hour in another room, and then returned, saying, "I am ready to go now." She went supported by a schoolmate on either side: stopping in the court, she turned to take a last look of the dear home where she had learned of Jesus, and, plucking some of the roses that bloomed by her side, passed on. On the preceding page that court is represented, as seen from the adjoining one. She suffered intensely for a few days. Her disease forbade her lying down, even at night. But still not a day passed that she did not gather some women about her, and point them to Jesus. Her teacher visited her frequently, and often found her with her Bible open, and several women around her bed, to whom she was explaining it. The praying pupils, too, often knelt with her at the accustomed throne of grace.

One Saturday in June, her father was asked if he could go to Tergawer — twenty-five miles distant — and preach. His reply was, "I will see what Sarah says." She said, "Go, father, and I will pray for you." Sabbath morning came, and her teacher saw that Sarah was almost home: she told her so, and once more committed the dear pupil to the Saviour who stood by. She had to return to her duties in school, but first said to her mother, "Send for me when the Master calls for her, for, if I cannot go over Jordan with her, I would at least accompany her to the swelling stream." In the afternoon her sufferings became intense; and losing herself for a moment, she said, "Call my father." They told her where he was. "O, yes, I remember. Don't call him. Let him preach; I can die alone." She then said, "Call Miss Fiske;" and her sister started to go. But the dying one remembered that it was the hour for prayer meeting, and beckoned her to return, saying, "She is in meeting now, with my companions. Don't call her; I can die alone." Perhaps, with that teacher present, her eyes had not so clearly discerned the Lord

Jesus. Her sufferings were now so great, she hardly spoke for an hour. Then she said, in a clear voice, "Mother, raise me, that I may commit my spirit;" for she would never approach her Saviour but on her knees. Supported, as she had been hundreds of times before, by that mother's strong arms, and in the attitude of prayer, she said, "Lord Jesus, receive ——" And there she stopped: prayer had ended. Instead of the closing words of the earthly petition was the opening of the new song in heaven. The Saviour did not wait for the close of her petition before he answered it. The teacher had just sat down with her pupils when the door opened, and a messenger said, "Sarah is asleep!" "Yes," thought she, gratefully, "till Jesus shall say, 'Awake!'" According to Eastern custom, Sarah was buried that same evening (June 13th), and the whole school followed her to the grave, which was close to that of Mrs. Grant. The first fruit of the school appropriately lies by the side of her who planted that tree in the garden of the Lord. At the funeral her teacher was just thinking that Sarah could help her no more, that her prayers and labors were forever ended, when she looked up, and her eye rested on the evening star looking down upon the grave. It was a pleasant thought that she, too, was a star in glory. She was glad that the first to love Christ was the first to go to be with him, and still loves to think of her as waiting for those who used to pray with her on earth. The Christian life of Sarah was short; but she did much, for she taught her people how

"Jesus can make a dying bed
Feel soft as downy pillows are." [1]

[1] For additional facts about Sarah, see Nestorian Biography, pp. 25–40.

After Sarah, like Stephen among the early disciples, had led the way into the presence of her Saviour, Blind Martha was the next to follow.

She was constrained by sickness to leave the school early in the spring of 1847, and go home to her parents in Geog Tapa. Though six miles distant, her schoolmates loved to walk out there to comfort her. They prized no recreation so much as the privilege of going to see her. They read and talked with her about her favorite portions of Scripture, prayed with her, and were never allowed to leave without singing "Jerusalem, my happy home." At such times, one of them said, "Her countenance always showed that her spirit was walking the golden streets." When asked about her health, she uniformly replied, "The Lord helps me;" and when urged to speak more particularly, would say, "Dear sisters, the Lord helps me, and that is enough." When, after five or six of them had prayed in succession, she was asked if she was not wearied, she would reply, "I know that I am weak, but prayer never tires me." So great a privilege was it deemed to be with her, that one morning, when a pious member of the Seminary at Seir was called to leave the village early, he said, "I cannot go till I have prayed with Blind Martha, and got from her manna for the road."

Her companions desired very much to be present when she went home; but this was not permitted. One morning in June, she said, at early dawn, "Mother, the day breaks; I think Jesus is coming for me now; let me go." But seeing no change in her appearance, her mother lay down again, and, when next she woke, found that Jesus had come, and taken her to be with him in his home above. What was that vision of the glory of Immanuel that prompted the cry, "Mother, the day breaks!" from one who never remembered to have seen the light? She became blind in infancy. A smile remained on her pale face; and well might the sight of Him who said, "If I go to prepare a place for you, I will come again and receive you unto myself," leave such a memento of the bliss.

Little Hannah, the youngest member of the school, was suddenly called home the following September, when only eleven years of age. When she first came to Christ, her teacher was awakened one morning by her asking at the bedside, "Is it wrong to wish to die?" "But why do you want to die?" "That I may go and stay with Jesus, and never sin again." This desire never left her. Once she said, with tears, "It seems as if I cannot wait so long to go to my Saviour;" and at another time, "I fear that I have sinned in not being willing to wait till Jesus calls me." Before leaving for vacation, each pupil put up her own things in a bundle, to be laid away till her return. As Hannah was at work on hers, she said to a girl near her, "Perhaps you will open this. I do not think that I ever shall. When you come together in the autumn, I trust that I shall be in the Saviour's school above." So strong was the desire awakened in her by Him who intended soon to gratify it.

While the cholera raged around her in August, she frequently said, "This may be my time to go to my dear Saviour;" and repeated it to her mother on the last morning of her life, but went out as usual to her work in the vineyard. About noon she became unwell, and said to a companion, "I am sick; perhaps I shall die soon." "Are you willing?" "O, yes, I am not afraid to go to Jesus." The disease made rapid progress, and again she said, "I am very sick; I shall die soon: shall we not pray together?" Her young friend led in prayer, and then called on her to follow; but her time for prayer was almost finished. She could just say, "Bless my dear sister; take me gently through the dark river;" when she sunk exhausted, and was carried to the house. A mother bent over an only daughter, and three loving brothers over an only sister; but they could not keep her back from Jesus. She sent for her companions, and they hastened to her bedside. She called for her Testament; but her eyesight was failing her, and she returned it, saying, "I can never use it more; but read it more prayerfully, and love the Saviour more than I have done." She lingered through the night, and rose with the dawn to her long-desired rest in the presence of her Redeemer.

It is remarkable that three timid girls should have been chosen to lead the advance of a great multitude of Nestorians through the dark valley into the light beyond. No member of the Boy's Seminary died till three years afterwards; and only two others of this before 1858 — a period of eleven years; but Infinite Wisdom chose, through such weak and timorous ones, to glorify the power of Christ to bear his people through the last conflict into everlasting rest.

CHAPTER XIII.

SUBSEQUENT REVIVALS.

DEACON JOHN STUDYING BACKSLIDING IN 1849. — WORK IN VILLAGE OF SEIR. — WIVES OF SIYAD AND YONAN. — KHANUMJAN. — WOMEN AT THE SEMINARY. — GEOG TAPA. — DEGALA. — A PENITENT. — SIN OF ANGER. — REVIVAL IN 1856. — MISS FISKE ENCOURAGED. — STILLNESS AND DEEP FEELING. — UNABLE TO SING. — CONVERSION OF MISSIONARY CHILDREN. — VISIT OF ENGLISH AMBASSADOR. — REVIVAL OF 1857. — LETTER OF SANUM.

THE first indication of a work of grace in 1849 was seen in the unusual seriousness of Deacon John. He had been reading Pike's Guide to Young Disciples, and the chapter on backsliding moved him deeply. For a long time, he went mourning his departure from God. One day he was reading aloud in the Seminary, when a missionary came in, and wondering to see him there, asked what he was doing. He replied, "I am studying backsliding; and O, sir, I love it very much;" meaning to say that he loved to study the way back to the enjoyment of God. This state of mind was followed by earnest effort for the salvation of others, and the hopefully pious first passed through a season of deep heart-searching and renewed consecration to God. Under an awful sense of the violation of covenant vows, for many days some of them did nothing but weep and pray. "How unfaithful have I been to my Saviour and to immortal souls!" was the cry on all sides.

One whose Bible was found blotted with tears, had been converted in 1846, and her grief was on account of her unfaithfulness as a follower of Christ. Having thus wept bitterly herself, she was well fitted to lead others to the God of all comfort. Her labors were unwearied, both in and out of school. Indeed, the mission was now so reduced in numbers, that much of the work in this revival was performed by the Nestorians, and they proved themselves very efficient. Naturally ardent, they preached Christ and him crucified with a zeal and faithfulness rarely witnessed in our own land; but their ardor needed careful guiding, for some were, at one time, entirely prostrated by excessive labor.

The pupils of the Seminary, during a short vacation, seemed like angels of mercy to their families and friends. In Geog Tapa, their meetings for women every evening had an attendance varying from thirty to one hundred. Many of these were glad to learn the way of salvation, even from children. Besides this, the older pupils, under the guidance of an experienced native helper, spent much time in personal conversation and prayer with their own sex, as did the members of the other Seminary with the men.

In the village of Seir, the work was very general. In addition to the labors of the pious students in the Male Seminary there, Sanum and Moressa labored from house to house among the women. But hear their own account of what they did, in a letter to Miss Lovell's school at Constantinople; —

"What shall we tell you, beloved, of the great love God has shown to our school and people? For two months we have had such delightful days as we never saw in our lives before. The work of the Lord has also commenced in the villages, and in many there is great inquiry for the way of life. The servants of God are so full of zealous love, that they preach till their strength and voice give way. But again they go on to preach, for the harvest is great, and the laborers few. How should we, with burning hearts, beg the Lord of the harvest to send forth laborers! Can we bear, dear sisters, to see the deadly wings of Satan's kingdom spread out and destroy those bought by the precious blood of Christ? Ought we not rather to wrestle like Jacob till we see the loving wings of the kingdom of the Saviour spread out, and impart life to wounded souls on every side? We hope that your waiting eyes may see greater wonders among your own people than we do here.

"Now we will tell you about the little village of Seir, which contains nineteen houses. God has visited every house; and because the women were much awakened, and had no teacher, the missionaries sent two of us there, not because we were fit for such a work, — for we are deficient in Godly knowledge, and every qualification, — but because God sometimes chooses the ignorant and weak to do him service. And what shall we tell you of the wonders God showed us among those poor women? There was no time in which they did not cry, with tears, 'What shall we do?' 'Woe unto us!' 'We are lost!' When we asked them to pray in meetings, they prayed as if taught of God. We wondered at them very much. In one house, we found a woman beating her head with both hands, crying, 'O my sins! They are so great! There is no pardon!' We tried to reason with her; but if we took her hands from her head, she beat her breast. She said, 'You told me, when you prayed with me the other day, to go to Christ; but he will not receive me, I am such a sinner.' With difficulty we quieted her, and told of the great mercy of the Son of David. We prayed with each woman of the village alone, and they with us, fervently and in tears.

"In one instance, we heard an old man praying earnestly in the stable, and his wife in the house. We waited till they had finished, before we went in, and there we found an old man, perhaps ninety years old, and his wife, also very aged. We spoke with them of the lowly Redeemer, and how he was ready to dwell with them, poor as they were. The tears rolled down their wrinkled faces, and made our own hearts burn within us. The old man prayed with us as if Christ stood right before him, and we prayed with them both.

"There were meetings several times a day, and when they closed, the voice of prayer might be heard on all sides, in the houses and stables. Every family now has morning and evening worship."

In this revival, the native helpers were very much interested for the salvation of their unconverted wives. The families of Siyad and Yonan live in Geog Tapa, and their first visits home were blessed to the conviction of their companions, who soon came to the school, begging to be allowed to stay and learn the way of life. Of course, they were not refused. The wife of Siyad had been a frequent visitor there, but such an opposer of religion, that her coming was always dreaded; but now how changed! Day by day her convictions deepened, till they were overwhelming. Tears were her meat, and prayer her employment, day and night, till, as she said, "The Saviour found her," and she was at rest. Three children and a daughter-in-law joined her in believing, and it was delightful to see the family, not long after, each in his or her turn, calling on the name of the Lord in one of the rooms of the Seminary.

Yonan, the junior teacher of the school, had been married by force two years before, by his wicked father; that, too, when his heart was fixed on another, every way fitted to be his companion. It was a severe trial; but grace triumphed, and his great desire seemed to be the conversion of the wife thus forced upon him. At midnight, he was often heard interceding for her, and, in the early part of the revival, the answer came. Miss Fiske will never forget the time when, in an adjoining room, she heard her for the first time praying with her husband. It gave her a new insight into the meaning of that scripture, "They believed not for joy." The new convert was very active among the women in her village; and when her father-in-law forbade social prayer in his house, she took her little company at sunset behind the village church, where even the bleak winds of February did not chill their devotions.

Khanumjan, the aged mother of John, though past threescore and ten, entered into the work with a zeal that might put to shame many younger women in our own land. She toiled to bring the more aged women right to the cross, taking them one by one into her own closet, that then and there they might accept the Saviour. Though herself unable to read, she did much for the preachers who went out to the villages, providing food for them on their return, and exhorting them to courage and faithfulness. No wonder she said to a visitor, "Three years ago, I saw Christ in heaven, and I have seen him there ever since; but now he sits by my side all day long." When she died, she said, over and over again, "I am going after Jesus."

In this revival, the encouragement to labor for woman was greater than ever before. After the middle of January, the Seminary was almost constantly thronged with inquirers. Day and night, it was consecrated by the prayers and tears of women seeking their Saviour. On

Friday, and on the Sabbath, many from the neighboring villages spent the time there between services. The room was filled with them; and even while they ate, they must have some one speaking to them of Jesus. Those who did so, often spoke with such tenderness as showed that Christ himself was very near. Sometimes the women could not eat any thing but the bread of life. At times, the anguish of some for sin was so overpowering, that the question, "Can a woman forget her sucking child?" might almost have been answered in the affirmative. In some instances, the scenes that took place were too much for frail nature to bear, and the laborers were ready to ask to be clothed upon with immortality while the Lord passed by. Those who spent the night in the Seminary slept in the large room on the lower floor, between the central door and that on the left, in the engraving; and occasionally the sound of their weeping and praying banished sleep from the rooms above them. Yet such hinderance to rest brought a refreshment all its own.

In Geog Tapa, the village ruler was found sitting at the feet of Jesus, and going with the preachers from place to place, to give greater weight to their words; and twenty-five young men, though they could not read, yet did what they could with untiring zeal.

There was an interesting work in Degala, so noted for vice that it was called the Sodom of the Nestorians. The first converted there was a young man employed in the Seminary. He passed through a severe mental conflict before his proud heart yielded; but when it did, he became a living sacrifice to God. One day he came to the teachers, saying, "I have a petition to make; will you receive it?" Supposing it to be some pecuniary matter, they replied, "Tell us what it is." He at once burst into tears, and covering his face with his garment, said, "My village is lost; my family is perishing, and their blood is on my neck; let me go to-night and beg forgiveness for my wicked example, and urge them to flee from the wrath to come." He obtained his request, and left, sobbing aloud. Next morning, he brought his wife and two other women to be instructed. About a week after, Deacon Tamo found in the village several inquirers, and one woman in agony on account of her sins. She had been notorious for wickedness, and so vile as hardly to find one who would associate with her, though now one of the most lovely Christians in any land. The next day, she came to the Seminary, and as soon as Miss Fiske sat down beside her, she threw herself into her lap, crying, "Do tell me what to do, or where to go, to get rid of my sins." She was pointed to the Lamb of God, and one moment her feet seemed to rest on the Rock of Ages, and the next a fresh wave of conviction swept her into the raging sea. So she vibrated between life and death. She was asked to pray. In all her life she had not probably heard ten prayers; but her strong crying and tears showed that the Holy Spirit was her teacher, and the helper of her infirmities. She had learned to pray where her Saviour found a cradle — in the manger — cast out and derided by her friends.

She was first awakened in the Seminary; for one day, as soon as she entered the door, a pupil, then under deep conviction herself, and to whom she was an entire stranger, seized her hand, saying, "My sister, my sister, what are you doing? We are all lost. We must repent, or perish." These words she could not forget, and from that hour sought until she found her Saviour, and then bore ill treatment with such meekness as won others also to Christ.

The desire of the converts for instruction was most

affecting. One of them wept bitterly when asked if she was willing to forsake every sin, saying, "What shall I do? I have one sin so strong that I fear I cannot leave it off." "What is it?" "I cannot live without these words of God. My husband will not let me go to hear them, and anger sometimes rises in my heart at this. Tell me what to do with this sin."

An account of the revival in 1850 will be given in the chapter on the prayerfulness of the Nestorians. After this were instances of conversion each year, but not so marked, or so general, as in 1849. So we pass over the intervening time to dwell a moment on the revival of 1856. That year, the pupils were very studious, and kind in their feelings towards each other and their teachers; but the winter was nearly over before any additions were made to the now diminished number of believers. The teachers mourned; still the heavens were brass, and the earth iron. Christians were lukewarm, and none seemed to have power with God.

Miss Fiske returned from the English prayer meeting Sabbath evening, February 18th, in that desponding state that sometimes follows intense and protracted desire, when its object is not attained. At such times, the sensibilities seem paralyzed, and emotion dies of sheer exhaustion. The pupils had retired; so also had Miss Rice; and she was left alone. Her thoughts brooded over the state of her charge, but she had no strength to rise and carry those precious souls to Christ. She could not sleep, and yet so shrunk from the duties of the morrow, that she longed for a lengthening out of the night, rather than the approach of dawn. Eleven o'clock struck, and there was a knock at the door. Could she open it? Must she see another face that night? She did open it, and there stood one of her pupils, not so without feeling as her fainting heart had imagined. Struck by the languor of her teacher's looks, she inquired tenderly, "Are you very tired?" "No, not very; why do you ask?" "I cannot sleep; our school has been resting on me all day, and I thought perhaps you would help me to pray." The spell was broken; the dry fountain of feeling gushed out afresh, and, with a full heart, she said, "Come in, thou blessed of the Lord." As an angel from heaven, that dear pupil strengthened her teacher that night, and together they carried the whole household to Jesus. When at length she retired, all was sweetly left with Christ, and he whispered peace. She could sleep now, and when morning came there was still peace. "Could ye not watch with me one hour?" was the word spoken to her as she arose; and hardly had she repeated it at morning prayers, before three, in different parts of the room, were weeping. She said little, for she felt it safer to go and tell Jesus their wants and their unworthiness. All day, the feeling in the school was subdued and tender. No one asked, "What shall I do to be saved?" but there was quiet at the table, and quiet in the rooms. The work was done willingly and well, but in silence, and the voice of prayer in the closets was gentle. Tuesday passed in almost perfect stillness. No one said even, "Pray for me." Towards evening, Miss Fiske said, "If there is one who wants first of all to attend to her eternal interests, I would like to see her at half past eight o'clock." At that hour, her door opened, and one entered alone; then another and another, each alone, till the room was full. She closed the door, but still they came. What were her feelings when she looked round on twenty-three, sitting with their heads bowed down in silence? She said little, for she felt that they wanted to hear God, rather than man, and the parable of the prodigal son that evening seemed to come fresh from the lips of Jesus.

Next day, each lesson was recited in its season, and recited well; but tears blurred many a page, and at recess not a few went to be alone with God. At eleven o'clock, Mr. Perkins came in as usual to sing with them. "Bartimeus" was the first hymn. All began it; but some voices faltered on the first stanza, more on the second, and soon the leader's voice was heard alone. He took up the Bible lying on the desk, and saying, "Perhaps some wanderer would like now to arise and go to her heavenly Father," he too read the portion of the night before, and led in prayer. The teachers had to lengthen the intermission at noon, because they could not bear to summon the pupils so early from their closets.

The mission met that afternoon in the Seminary. Mr. Stoddard came down from Seir covered with snow, saying, in his pleasant way, as he opened the door, "We have snowed down this time;" but when he learned the state of things, he said, very tenderly, "You must have thought my speech untimely; I did not know God was so near; but my heart is with you, and I hope we both shall have a large blessing." That meeting was almost all prayer, and the weeks that followed it witnessed a work silent but deep. It was characterized by humble contrition, and much simple dependence on Christ. Most of those twenty-three, before the close of the term, were hoping in his mercy.

Three missionary children were among the converts in this revival, and their conversion did much good to the Nestorians; for, though they had felt their own need of regeneration, they were in doubt about the children of pious parents; but when they saw the children of missionaries weep over sin, and come as lost sinners to the

Saviour, they understood as never before that the entrance into the kingdom was the same for all.

At this time, the English ambassador passed through Oroomiah; and though, when he and his suite visited the Seminary, there was some apprehension felt as to the effect it might have on the religious interests of the pupils, they not only did themselves credit, in the examination he made of the school, but returned from the interview with their relish for spiritual things undiminished. Indeed, the event, which ordinarily would have been more than a nine days' wonder, caused scarce a ripple on the deep current of spiritual emotion.

The Seminary was again blessed in 1857, and the year following Miss Fiske returned from Seir after the funeral of Harriet Stoddard to welcome several who had entered the fold of the good Shepherd during her absence.

The labors of Miss Rice, who had charge of the school (while she was away,) have also been blessed in each of the four succeeding years. During that time, eighteen of the pupils have been received to the communion. The revival in the winter of 1861–62 was, however, more interesting and extensive.

At one meeting in the Male Seminary, the young men burst into tears while singing the hymn, "Alas, and did my Saviour bleed?" and soon after, in the Saturday evening meeting, Miss Rice's whole school were bowed in earnest prayer, and did not move for some time when requested by her to retire for private devotion. On this occasion, Mr. Cobb writes, "It was my privilege to speak a word to them, and I can truly say that I never saw such a scene before, as, with heads bowed down on their desks, unable wholly to repress their sobs, they listened, and again engaged in prayer." Even then, it was only after repeated requests that they went to their own rooms, where many continued their supplications far into the night.

The interesting scenes of these awakenings are thus gratefully recalled by Sanum, a convert of the first revival, in a letter dated Salmas, June 6th, 1859:—

Beloved Teacher, Miss Fiske: I received your priceless letter with many tears of joy, and when I read your loving, motherly counsels, my heart was full; it was drawn to you with inexpressible love; and when you reminded me of those blessed revivals, my eyes were darkened with floods of tears, so that, for a time, I could not read. How can I ever forget the first night that you met me, after the Lord had touched my heart, in that blessed room? or how many times you took me by the hand, and led me to the throne of grace? Often I was in the dark, and the Lord, through you, was pleased to give me rest. Can I ever forget, when the hand of the Lord rested on me in the death of my dear children,[1] how many times you came as an angel of peace to wipe away my tears? Shall I ever forget the Lord's coming among us by the still rain of the Holy Spirit? or those meetings of the sisters for prayer? or those tearful pleadings in the closets? Can I ever forget the fervent supplications and preaching of blessed Mr. Stocking, and how he begged us to flee from the wrath to come? If I forget these, let my right hand forget her cunning, and my tongue cleave to the roof of my mouth.

It is a year, my beloved, since I have been able to go to Oroomiah. I have sorrowed greatly to be cut off so long from the supper of our Lord, and them that meet around his table. Perhaps it is because I am not worthy

[1] Page 165.

of the blessing. The Lord mercifully grant that I be not cut off from the heavenly supper of the Lamb.

Our work here is much as before. I grieve to say that there are few with whom I can pray, and in the few cases where I can do so, it must be done as by stealth. But there are those with whom I can talk. Hoimer and I have a meeting for the women every Sabbath, and on other days. Every Tuesday, Hoimer, Raheel, and I have a little meeting together, and it is very pleasant, but will be more so when the Lord shall increase our number. O that we longing ones might see that day, and our troubled hearts rejoice!

During the nineteen years since the Seminary was established, it has enjoyed, in all, twelve revivals; and though it is not desirable to count up the results of human labors, it is due to the praise of divine grace to record, that out of those who have been connected with it, as many as two thirds have, in the judgment of charity, been created anew in Christ Jesus.

CHAPTER XIV.

DARK DAYS.

SEMINARY BROKEN UP IN 1844. — DEACON ISAAC. — PERSECUTION BY MAR SHIMON. — FUNERAL OF DAUGHTER OF PRIEST ESHOO. — DEACON GUWERGIS. — ATTEMPT AT ABDUCTION OF PUPIL. — PERIL OF SCHOOL. — MRS. HARRIET STODDARD. — YAHYA KHAN. — ANARCHY. — LETTER FROM BABILO.

THE Nestorian mission has encountered less opposition than other missions in Western Asia. Yet here, also, they who would live godly in Christ Jesus have suffered persecution. On June 19th, 1844, the brothers of Mar Shimon issued this order: "Be it known to you all, ye readers at Seir, that if ye do not come to us to-morrow, we will excommunicate you from our most holy church; your finger nails shall be torn out; we will hunt you from village to village, and kill you if we can." Miss Fiske was spending the summer there with her pupils, and it was not deemed best to provoke further trouble by retaining them. When told of this, they all wept aloud. Nor did they weep alone. Their teacher, and the family of Mr. Stocking, in which they lived, could not restrain their tears. It seemed as if the girls would never tear themselves away from their teacher; and when at length they departed, again and again the lamentation arose, "We shall never hear the word of God again." Miss Fiske laid them at the feet of Jesus, trusting that he would bring them back to her, and others with them. A German Jew, who was present, said in his broken English, "I have seen much bad to missionaries in other countries, but nothing bad like this, to take little children from words of Jesus Christ."

Even Deacon Isaac, a brother of Mar Shimon, who was prominent in the act, was ashamed of it. On a visit to the school, eight years afterwards, he asked leave to speak to the pupils, and said, "My young friends, I want you to do all you can to help your teachers, for I once troubled Miss Fiske, and it has made my life bitter ever since." Here the good man broke down, and there was not a dry eye among his hearers; while he added, "I have vowed before God that I will do all that I can to help her as long as I live." And all who know him can testify that he has kept his word, ever since his conversion in 1849. When he first began to be thoughtful, he heard that one of the pupils was in the habit of praying for him. He sent for her, and insisted on her praying with him; and though he was the most intelligent of the Nestorians, and possessed of rare force of character, and Sarah was more noted for devotion, than for her mental powers, yet he learned from her in a most childlike spirit; and that scripture which says, "A little child shall lead them," found in this case a beautiful illustration.

He has been occasionally employed in the school, and always proved a very useful and acceptable teacher. When he bade Miss Fiske good by, in 1858, he said, "You may rest assured that I will do all I can for the women till you come back;" and the next Sabbath found him teaching a class of adult females. In our favored land, the grace of God has made it nothing strange for the governor of a state to be a teacher in the Sabbath school; but one who has not lived in Persia can form no idea of what it is for a brother of Mar Shimon to teach a class of women. He has great skill in bringing out the meaning of Scripture, and is every where exceedingly acceptable as a Bible teacher. Along with unfeigned piety, he has more real refinement than any of his countrymen, and few Nestorians can show kindness with such true delicacy of feeling.

The health of Miss Fiske was so impaired in the spring of 1848, that she reluctantly yielded to the advice of the mission, and went with Mr. Stocking to Erzroom, to meet Mr. Cochran and family, then on their way to Persia. When they returned, they found Mr. Stoddard's health so seriously affected by long-continued over-exertion, that he only awaited their arrival to leave for Trebizond. Little did they dream that it was Mrs. Stoddard's last farewell to the scene of her labors.

Nor was this all. The patriarch Mar Shimon, who had long worn the guise of friendship, now threw off the mask. He broke up schools in small and distant villages, and secured the beating of a man by the governor on the charge of apostasy. The Female Seminary was honored with his special anathema. "Has Miss Fiske taught you this?" was his frequent demand of those who fell into his hands, followed by such reviling as only an Oriental could pour forth.

On the morning of July 28th, the infant daughter of Priest Eshoo, named Sarah, after her sainted sister, lay on her death bed; and to punish her father for his preaching, Mar Shimon forbade her burial in the Nestorian grave-yard. He collected a mob ready to do his bidding as soon as she should die; but she lingered on, and so disappointed him for that day. Next day she died, and at once he anathematized all who should assist in her burial. A pious carpenter, however, forced his way through the mob, and made her coffin. He remained steadfast throughout the storm, replying to every dissuasion of his friends, "I must go forward, even to the shedding of my blood."

The missionaries appealed to a former governor, who owned that part of the city, for leave to bury in the cemetery used by the Nestorians from time immemorial; but the patriarch paid no attention to his messages, and the child remained unburied. Miss Fiske wrote, "As we look out on this troubled sea, and sympathize with these afflicted parents, we love to look up and think of the dear child as sweetly resting on the bosom of the Saviour. May the Sabbath bring us a foretaste of heavenly rest." But it found them still "where storms arise and ocean rolls." The governor sent men to demand the digging of a grave, which the mob would not allow. Meanwhile, the profligate Mar Gabriel craftily suggested that a promise from the priest not to preach any more, might end the trouble. "Never," was the prompt reply. "Let my dead remain unburied, but I will not go back from the service of the Lord." This so enraged the patriarch, that, for the sake of peace, the governor advised to bury the body in one of the villages. The sorrowing parents then locked their house, and leaving their babe alone in its slumbers, went to the chapel. There they found comfort from a sermon on the text, "Through much tribulation we must enter into the kingdom of God." About twenty men returned with them to the house. Then one bearing the little coffin went before; the rest followed, singing the forty-sixth Psalm. Even Moslems gazed with wonder, as they passed close by the door of the patriarch, and went out of the city gate. The engraving (page 154) gives a very good representation of this gate. On the green hill-side at Seir the little one was laid to rest, and the father, thanking the company for their kindness, hastened them back, to be in time for the afternoon service.

In the mean time, Mar Shimon sent far and near, forbidding all intercourse with the missionaries. At Geog Tapa,

SEIR GATE, OROOMIAH.

in the absence of the Malik, he ordered an old man, who formerly held that office, to summon the people before him. Only a few vagrants obeyed, and these he commanded to break up the schools, and prevent preaching in the church. So, that evening, when John commenced preaching, they proceeded to execute their orders; but, afraid to face the determined people, they deferred the attack till the hearers passed out; and then, like stanch old Puritans, hardly noticing them, the congregation wended their way homewards, singing psalms as they went.

The patriarch now excommunicated Mar Yohanan, and made common cause with the French Lazarists. He even wrote a fraternal epistle to the pope, ready for any thing, if he could only crush the mission. His attendants marched about the mission premises with loud threats; pious Nestorians were knocked down in the streets; while his brother Isaac went to a distant village, to show that he had no sympathy with such iniquity.

Soon after, the carpenter who made the coffin was severely beaten by his own father for attending a prayer meeting. As the blows fell thick and fast, he cried, "Must this come from my own father?" But he remained firm, and next day went to the chapel pale and weak, but filled with holy joy.

Deacon Guwergis, prevented from going to the mountains, — for the Koords sided with Mar Shimon, — fearlessly encountered the revilings of the patriarch in his own house, and told him that he hoped to continue preaching till he died. His countenance must have shone like Stephen's, for his persecutor said to one of the attendants, "See how his face glistens. If he is so bold here, what will he be in the mountains?" Well might a missionary write, "What a blessing are such men! The sight of them is worth ten thousand times the sacrifices made by us all."

Though this was vacation, fifteen of the pupils remained in the Seminary for protection during the storm; yet even there they were not wholly safe. On the 25th of August, a messenger came in haste for one of them, saying that her dying brother wished to see her immediately. As the man was her relative, the girl was ready to go at once; but providentially Miss Fiske learned that the brother was well, and the messenger had been seen last with Mar Shimon. So he left, chagrined and enraged at his failure. The patriarch had told him to be sure and hide his purpose from that Satan, Miss Fiske, and in case of failure, to take the girl by force. But the teacher had had some experience in guarding her fold, and both she and her pupil were thankful for the deliverance. Next day, Mar Shimon forbade preaching in Geog Tapa; but if the church was closed, the house-tops remained open. The same day, the school in Vizierawa was repeatedly dispersed, but each time reassembled by the teacher.

The 28th of this month was such a day as the mission had never seen before. In the forenoon, the teacher from Charbash fled wounded from the servants of Mar Shimon to the mission premises. Scarcely had he entered, when his brother came in, having escaped from similar violence. The Moslem owner of the village had to put a stop to the tearing down of their house.

Miss Fiske and Miss Rice had just sat down to dinner with the school, when the cry, "A man is killed!" was followed by a rush from all parts of the yard. A mob at the gate was trying to break in and seize the native helpers. Mar Yohanan was wounded, and all was confusion. The teachers exhorted their little flock not to count their lives dear to them, for Jesus' sake. Happily, they were not called to such a test of discipleship; but the sympathies of the Moslems were plainly with Mar Shimon, and no one knew what a day might bring forth. That tried friend of the mission, R. W. Stevens, Esq., English consul at Tabreez, feared lest the missionaries should fall by the hand of violence. Miss Fiske writes, "Our native friends will doubtless suffer much, and we rejoice to share with them. We hope that fears on our account will not be realized. Still there is danger; and we try to be ready for life or death, as our Father sees best. Though in a land of violence, we are not unhappy; we trust in God, and hope this vine is being pruned that it may bring forth more fruit. We would have all the gracious designs of God fulfilled, even though we should be cast down."

The same day came tidings of the death of Mrs. Stoddard, at Trebizond, and Miss Fiske wrote that night an account of it to her former teacher, at South Hadley, adding, "Precious sister: she died far away; but my Father knows why I might not stand by that dying bed, and I would submit, though my heart bleeds. *Our* homes are sad to-night, and there is many a weeping eye among those for whom she toiled so faithfully. From my first acquaintance with her, she has been to me all that mortal could be. Her heart was tenderly alive to the spiritual interests of the dear Nestorians; and to them she devoted all her powers. It was she who first taught their daughters to sing the songs of Zion. Few, probably, have accomplished so much in so short a life. Her family, the mission, the Seminary, and all about us, shared in her untiring labors. As truly as of dear Mrs. Grant may it be said of her, 'She hath done what she could.'

"Like Mrs. Grant, she was the youngest member of the mission at the time of her death. When she left her native land, some almost regretted that so frail a flower should go forth to encounter the hardships of missionary life; but she did much, and did it well. The Seminary in Seir still bears the impress she stamped upon it. Her memory is not only fragrant to-day among the Nestorians, but it draws them nearer to Christ, and renders them more efficient in his service."

Mar Shimon now made common cause with the Persian nobility. The English and Russian ambassadors had procured the appointment of Dawood Khan as governor of the Christians in Oroomiah, in order to protect them from illegal oppression. The nobility of course opposed this; and Mar Shimon, by promising his aid in the removal of the protector of his own people, secured their coöperation in his wickedness. The converts were now insulted at every turn. They could hardly appear in the street, and the authorities afforded no redress. The missionaries had no earthly friend nearer than Mr. Stevens at Tabreez, who did all he could for them; and the pious natives felt shut up to God as their only refuge.

Yahya Khan, the governor of the province, now wrote urging on Mar Shimon, and ordered his agent in Oroomiah to aid him to the utmost of his power. As Yahya Khan was brother-in-law to the king, he was able to do the mission much harm at the court; and the patriarch, encouraged by such a coadjutor, set himself with renewed zeal to destroy it; but in September, the prince royal summoned him to Tabreez, and, the nobility hardly daring to resist the order, he was reluctantly preparing to comply, when news came of the death of the shah, and all was confusion. The missionaries had been praying for help against their dreaded enemy, Yahya Khan, and lo! his power to harm them perished with his master.

The night after the news reached Oroomiah, anarchy reigned, and all kinds of crime abounded. Five men were killed near the mission premises, and the firing of guns was heard all night long; but though outside were robberies and murders, within that enclosure all was peace. Though its inmates knew that the fanatical population would gladly stone them, yet they felt it a privilege to labor on under the care of the Keeper of Israel.

In Persia, no king, no government; so besides this anarchy in the city, the Koords came down and plundered many villages, burning the houses and driving the people for shelter to Oroomiah. These strokes fell most heavily on the Moslems, many of whom were robbers themselves. The fear of an attack on Seir was at one time so great, that the ladies were sent off, and the gentlemen remained alone to guard the mission premises; but both in Seir and the city the houses of the missionaries were thronged by multitudes seeking relief, and each approaching footstep announced some new tale of woe.

Mar Shimon, after the death of the king, prudently retired into Turkey, and his servants were put under bonds to keep the peace. The Koords, however, drove him back, later in the season, but stripped of his power to persecute. It may sound like the close of a tale of fiction to add, that the next time Miss Fiske met the patriarch was in Gawar, August, 1851, when he rode up to the tents of the missionaries to inquire after their health, before he went to his own. He staid an hour and a half, appearing more free and social than ever before; and when they returned his visit, he came out of his tent to meet them, and treated them with unusual respect, saying, in the course of the interview, "I fear that Miss Fiske is not happy here: she does not look well." On being assured that she was both well and happy, he said to his attendants, "This lady is happy only as she has a number of Nestorian girls around her, eating care * for them, teaching and doing them good." So, when our ways please the Lord, he maketh even our enemies to be at peace with us.

Babilo, the carpenter, who made the coffin for the child of Priest Eshoo, was taught to read by the younger girls in the Seminary after school hours, and thus writes to Miss Fiske, November 20th, 1859: —

* This is the Nestorian idiom. We say, "taking care of them."

"I remember how, thirteen years ago, in that trouble with Mar Shimon, when my father beat me for attending meeting, and men despitefully used me, dear Mr. Stocking and you comforted me in the great room. I shall never forget your love. Give my love to your dear mother, who so loved us that she willingly gave you to the Lord, as Hannah did Samuel.

"If you inquire about my work in the city Sabbath school,—I teach a class of ten women; three of them, I trust, are Christians. When I read your letter to them they greatly rejoiced. I reminded them of the meetings you used to have for them in your room, and their eyes filled with tears. In the afternoon I went to Charbash, and read your letter to the eighteen women in my class there. They, too, were very glad. Five of them, I trust, are Christians. We are now studying Second Timothy. After the lesson, I question them on Old Testament history; and then I teach the women and their children to sing."

CHAPTER XV.

TRIALS.

EVIL INFLUENCE OF HOMES. — OPPOSITION IN DEGALA. — ASKER KHAN. — POISONING OF SANUM'S CHILDREN. — REDRESS REFUSED. — INQUISITOR IN SCHOOL. — TROUBLES AT KHOSRAWA. — LETTERS FROM HOIMAR.

BUT, aside from open persecution, there is a constant danger arising from the people themselves. The teacher in a Christian land can never fully understand the feelings of the missionary teacher. The one sends forth his pupils to meet Christian parents, brothers and sisters, who, with more than a teacher's love, lead the young convert by still waters, and establish him in holy feeling; but the flock of the other goes out often into families where every soul would gladly break the bruised reed and quench the smoking flax. He can sympathize with Paul in his anxiety in behalf of those for whom he had labored in the gospel.

Sometimes the pupils of the Seminary so dreaded the scenes of home, in vacation, that they preferred to remain in the school.

In April, 1849, Miss Fiske visited the village of Degala. As it was a holiday, most of the women had gone out for amusement; but a little company of twelve praying ones gathered around her, and listened in tears while she spoke of Jesus and his love. Their fervent prayers for neighbors and friends made her feel that a blessing was yet in store for Degala. These women suffered all sorts of insult for their attachment to the truth; they were often beaten and driven from their homes by their husbands. While the pupils of the Seminary were here, some of their own sex did all they could to annoy them. But read an account of their trials from the pen of Sanum, of Gawar. She writes to a friend in this country, —

"I had bitter times this vacation, for our neighbors are all very hard-hearted, not listening at all to the words of God. When I opened my Testament to read to them, they would shut it, and begin to quarrel about the forms of religion. I entreat you to pray for my village, that I, so unworthy, may see its salvation.

"One day, Miss Fiske went to the village of Degala, where is a band of women who greatly love the Lord. They gathered about her, and she had a very pleasant time. All these were inquiring what they should do to be saved. She could not stay long with them; but they were so humble that they asked to have some of the girls sent to them. So four of us, though so weak, ventured to go in the name of Christ. We found these sisters in great distress, being reviled and beaten by wicked men, for Jesus' sake.

"We were speaking in an upper room there on a feast day, and the women with us were weeping very much, while others, afraid to come in, seated themselves on the terrace by the window. Suddenly a wicked man came with a rod, and drove all those away who were without. Poor souls! how my heart burned for them! One, who had not been used to come to meeting, came that day for sport. She wore many ornaments, but as soon as she heard the words of God, her tears began to flow. After meeting, she arose up quickly, and threw aside her ornaments, and followed us wherever we went. We were having a meeting in another house, when a quarrelsome woman entered, having a large stick in her hand, and began to beat her daughter and daughter-in-law, and she carried off her daughter; but the other remained, though sorely bruised, saying, 'I will spill my blood, but will not leave the place of prayer.' The women who fear God wept much because this woman did so.

"We went to the sacrament, and there was a company of women who separated themselves from the others, and were weeping in one corner of the church. Some very bad women came to them, and said, 'Let us rise up and dance, because they are weeping.' Another, in anger, took the sacrament from the mouth of one of them, and gave it to her little granddaughter. There was much confusion in the village, and they seemed like those who cried, 'Great is Diana of the Ephesians.' One said, 'I wish neither Satan nor God, but only Mar Shimon.' Once, when we were assembled with the women, and Moressa was speaking, a wicked man fired a pistol to frighten us. But the women encouraged us, saying, 'Go on, and speak louder, that he may hear.' And when he heard my sister speak of the wickedness of man's heart, he cried out, 'Those words must have been for me. She must have known that I was there.'"

It does not fall within the object of this volume to give any detailed account of the proceedings of Asker Khan, who for several years sought to wear out the saints of the Most High, causing the native helpers to be beaten, fined, and annoyed in many ways, and then arrogantly denying all redress. Encouraged in his persecutions by the prime minister, he was able to defy all interference. Indeed, during part of the time, the English ambassador was constrained to leave the kingdom, and the Russian ambassador, though personally disposed to do all in his power for the mission, was yet officially unable to help.

At one time, he gave orders that no school should be opened without his sanction, and that all the teachers must report to him; and in case of disobedience, he threatened them with fines and imprisonment.

It may show in what estimation the influence of the Female Seminary was held by enemies, when we find him issuing his command, "Allow no girls to attend your school; schools are for boys alone;" and claiming credit for great forbearance because he did not at once break up the Seminary. That which called forth such opposition from enemies was surely not inefficient. There must have been a power for good manifest even to Moslem opposers, that taught them where to strike so as most effectually to destroy. But there was a Power above them that said, "Thus far, and no farther." "The bush burned with fire, yet it was not consumed."

The evil wrought by Asker Khan was not confined to his own doings. His hostility, in a position so commanding, emboldened every Shimei to curse. In Ardishai, two or three unprincipled drunkards, with their dissolute bishop (Mar Gabriel), saved themselves from Mohammedan rapacity by taking part against the converts. These last were made examples of, to deter others from attending preaching or sending their children to the schools. One poor widow, with four children, — a most consistent Christian, — was driven from her house by her father-in-law, because she allowed her oldest daughter to attend the village school. As many as thirty families, unable to endure persecution any longer, fled from the village; and Priest Abraham himself, after suffering much, was compelled to leave, though his congregation was from one hundred and fifty to two hundred every Sabbath.

In Dizza Takka, on the evening of April 20th, 1856, Sanum, who graduated in 1850, had arsenic put into the supper which she carried to a neighbor's tandoor (native oven) to be warmed. Happily, Joseph, her husband, was delayed beyond his usual hour, so that he was uninjured; and the quantity of arsenic was so large, that, by the prompt use of remedies, the mother's life was saved, though her innocent children suffered severely, and, after lingering a few months, both of them died. She rose from weeping over their graves to serve her Master more faithfully than ever. But Asker Khan,—though the arsenic was found at the bottom of the pot, though a portion of the contents, given to a cat, speedily produced convulsions and death, and though a Jewess testified that "the neighbor" had recently applied to her husband for arsenic, and no one else had access to the vessel where it was found,—instead of investigating the case, insulted Joseph and his friends, and caused his aged father to be beaten; at the same time telling the people of Dizza Takka to shoot Joseph if he went to their village again. Such conduct emboldened the enemies of the truth to complain against the more enlightened of their clergy who had renounced many sinful customs, as forsaking the religion of their fathers; and, with blasphemous threats, they were ordered to do the bidding of their accusers.

On the 1st of June, an order from the authorities at Tabreez to Asker Khan was presented to him by the missionaries, which, after a calm recital of the facts in the case of poisoning, proceeded thus: "As the person who did this act is a criminal, and, if unpunished, the affair may lead to the destruction of life, it is necessary that you, high in rank, take the attitude of investigation, and having discovered the criminal, that you punish him, with the knowledge of the Americans, and so act that no one, Christian or Moslem, shall dare to repeat such a crime." This order was obtained through the kind offices of the Russian ambassador; but the criminals were only detained a few days, and not pressed at all to a confession. Asker Khan then proposed, as they had not confessed, that the missionaries should intercede for their release. Of course, they refused. Then, saying "that if he had known that, beforehand, he would not have touched the matter, and that he could defend himself at Tabreez," he dismissed the accused, and it was in vain for the missionaries to prosecute the matter further.

Indeed, the opposition at this time was more serious than at any previous period, and for a time it seemed as though the seminaries, and especially the Female Seminary, would be destroyed.

In the autumn, a commissioner, sent from Teheran to examine into the proceedings of the mission, made an inquisitorial visit, and went all through the building, peeping into the chambers, and making himself and suite every where at home. Coming into the recitation room, where most of the girls were engaged in study, he selected a large, robust pupil, who could speak Turkish, and questioned her as follows: —

"Are you allowed to follow your own customs?"

"We follow all that are good, but not such foolish ones as you would not wish us to follow."

"Do these ladies let you see your friends?"

"Certainly; we always see them when they come here, and we go home three times a year, staying, at one time, three months."

"What do you do when at home?"

"We work in the fields, and do any thing that our

friends do. Our teachers tell us to help our friends all we can, and are displeased if we do not."

"Can you work, or have you become Ingleez?" (English.)

"Look at me; I am strong; I can carry very large loads."

"What do you do here?"

"We study, and learn all wisdom."

"Are you allowed to use your own books?"

"Certainly; the principal book of our religion they have printed for us, and we use it more than any other."

"But have you not left the books of your fathers?"

"The book I spoke of is our sacred book, like your Koran, and we use all others that agree with that."

"Do you fast?"

"One day at the beginning of the year, and other days afterwards."

"But have you not forsaken some of your church fasts?"

"None that are written in that book. I keep all those very carefully."

"What! twice in the week?"

"No; for that is not required in the book."

"But your people do."

"Yes; not being readers, they do many things that are not written in the book."

"Would your teachers allow you to fast?"

"O, yes; but we don't want to fast more than our book requires."

"What are your prayers?"

"Those taught in the book."

Then followed questions about dress, employment, and such things, all of which she answered in the same manner. The teacher was very thankful that the Master had neither left to her the selection of the witness, nor her preparation for the examination. But the examiner expressed very decided disapproval of female education, and held up their previous condition as their only proper one. The truth was, the Moslems were angry that their rayahs were being elevated, and they were specially indignant at the education of women.

So the opposition went on. Messrs Stoddard and Wright proceeded to Tabreez, and secured orders for redress; which, as usual, were counteracted by secret orders to the contrary. The native helpers were now beaten because they were in the employ of the mission: some were thrown into prison, and threatened with being sent to Teheran in irons. But when the Lord saw that the wrath of man had proceeded far enough, he restrained the remainder thereof. For one of the leading spirits in this onset on the mission fell under the daggers of the Koords, and his death at once called off attention from missionary operations to other things.

Again, in January, 1858, two pious residents at Khosrowa, in the province of Salmas, were shamefully oppressed; and when application was made for redress, Asker Khan not only refused to adjudicate the matter, but beat one of the complainants so severely that he was confined to his bed for weeks. Still later, after urgent importunity from Nestorians and nominal Papists, two very able and excellent men, Deacons Joseph and Siyad, were sent to labor in that distant province. On one occasion they entered the village of Khosrowa to purchase fuel, and were quietly passing along the street, when a mob stoned them out of the village. Shortly after, Deacon Siyad was expelled from the district so suddenly that he had to leave his wife, Merganeeta: she, too, was driven away alone; but Hoimar, a pious woman residing there, went with her. The first night they spent in a field, and the next day they sought refuge in an Armenian village; but, driven from thence, the persecuted wife fled to Oroomiah. After long effort, an officer was sent from Tabreez to Salmas, and ample promises of full redress were given, ending, as usual, in nothing. A mob, headed by a French Lazarist and native bishop, rescued the offender, and the officer desisted from further procedure.

The reader will be interested in the following extract, from a letter of Hoimar to Miss Fiske, in 1859:—

"I cannot tell you how glad I am to hear that your health is better. O that quickly you might meet us, if the Lord will! Till death I can never forget your love, nor your reminding your pupils to ask the Lord to support a poor, ignorant one like me. I do not believe your thoughts can ever rest about your little company of Nestorians. If a mother leaves a nursing child, she cannot rest till she returns to it. If you are far from us in body, I know your spirit is with us. If Jonah mourned over the gourd for which he had not labored, how shall not you mourn after those for whom you have labored?

"If the breezes did not bring the cry of 'Salvation' over the ocean, our desolations would cry out. But thanks to Him who favors those that leave their native land to labor among the ignorant. Yet what shall this people do? The beast having great iron teeth still reigns here; but it may be the Lord will speedily destroy him with the breath of his mouth. I trust that you will ever remember in your prayers one who will remember you in her weakness till death."

Two years later brought the following, with its graphic delineation of the trials that such as choose the better part may meet with yet for years to come:—

Beloved Miss Fiske: Almost every day of this summer has been a bitter day. For my mother had become willing to give Raheel (Rachel, sister of Hoimar) to the Papists, and she had prevailed over my father to do the same. And now I will tell you how Goliah fell upon the earth, and he that had no weapons overcame; but it was from the power of God. The arrangement had all been made by my parents, and the betrothal feast made ready. Sanum and I were in Oroomiah, but Deacon Joseph was in Salmas, and we had also this comfort — my oldest brother stood firm, saying, "Fear not; till death *I* stand." Raheel also was firm, hoping for help. With entreaties and tears, I asked Deacon Isaac to go to Salmas. He went, but Raheel knew it not. She was very sorrowful, for only an hour remained to the time fixed for putting the betrothal ring on her finger. The hope of her life seemed to hang on a hair. She went to the vineyard, and prayed God to deliver her; then returned sorrowful to her room. She hears them say, "They have come!" and locks her door. They ask her to open it, but she opens it not. Just then, Deacon Joseph goes to the window, and, seeing that Deacon Isaac has come, says, "Open; be not afraid." Deacon Isaac sits down with the Papists who have come to the betrothal. My father leaves it with him, and he says, "Very well; I have only now come; I must have time to examine into this business. To-morrow I will give you an answer." He talks with my father, saying, "How can you give your daughter to the Papists? The missionaries are not willing, our people are not willing, I am not willing; and more than all, the girl is not willing." My father at length said, "She is your daughter, not mine; do as you please." Then Deacon Isaac sent word to the Papists, "There is no possibility of your carrying this forward. I have questioned the girl, she is not willing; speak no more about it." The deacon then asked my father to let her go to the city to school again. At first he consented, but finally left it with her mother, who did not let her go. The deacon left displeased. When I heard this, I arose and took Mar Yohanan's brother, and went to Salmas, thinking I might possibly bring Raheel. While yet a good way from the village, like Canaan's spies, we sent for my oldest brother (who is, as we trust, a Christian). He gave us good news, and said, "Raheel is all ready to go to school." As the Lord favored Eleazar about Rebecca, so he favored us; and the next morning my sister and Deacon Joseph returned to Oroomiah, while I remained to meet the wrath of my mother. As soon as Raheel was gone, she left, and as yet we know not where she is. Truly, great is the power of prayer. So God brought to nought evil counsels, scattered fearful, dark clouds, and caused the light of joy to rise upon us. But I am very sad about my mother, because she has turned away from the fear of God, and is fleeing from life. My father and husband still get intoxicated. I trust that you will multiply your prayers for them; and ask your friends to do the same, and to pray for me, and our village and country. Give my love to all your friends.

From your lover, HOIMAR.

We shall hear from Hoimar again, in connection with the communion.

CHAPTER XVI.

PRAYERFULNESS.

LANGUAGE OF PRAYER. — PRAYER ON HORSEBACK. — OLD MAN IN SUPERGAN. — MAR OGEN. — EARNESTNESS. — FAREWELL PRAYER MEETING IN 1858. — LETTER FROM PUPIL. — SPIRIT OF PRAYER IN 1846. — WOMAN WHO COULD NOT PRAY. — "CHRIST BECOME BEAUTIFUL." — CLOSET IN THE MANGER. — MONTHLY CONCERTS. — PRAYERFULNESS IN 1849 AND 1850. — SABBATH, JANUARY 20TH. — INTEREST CONTINUED TILL CLOSE OF TERM. — FAMILY MEETINGS. — AUDIBLE PRAYER. — ANSWER TO MOTHERS' PRAYERS. — CONNECTION OF REVIVALS WITH PRAYER AT HOME.

THE Nestorian converts have been noted for their spirit of prayer.

In 1846, the prayers of the hopefully pious in the Male Seminary were very remarkable. Several rooms were appropriated to devotion, and there one might hear the voice of supplication from morning till night. Many spent several hours a day in this holy employment; and one needed only to listen to know that their prayers came from the depths of the soul. At one time, they beg that the dog may have a single crumb from the table of his master; again, they are smiting on their breasts by the side of the publican. Now they are prodigals — hungry, naked, and far from their Father's house; and now they sink in the sea, crying, "Lord, save me; I perish!" or, as poor outcast lepers, they come to the great Physician for a care. This one builds on the Rock of Ages, while the torrents roar around. That one washes the feet of Jesus with his tears, and wipes them with the hair of his head; another, as a soldier of the cross, plants its blood-stained banner in the inner citadel of his heart. Their ardent feelings found such appropriate expression in their Oriental metaphors, that one might learn from children to pray as he never prayed before.

On the reopening of the Seminary that spring, the first desire of the pupils was to enter their closets and commune with God.

Riding out one evening, Mr. Stoddard saw three persons before him on the way to Seir. Their horses went from one side of the road to the other, at random; and their own heads were uncovered to the cold March wind. At first he took them for dervishes; but on coming nearer he heard the voice of prayer, and found they were Nestorians. The eyes of all were reverently closed, and when one finished the other continued their supplications. He turned aside, and left them undisturbed. On another occasion, when John and Moses were riding to Geog Tapa on the same horse, they again engaged in devotion; but as the horse was unruly, they each prayed in turn, while the other held the reins.

Sometimes the language of their prayers is very broken. Mr. Stoddard once stood in the church in Supergan, twenty miles from Oroomiah, while prayers were read in the ancient Syriac, and overheard an old man, very ignorant, praying back in the congregation by himself. He had, perhaps, never heard five prayers, in his whole life, in a language he could understand; but reverently, and in a low tone, commingling the memories of old forms with the utterance of new desires, he was saying, "Our Father in heaven — always going after Satan — O Lord Jesus Christ — hallelujah — forever and ever, Amen!" It was incoherent, but comprehensive. He addresses God as his heavenly Father. He confesses his sins. He appeals to Christ as his only helper. He praises God for his unspeakable gift, and then closes in the usual form.

The pious Mar Ogen, of Ishtazin, when in great pain, and hardly able to move, often broke out in words like these: "O Lord Jesus, thou art the King of glory, the King of kings and Lord of lords; thou art great, and holy, and merciful. I am a sinner, condemned. My face is black, my bones are rotten. O Lord Jesus, have mercy upon me, poor, and blind, and naked, and miserable. O Lord Jesus Christ, I am vile, I am lost; but do thou remember me."

No language expressed their sense of guilt better than the words, "All our righteousnesses are as filthy rags." In the fervor of their desire for Christ, and grace through him, they would say, "Blessed Saviour, we will cling to the skirts of thy garment, and hope for mercy till our hands are cut off." A common petition was, "O Lord, we pray that we may never deny thee, even to the blood of our necks" — most expressive words, in a land where so many criminals are beheaded.

One prayed for our country, when he heard of the southern rebellion, thus: "O God, pour peace into that land. Permit them not to fight with each other, but with Satan and their wicked hearts, and may they fight spiritually to subdue the whole world to Christ."

During one of the revivals in the Female Seminary, the prayers of the pupils were exceedingly earnest. A member of the mission, having occasion to open the door of a room where a few of them were together, heard as follows:

"We are hanging over a lake of fire, with a heavy load upon our backs, by a single hair, and that is almost broken. We are in a ship burned almost down to the water; the flames are just seizing upon us. O God, have mercy. Jesus, Son of David, have mercy. O Lamb of God, have mercy on us." "No wonder," a missionary wrote, "I sometimes think that it is pleasanter to pray in Syriac than in our own language, because I have such fervent-minded ones with whom to pray."

The day Miss Fiske left Oroomiah, a large number of women and girls gathered around to bid her farewell. They said, "Can we not have one more prayer meeting before you leave?" They were told that they might meet in the school room. "But may it not be in that Bethel?" they asked, referring to the teacher's own room. She told them she could not lead their devotions then. Their reply was, "You need not do it; we will *carry you* to-day." Seventy were soon assembled in her room. They sung, "Blest be the tie that binds," and offered six prayers. One asked that when Elijah should go up, they might all see the horsemen and chariot, and all catch the falling mantle; not sit down to weep, or send into the mountains to search for their master, but take up the mantle, go, smite Jordan, and, passing over, go to work. She then reminded the Saviour that he had promised not to leave them orphans (John xiv. 18, Greek and Syriac), and begged him not only to come to them, but to abide with them when their teacher was gone. Her thoughts then turned to the departing company, who were to take their long land journey of six hundred miles on horseback. She asked that the sun might not smite them by day, nor the moon by night. Theirs was a desert way, and the Lord was entreated to spread a table for them through all the wilderness, and, when they should pass over the narrow, precipitous roads, to give his angels charge to keep them in all their ways, and bear them up in their hands, lest they dash a foot against a stone; and when they should go through the rivers, not to let the waters overflow them. The company would lodge by night in tents, and it was asked that the angel of the Lord might ever encamp round about the moving tabernacle. Borne in mind as they should pass on, first to the steamer, and then to the sailing vessel, she asked that when they should be on the "fire ship," the flame might not kindle upon them; and when on the "winged ship," where the waves would go up to heaven, and down to hell, that He would keep them in the hollow of his hand, and bring them to the desired haven. She then asked that all her teacher's friends might be spared till she should reach them, especially the aged mother, and that when she should fold her daughter in her arms, she might say, like Simeon of old, "Now lettest thou thy servant depart in peace." Here she paused, and Miss Fiske thought she had finished; but soon she added, "May our teacher's dust never mingle with a father's dust, or with a mother's dust; but may she come back to us to mingle her dust with her children's dust, hear the trumpet with them, and with them go up to meet the Lord, and be forever with him." Nor did their prayerfulness cease after their teacher had left them.

There was a pupil in the Seminary, who, before conversion, was exceedingly obstinate and rude; but afterwards, in writing to Miss Fiske, she uses expressions like these: "I remember how you used to put your arms about my neck, and tell me how Christ became obedient unto death; not for friends, but for enemies like me. Especially do I remember how you spoke of that love which saw a remedy in its own blood, when there was no help for a lost world.

At that time I did not understand it, but now I know not how to express my gratitude. I know that you are very happy with your aged mother, though your heart is here; and she is happy, too, that she sees your face. Yet these earthly meetings, though so pleasant, are but for a season. But how delightful will be that meeting with the holy angels, with the risen Lamb, and with God our Father! and if separations are so trying here, what must be those of the last day? May I not then be separated from you. If I should be, I know you will say, 'Holy, holy Lord God, just art thou, for she has been taught.' We miss you much; but the Teacher who is better than any earthly instructor, came and taught us this winter (1858–1859). The Lord Jesus has been the gardener of our school. He has come down and watered it with heavenly rain. He has truly fulfilled his promise, 'I will not leave you orphans; I will come to you.' He said, 'Wait for the promise of the Father.' We waited for his coming, and he turned himself quickly, and we had delightful seasons. Our times of prayer were longed for. We prayed more than we did any thing else. When we retire from the school room now, in many places two girls are found praying together. In my village I meet the women together and alone. I also have precious seasons, praying with a company of girls; and I have selected two women to pray with and for till they shall be Christians. I hope that they will choose Christ for their portion. Some of the women of our village, like Mary, sit at Jesus' feet. One Christian mother had an only son, and very wicked, who trod the Sabbath under foot, and was wholly given up to his own pleasure. She set apart a day for fasting and prayer in his behalf, and soon the Lord met him in his evil way, and now he is a decided Christian."

But let us leave these general views, and look at this prayerfulness more in the order of its manifestations.

During the revival in 1846, two of the pupils spent a whole night in prayer for the conversion of their brothers, first one leading in devotion, and then the other, till morning. Like Jacob they felt, "We will not let thee go except thou bless us." While the missionaries admired their pious zeal, it is proper to add, that they generally insisted on the observance of regular hours of sleep, as conducive alike to bodily and spiritual health. Yet one writes on a similar occasion, "Sometimes, in my anxiety, I have gone to their cold closets to persuade them to leave; but the fervor of their prayers has oftener driven me to mine, than it has allowed me to call them from theirs."

Twice, and even three times, a day, were not enough for them to retire for communion with God. Many spent hours every day at the mercy seat. There were but few closets, and this was a great trial to them. Often three or four of them might be seen sitting, in tears, waiting their turn to go in to the mercy seat. Would that they might have had some of those closets at home that are never entered! At another time, the Bible of one of the girls was found on one of their wooden stools, open at the fifty-first psalm, and the page blotted with weeping, as she read it preparatory to retiring for prayer. Her teacher could put her finger on no part of those large pages without touching a tear.* Still later, when news of the death of Munny, of Ardishai, by the accidental discharge of a gun, reached Miss Fiske in America, her first thought was, "Dear child, I shall never again break off your communion with Jesus;" for she remembered that when once she begged her to leave her closet and get rest for the Sabbath, her reply

* See page 138.

was, "O, I am so sorry that you spoke to me! I was having such a good time with my dear Saviour." Only a few days before her death, while in the vineyard with her brother, she suddenly clasped her hands, and exclaimed, "Blessed Mr. Stoddard! when shall I see him? and when shall I see my blessed Saviour?"

A poor woman, came to the Seminary one day, weeping for her sins, and seated herself on the floor. The teacher was soon at her side, telling her of Him who was wounded for our transgressions. She prayed with her, and then asked her to pray for herself. "But I can't pray; I don't know your prayers." "Hatoon, don't try to pray like me, or like any body; but just tell God how you feel and what you want." "May I tell God just what is in my heart?" Being assured on that point, she fell on her face, weeping aloud, saying amid sobs, "O God, I am not fit even for an old broom to sweep with," and could say no more. This was doubtless the most worthless thing the poor woman could think of in her humble home. But it was not long ere she could join others in their little meetings for prayer; and she still lives, honoring the Saviour, whom she loves. She is the mother of two of the most useful graduates of the Seminary.

Again: a pious man brought his wife to spend a few days in the Seminary, when she was somewhat thoughtful, and left her nearly a week. Let Miss Fiske describe their meeting. "He came for her at noon, and I was conversing with him in my room, when she passed out from her closet without seeing him. [The small upper window to the left, over the central door, marks the closet.] But he saw her, and reached out his hand, saying, 'My beloved, come here.' She placed her hand in his, looked up in his face, and answered his 'Is Christ become beautiful?' with a gentle 'I think so.' The tears of both fell fast, while he led her, without leave, into my chamber, that they might unite in prayer. But I was glad to have them offer their first *united* prayers there. It was ever after a more sacred place."

Miss Fiske spent most of the vacation, that followed the first revival, in 1846, with Mr. Stoddard, in the villages, where her pupils aided her much in labors among the people. After a very pleasant evening spent in Geog Tapa with those who were seeking Jesus, Hanee, the pupil with whom she staid, came and asked, "Would you like to be alone?" It was the first time she had ever been asked such a question by a Nestorian, and it awakened feelings similar to those that filled her heart when first she heard the voice of a Nestorian woman leading in prayer. To use her own words, "I followed the dear child, and she led me to the best closet she could give me — a manger, where she had spread clean hay; and she said to me, as she turned to leave, 'Stay just as long as you like.' You may well suppose it was a precious spot to me. It was my own fault if I did not there meet Him who was once laid in a manger for us."

The members of the Seminary were especially interested in the monthly concert, which was held in Oroomiah, on the first Monday of the month. On that day they generally wanted two or three meetings; and in 1846 it was often difficult to persuade them to study at all. From the rising to the setting sun, the voice of supplication for a dying world continually fell upon the ear. At one time, all united in pleading for a world's redemption; then, in little companies of five or six, they urged the request; and again, each, alone in her closet, still pressed the same petition.

Previous to 1846, so few of the Nestorians knew how to pray, that religious meetings were for instruction rather than prayer; but now it was a delightful privilege to unite with them in pleading for the conversion of the world to Christ. Never were their petitions so full of unction as when offered for this object. In April, Miss Fiske's pupils, not satisfied with an extra meeting by themselves, though continued till near sunset, were induced to close it only by the promise of having a similar meeting next day. No wonder their teacher never enjoyed a monthly concert in America as she did that one. It was indeed a rare privilege to unite with such spirits in its observance.

The pupils wrote to the Seminary, at South Hadley—"Dear sisters, we love the monthly concert very much. Three hours on that day we meet together to pray that the kingdom of God may come among us, and among all the nations of the earth. It is a very sweet day to us, and we love none so well, except the Sabbath."

In January, 1849, they spent day and night in weeping and prayer, mostly for themselves, as unfit to pray for others. The same was true of the Male Seminary. The teachers, the older pupils, and Deacons John and Guwergis spent nearly the whole of one night in prayer; and so burdened were they with the lost condition of their people, and their own unfaithfulness, that almost all of them gave up their former hope in Christ, and sought anew for pardon. The voice of praise and prayer was now heard, not only through the day, but frequently during the night.

Up to January 29th, only two or three of the unconverted in the Seminary showed any concern for salvation. Most of them were so careless and trifling, that their teachers were almost heart-broken; but when the retiring bell rung that night, many were so distressed for sin that they could not heed it. The pious were pleading in behalf of those out of Christ, and many of these last were crying for mercy. One prayer commenced, "O Lord, throw us a rope, for we are out in the open sea, on a single plank, and wave after wave is dashing over us." So they continued till near midnight, when their teachers constrained them to retire.

At the beginning of February, the other Seminary witnessed a remarkable outpouring of the spirit of prayer. Every spare moment of the previous day, and much of the night, had been devoted to fervent intercession by those who feared that the Spirit of God was about to leave them. So intense was the feeling, that the ordinary services were suspended, and at once every closet was filled; yet a majority had no place for retirement. One of them proposed prayer in the yard, and there, on that wintry day, for an hour, their earnest cries went up to heaven. All of the careless were deeply moved, and many dated their conversion from that day.

The work extended to Geog Tapa, Seir, and other villages. From Degala, Deacon Joseph wrote, "Whenever I went home, I found our house a house of mourning. After the lamp was put out at night, I could not sleep for the sounds of prayer and weeping on all sides. In some houses, very young children had heard their parents pray so much, that they also did the same. The women, too, had frequent meetings by themselves. One day I led some men to a place where they could hear women praying within the latticed window of a house, and, trembling, they begged me to teach them also how to come to God."

The missionaries avoided all stirring appeals to the passions, among a people so excitable, though the ready performance of every duty manifested the sincerity of the praying pupils, while it made the labors of their teachers pleasant.

There was not that agonizing wrestling in prayer on the

first Monday of 1850 that had marked the same day the year before; but the following week was characterized by unusual tenderness in both Seminaries, and two of the older pupils of the Female Seminary found no rest except in their closets.

On the evening of the second Sabbath in January, Miss Fiske was not able to attend the prayer meeting, and remained in her room alone. The gentle opening of her door announced that the meeting was over, and a little group passed on hastily, but quietly, to the rooms beyond. She had just risen to follow, when she heard several voices in earnest supplication. She turned to the stairway, and there also the sound of fervent entreaty came up from many closets, while some groped about to light their lamps, or stirred the dying embers of their fires. What meant this simultaneous movement to the mercy seat? There had been nothing unusually exciting in the meeting, and she sat down with the sweet assurance that it was from above. It was late before the suppliants left their closets, and retired in perfect silence; but morning found them resuming the same loved employment, and good news came of similar blessings from the Boys' Seminary.

That week was one of deep solemnity. The pious pupils devoted every leisure moment to prayer. Their domestic duties were performed faultlessly, and much earlier than usual, and then they sought their closets. Some spent five hours each day of that week in those sacred retreats, and when urged to leave for needed sleep, the reply was, "For weeks we have slept, doing nothing for God and souls. How can we sleep until forgiven?"

Saturday afternoon, several begged leave to give themselves entirely to prayer for a blessing on the morrow; and never did the teachers more gladly welcome the approach of holy time. A blessed Sabbath followed such a preparation day. During morning service, almost all were in tears. At dinner, many seats were vacant. It may seem an exaggeration, but it was literally true, that no voice was heard all that day save the voice of prayer. Miss Fiske has never known such a Sabbath before, nor since. In the afternoon, the feeling was overpowering. There was no request for prayer, but unbroken stillness and the perfect performance of every duty, without a word being said. At the supper table, every face seemed to say, "Our meat and drink are not here." Some asked to be excused, but at length all were seated; and the scene that followed can never be forgotten. All who were previously interested, and more beside, wept tears of silent sorrow. The blessing was asked, and the steward * began to help them, himself in tears; but no plate was touched, for even the uninterested gazed in silent wonder. Their teacher urged them to eat; but one, seizing her hand, said in a voice too low to be overheard, "You would not ask *me* to eat if you knew my heart." The reply was, "I feel just as sure that the Lord would have you eat, as that he would have you pray." They were then besought to eat, so as to have strength to pray. This touched a tender chord, and so succeeded; and then they silently withdrew to make that use of their renovated strength. Each hour that night found some at the mercy seat, feeling that to leave off at such a crisis might lessen the blessing.

Two months now passed on, each day furnishing new evidence that those prayers were heard. There was less of excitement, but no diminution of interest, to the close of the term. The uniform and sustained prayerfulness of those months surprised the beholders. The voice of sup-

* Yohanan, father of Esli. See page 67.

plication was the latest sound of evening, the watchword of midnight, and the lark song of the dawn. One pupil, nine years of age, after spending two hours in her closet, consented to retire only when allowed to rise and pray if she awoke during the night; and she was sure to wake. About three o'clock every morning, her earnest pleadings roused her teachers from repose.

The hours of social prayer were full of tenderness. Those who heard the pupils pleading far within the veil, close by the mercy seat, almost forgot that they were yet on earth. The school, their parents and relatives, were all affectionately remembered. The hour always seemed too short, and often closed with such expressions as these: "If we have not been heard here, we will go to our closets, and if not heard there, we will return here, and again go back to our closets, and so continue to plead for these loved ones to the last." These meetings, though varied in character, were always of thrilling interest. Now there was an overwhelming sense of sin, as committed against a holy God, and then, as a ray of hope appeared, a weeping voice would implore, as on one occasion, that "the Holy One would walk over the hills of Judea, find Golgotha, and let them live." Again, the sight of manifold transgressions prompted the cry, "But we fear our sins have covered Golgotha from thy sight, and then are we forever lost." Another part of the same prayer contained the entreaty, "Lift not the mercy seat from off the holy ark, to look on the law we have broken, but look into Jesus' grave, and bid us live."

In the daily family prayer meetings every inmate of the room was specially and tenderly remembered. Once, when a father had come for his daughter, and Miss Fiske went to find her, on opening the door she heard a prayer for one who had shown little feeling; and in pleading the sufferings of Christ on her behalf, each petition seemed to rise higher, till every face was turned upward, as if to see him; and the one who led in devotion involuntarily stretched out her hands to lay hold of him, saying, "Come, Lord Jesus, and save our perishing sister; but if she will not receive thee in this life we must forever rejoice in her destruction" — a striking illustration of intense spiritual emotion, bringing the heart into sympathy with the whole truth of God. (Rev. xix. 3.)

These labors for their impenitent associates, and for those women who came to the Seminary, were full of Christ. The hour between supper and the evening meeting was usually spent in personal labor from room to room; and the entreaties and prayers, then audible on all sides, made it delightful to be a stranger in a strange land for Jesus' sake. It was scarcely less affecting when superstitious grandmothers, worldly mothers, and giddy sisters were prayed with and entreated to come to Christ.

The audible prayers of the pupils may trouble some readers, but not more than they troubled their teacher. She desired more silent devotion; but Mr. Stoddard, himself in the habit of praying aloud, looked on it with more favor, and feared to have it checked. Soon after his own conversion, a friend remarked to him, "I think you had better not pray quite so loud;" and for days after it he could not pray at all. He had never thought of others while communing with God, and he was troubled that others should think of him. Even to the last he continued the practice of praying audibly.

Miss Fiske sometimes spoke to her pupils on the subject. There was one who spent hours daily in her closet, but her teacher heard all she said. So, on a fitting opportunity, she suggested to her, in a gentle way, that she might modify the practice. "I will try to pray in a lower voice," was the reply; "but I never thought of any body's hearing me." That night her voice was more subdued, but her prayer was very short; and soon after midnight her teacher was awakened by the voice of prayer out on the roof. She stepped out quietly; and there was her pupil wrapped in a blanket, and thanking the Lord for such a place to pray. She continued her devotions till near morning; and the kind teacher had no heart to interfere any further. Mr. Stoddard was much amused with her success; and it may teach all of us, in this matter, to suffer the Holy Spirit to divide to every one severally as he will.

On another occasion, not liking to assume the responsibility herself, and yet fearing for the health of her pupil, who generally spent a long time in fervent devotion, she led the physician to the outside of the door; but he, too, after listening for a while, did not venture to interrupt such communion with God. Sarah of Tiary was within.

Meetings were held three days in the week with the women in the neighborhood, and were well attended. The older pupils were allowed to assist in these in order to form habits of doing good for after life; and they did so to edification, both leading in prayer and addressing the beloved mothers — as they called those older than themselves — tenderly and in fitting words.

It was of such a work that Miss Fiske wrote at the time, "We cannot speak confidently of its fruits at this early date, especially as many of our dear charge are so young; but we can say what present appearances are; and while we daily try to obey our Saviour's command, 'Feed my lambs!' we trust that friends at home will hear no less distinctly the same voice, saying, 'Pray for my lambs in

Persia.' All those whom we regarded as Christians have shown themselves most faithful to their Master during this season. Others, of whom we were less confident, have seemed to pass through a previously untried experience, and, we tremblingly hope, have laid hold of eternal life. The same is true of several never before convicted. Among these last is a little girl who was suddenly awakened, with as clear convictions, apparently, as I ever saw in any; and her final trust in Christ as implicit. For several days she would say, with tears and sobs, 'I have never yet loved the Saviour; but O, I do want to love him now.' Her mother is one of the few converted in Geog Tapa before the first revival. She has suffered almost every thing for Christ. Often, on returning late from meeting, she has found herself shut out for an hour in a piercing winter wind, before her husband would open the door. At other times she has been beaten, but never denied Him who bought her. The pious natives often say that in the conversion of her daughter, she now receives the reward of her years of prayer and faithful endurance. The last days of the term bound the dear pupils very closely to each other, and we trust to Christ. When the hour of separation came, a prayer meeting was held in each room, and continued to the last moment. Those without hope clung to their praying sisters, with tears and entreaties for prayer. The hopeful converts went forth with a holy, chastened gratitude and trust. We tremble for them among their wicked friends, but rejoice that Israel's Shepherd will keep his own."

Their prayer was, "May we not carry to our homes the poison of the second death in our hearts, but bear to them the seeds of eternal life."

But the rich blessings bestowed in Oroomiah were not

all in answer to prayer ascending from that place. There was a connection between them and prayer offered in our own country, of which David would say, "Whoso is wise, and will observe it, even he shall understand the loving kindness of the Lord." Most of the revivals in Oroomiah commenced on the day of the monthly concert of prayer, and several on or immediately after the first Monday in January — a day specially set apart to prayer for missions. But there was a special centre of prayer for the Female Seminary in the institution at South Hadley; and pious hearts loved to watch the connection between the two. While the two inquirers, on that first Monday in 1846, were making closets for themselves with the sticks of wood in the cellar, some of Miss Lyon's pupils distinctly remember how she said to them that morning, "We must pray more for Miss Fiske and her school." They did so; and they remember, too, how the good news of the revival cheered them, when it came.

The earliest indication of interest, in 1847, was on the first Monday in January; and letters afterwards told of special prayer for the school offered that day in South Hadley. Almost every letter written during the winter of 1849 contained similar information. The revival of 1856 came suddenly and unexpectedly; but when, on the night of February 17th, one of the praying pupils could not sleep, because, as she said, "the whole school was resting on her," and at midnight went to her teacher to ask her help in prayer, subsequent letters from America showed, that on that night she wrestled not alone. In 1857, the first inquiry for the way of life was on the last Thursday in February, the day of prayer for institutions of learning. Miss Fiske returned from the February concert of prayer, in 1858, feeling depressed on account of the want of interest in the school, and in half an hour was called to see two of her pupils, who felt that they could not remain the enemies of God. In the first week of February, 1859, meetings were held every evening in the Seminary at South Hadley to pray for the school in Oroomiah; and a letter from Miss Rice, written that week, says, "God is with us; souls are seeking Christ; and I am so strengthened for labor, that I am sure Christian friends are praying for us more than they did last month." Do Christians in this country realize as they ought the connection between their prayers and the blessings bestowed on the opposite side of the globe? Do we go to the monthly concert believing that prayer, offered then and there, will, through infinite grace in Christ Jesus, result in the salvation of souls and the advancement of his kingdom? Such facts as these ought surely to increase our faith. Well might a missionary say, "I have so often felt sure that I was reaping in answer to the prayers of those far away, that on this subject my heart is full, and my first and last word to friends is, 'Pray for us.'"

CHAPTER XVII.

FORERUNNERS.

MOUNTAIN GIRLS IN SEMINARY. — PRAYING SARAH. — RETURN TO THE MOUNTAINS. — VISIT OF YONAN AND KHAMIS, IN 1850. — OF MR. COAN, 1851. — OF YONAN, AGAIN, 1861. — SARAH'S LETTERS.

But rich as are the benefits conferred on the females of the plain, the influence of the Seminary is not confined to Persia. It has climbed the rugged steeps of Kurdistan, and pours into its wild glens and secluded hamlets the same spiritual blessings. It is delightful to trace the way in which God has led to results, as yet only beginning to appear, among the mountain Nestorians.

As the Seminary could not enter the mountains, Providence brought the mountains to the Seminary. In 1843, Badir Khan Beg sacked and burned the villages of Tiary, and the homeless fugitives who escaped the sword fled to the plains of Assyria and Azerbijan. Towards the close of that year, a miserable group presented themselves at the Seminary door for charity, asking for the lady who teaches Nestorian girls. The quick eye of the teacher detected three in the company before her, and replied, "Silver and gold we have not, but such as we have we will give you — a home for these children." This sent them away sorrowful, for it was not what they wanted. But while the parents retired to the shade of the tall sycamores to debate the matter, the little ones, attracted by kindness in a stranger, staid with their new friend. By and by the parents came back, and, falling on the necks of their children, told them they might stay, till they returned to Tiary. The teacher never heard a more gentle and subdued "thank you" than this announcement called forth from those mountain girls. This was the first movement of the school towards the evangelization of Kurdistan, and it will be seen how Providence led the Seminary at Seir in the same path.

The girls were taken in, washed, and clothed; and though at first they knew no more of good manners than of the alphabet, they made commendable progress in both. Better than that, Sarah and Nazee became hopefully pious in the revival of 1846, and Heleneh three years afterwards.

The last days of the spring term, in 1849, as we have seen, were full of interest. The teachers did not understand it then, but now they see that God was preparing his first messengers to the rude mountaineers for the work before them. Among a company of praying ones, Sarah had long been known as "the praying Sarah." She was the pupil whom Deacon Isaac invited to come and pray * with him; and the strong man bowed before the simple piety of that mountain girl. Her mind was not so gifted as many of her associates. She comprehended truth with difficulty, but she prayed with all prayer and supplication in the spirit. At this time an unusual spirit of prayer was imparted to the school. The prospect of vacation, instead of diverting the mind from devotion, seemed to produce intenser earnestness. The voice of prayer fell on the ears of the teachers at all hours, except the most silent watch of the night. After the evening meeting, some spent two hours in their closets, and others of the older pupils could not

* See page 151.

leave till they had prayed with each one in the school alone. On the last morning of the term, they separated with many tears and fervent supplications. The quiet of the hour seemed a foretaste of the rest of heaven. Not a loud voice, heavy step, or harshly shutting door was heard in all the house. All was so sacredly quiet that the still small voice might be heard the more distinctly. The teachers sent out the lambs from the fold with feelings of peculiar anxiety. Some were to go into families where every soul would gladly undo in them the work of the Spirit; others to villages where not one heart could enter into their feelings as the followers of Christ; and as they went forth, their teachers prayed, from full hearts, that the Shepherd of Israel would himself be to them for a little sanctuary in the places where they went.

While their thoughts were on such of their flock as belonged to the plain, the thoughts of God were on those also whom he was about to send forth to a life-long separation from these means of grace. As late as ten o'clock, on the evening after the close of the term, Miss Fiske heard the voice of prayer for the absent ones, and fearing that the occupant of the closet was transgressing the laws of health, she approached the door, intending to enter, and advise her to retire; but as she listened to her strong crying, with tears, for each of the school by name, she could not find it in her heart to disturb the intercessions of Sarah. She was then a great bodily sufferer, but very patient, and for a long time had not spent less than four hours daily in her closet. The next day her disease assumed a serious form, and for more than a week she hovered on the borders of the grave. Several times she appeared to have drawn her last breath. But though her sick room seemed to all like the gate of heaven, and though to her the dark valley was all light, and she longed to embrace the messenger who should lead her through, it was not her Father's will to call her then. She was at first disappointed at the prospect of coming back to the world; yet still she sweetly said, "Thy will be done," as God restored her to health, with its responsibilities and temptations.

April came, and a scarcity in the plain, occasioned by locusts, drove the fugitives from Tiary back to their mountains. The teachers hoped the girls might remain, and besought their parents to allow them to do so, but in vain. They were only too glad to get their daughters away from influences which in their blindness they abhorred. But God intended through these daughters to lay the foundations of many generations, and build again the old waste places of those mountains.

It was hard for them to go. How could they leave their Christian home, and the means of grace they had enjoyed so much? It was no less hard for the teachers to think of those lambs as about to be left at the mercy of wolves, in rocky glens, so far away that no cry of distress would ever reach them. Yea, even if those loved ones died, long years might pass ere their friends could hear of their death. Those were days of sadness, and communion with God was the only comfort of all, and especially of Sarah.

On the day of their departure, the whole school came together, in the room of the teachers, for the parting prayer. All was silent, till the three asked to go and bid a farewell to their closets. They went, and only He who seeth in secret knows how they prayed. They returned weeping. A few words of comfort were uttered, and the teachers commended them to God. They rose from their knees, but only to kneel again; for one of the pupils proposed that all who would pledge themselves to remember their Tiary sisters in every prayer should join hands around them, commend them to the good Shepherd, and give to him their pledge. About twenty thus enclosed the departing sisters, and so they continued in prayer until the last moment. As the dear ones passed out, they could not speak, they whispered but one word, — "the promise," — and so they went. For years after, no prayer was heard within those walls that did not contain a petition for "blessings on our Tiary sisters."

Many a time had her teacher noticed the large folio page of Sarah's Syriac Testament wet with her tears, and after she left, found the whitewash of the wall in her closet furrowed with the same. It opened out of the passage behind the door on the left of the engraving. She did not tell this to the school, lest superstition should attach an idolatrous sacredness to the place; and yet she could not obliterate marks that to her own heart were so full of comfort. Sarah had gone but a little way before she pleaded with her parents to stop, and allow her to retire a little from the road for prayer.

And so, weeping and praying as they went, these lambs were led into the dark recesses of a den of lions. We shall see persecution raging, pitiless as the mountain storm, and long continued. But we shall also see the Hearer of prayer preserving them unharmed; and if we hear more from the others than from Sarah, it may be that the revelation of the answers to her prayers is reserved for that day which shall unfold displays of grace too glorious for comprehension here.

Nothing was heard from them till October, 1850, when Yonan and Khamis entered those rocky fastnesses to gather tidings of them. They spent the first Sabbath of the month in the house of Nazee; but she was absent. They say in their journal, —

"We preached three times to large assemblies. They brought us Nazee's Testament to preach from, and seemed accustomed to the sound of the gospel. In respectful attention to the word, as well as in knowledge, they were far superior to other villages in Tiary. This we knew was the result of her teachings. Monday we waited her return. She came about noon. How can we express the joy of that meeting! We spent another night there, the most of it in sweet Christian conversation with Nazee. We were surprised at the respect shown to her, and the restraint felt in her presence. If any chanced to swear, he at once went and asked pardon for thus injuring her feelings. Tuesday we had to leave, lest we should be detained by the snow till spring. We longed to pray with her before we left, but custom here forbade it; yet she accompanied us a little on our way, which gave us an opportunity to mingle our prayers and tears together. As we bade her farewell, she said, weeping, 'Here is my love for my teachers, for my sisters in the school, for the missionaries, their children, and all that know me. Tell them to remember me in their prayers, that God may keep me in this place of temptation.' We left her looking after us, and wiping away her tears, till we were out of sight.

"We went that day to the village of the other two. As soon as Heleneh saw us, she began to weep, thinking of the past. Sarah we did not see; she was in another village, very anxious to come, but her wicked husband, whom she had been forced to marry, would not permit it. We spent the night with Heleneh, and preached to a large company. Next morning we left, and she too, with tears, begged that all her friends in Oroomiah would remember her in their prayers."

Was Sarah prevented from seeing her Christian friends,

that God might show hereafter how, without even that help, he could answer the prayers of others for her, and her own?

The next we hear of them is through Mr. Coan, who visited Tiary in August, 1851. The writer can understand his account of crossing the Zab, as the bridge was in the same condition when he crossed it with the late Dr. Azariah Smith, August 31st, 1844. But hear Mr. Coan:—

"A toilsome day, over the roughest of roads, brought us opposite Chumba. The bridge had been swept away, and fording such a torrent was impossible. Two long poplar trees spanned the flood; and we crossed on them, bending under us at every step. Nazee was on the bank, ready to greet us. After a few words of salutation and kind inquiry, she hastened to prepare a place for us; and while doing this, the malik took us to his house. She was much disappointed, but followed, anxious to treasure up every word. After supper, we spoke long to the company assembled on the roof. It was affecting to see how eagerly she listened. She staid after the rest, for religious conversation, till near midnight, when she apologized for keeping us up so late. She is cruelly persecuted by her wicked mother and ungodly neighbors; for she is a shining light, by which the dark deeds of the wicked are reproved; and hence their hatred. When Mar Shimon's attendants come, they treat her with wanton cruelty. Some friends in America had sent her several articles of clothing; but her neighbors came together and tore them in pieces before her eyes. She bore it meekly, and only prayed for them. She expected fresh insults because of our visit, but prayed that nothing might separate her from the love of Christ. Long before day, she again sought to improve every moment for Christian conversation. We tried to comfort her:

and her eyes filled with tears of gratitude. She received a copy of the Gospels with joy. When we left, she followed us, lonely and sad, to the river side. I opened her Testament, and pointed to Matt. xi. 28: 'Come unto me, all ye that labor, and are heavy laden;' but her voice choked, and tears prevented her reading. We kneeled by the roaring Zab, and in broken accents commended her to Him who will keep her, for his promise is sure."

For ten long years we hear nothing of either of the three; till, in September, 1861, Yonan — the same who found them in 1850 — and another preacher visited the mountains. In a village of Tiary, some two thousand people were keeping the feast of the cross — eating, drinking, dancing, and carousing. They sat down among the quietest of the crowd. Heleneh came up and saluted them. Though she had not seen her teacher for eleven years, she recognized him at once. They talked from morning till near sunset. As they spoke of old friends, Yonan asked, "Heleneh, do you remember where our Lord was crucified?" "On Calvary. Can I forget *Calvary?*" as though grieved that he should think she could forget. Yonan gave her a kerchief for the head, saying, "Take this, and remember me by it." "Shall I remember you by this?" was the reply. "I will remember you in my prayers." "Do you pray, Heleneh?" — She was the last one converted, and left Oroomiah soon after her conversion; so he wanted to know whether she still held on her Christian way. — "Always," was the answer. They sought a place to pray together; and though they might not go away alone, yet there, in sight, but not in hearing of the crowd, they approached the mercy seat, the spectators little dreaming of the nature of their intercourse. It was delightful to find that she had not forgotten the language or the spirit of devotion.

The accompanying sketch of a Tiary girl will show how the kerchief is worn. It also exhibits the mode of using the Oriental spindle, which is probably a fac-simile of the article mentioned by Solomon. (Prov. xxxi. 19.)

A TIARY GIRL.

The other two were not at the feast; so, next day, they left to seek them at their homes. Nazee was absent, but came home in the morning — a widow with two children. She was delighted, and even her children seemed to recognize in the strangers their mother's friends. She was poor; her house had been burned, and almost all it contained; but a stone was on her Testament, and that was saved. They talked long with her, and gave her a copy of the Rays of Light (the monthly periodical issued by the mission), and a pencil to write to her friends. She gave them letters written ten years before, which she had penned in secret, and carried about with her ever since, waiting an opportunity to send them.

The next day, another long journey brought them to the home of Sarah; she saw them coming and hastened to meet them; but that very night she had to leave for a distant village: yet not till in answer to prayer they had an opportunity to pray together; and the friends left that village happy; for, as Yonan said, they "found her, like the others, having the love of our Christ in her heart."

That solitary disciple, through those long years of seclusion, never hearing the voice of Christian fellowship, or knowing whether her pious friends were alive, or if her sisters still remembered their pledge, was yet kept of God according to his promise; and it is interesting to see that she does not once allude to her persecutions in her letters, but only solicits the prayers of her friends for her relatives and neighbors; and then, while both Mr. Coan and her teacher testify to her usefulness, with what humility does she allude to herself, and "the very little she has made known of the Lord Jesus Christ."

Extracts from the letters that she kept so long here follow. The first, to friends in Middlebury, Vermont, is dated September, 1851, and reads thus: —

"To you, dear friends, I write a letter unworthy and imperfect, in which I make known to you my lost condition and my present abode. Know ye that a little more than two years ago I left the Seminary, and came with my friends to our country. I did not wish to leave so soon, for I had learned but very imperfectly what the Scriptures teach about our Lord Jesus Christ. But my mother was not willing I should remain, for her heart is yet hard and dark. Know, then, dear sisters in Christ, I dwell in Tiary, in the village of Chumba, about six days' journey from Oroomiah. Again, though so far away, know ye, that your letter reached me in May. It was translated and sent to me by Mr. Perkins, our beloved father, whom we are unworthy to call such. My dear sisters, when I took your letter in my hands and read, my heart longed to fly and sit down by you, and behold your faces in the body; but I said, "The will of the Lord, not mine, be done." When I look within myself, and see not a place worthy to cherish gratitude to God for his great mercy and grace, which he hath wrought for us, sinful and unworthy, I liken myself to the slothful servant, who did not the will of his Lord. Yet, O, my sisters, though I have not done the will of my Saviour, I have hope in him that I shall do it, and serve him henceforth so long as I am in this world — fleeting as a dream in the night.

Though our country has been, in time past, greatly afflicted by the Koords, yet God has spared many of us, who had sinned and trodden under our feet the blood of his holy Son. But do not marvel that we have sorrow from the scourge God brought upon us for our sins. No. Still every day we provoke our Maker more and more. Then ought we not to mourn over this people, lost and fallen under the yoke of Satan? For should you go through all Tiary, you would not find one soul that fears the Lord, but all bound in fetters not to be loosed. If God do not loose them, quickly will they perish; and not this country only, but many others, sit under the shadow of death and walk in darkness, going to destruction. Then, dear sisters, though unworthy, we should increase our painful efforts, and our prayers to God, that speedily his kingdom may come and his will be done on earth as it is done in heaven, that all regions may know him and praise him forever. Beloved sisters, I am unworthy to thank you, and still more to thank God, who has disposed you to show such kindness to my poor body, and yet more to my perishing soul, with words so gentle and full of love; yet greatly do I thank you.

Again, dear friends, I have one request to make—that every time you bow before God, the Father of our Lord Jesus Christ, and of all who love him, you will remember me in your prayers, for I am very needy, and there is great danger that my soul will perish forever. Remember also my mother, and all my friends, sinners, and on their way to destruction. Know ye, further, that I conceal the writing of this because they would not allow me openly to write, for they are very foolish and benighted. Accept, then, this poor letter, as a token of friendship and gratitude, in the love of our Lord Jesus Christ.

From your unworthy and sinful sister,

NAZEE, of Tiary. Amen.

The following are extracts from another letter to the same persons:—

"Though we are far from each other in this evil world, yet I hope that our Lord Jesus Christ will make us pure from sin, and worthy of his kingdom, where we shall see each other with that light which shall not end, in the joy of the holy angels. Ah, my friends, how great are our mercies and we how unworthy, but especially I!—unworthy of the gift of the gospel of God, which I have received, that I might make it known to lost souls around me. But know ye, very little have I made known about our Lord Jesus Christ. Now, dear friends, I desire to speak of him to lost souls, in the imperfection of my mind. But many do not desire even to hear of the sound doctrine of the Lord Jesus Christ, and yet think to gain heaven, while they practise in this world according to their wicked desires. And for this reason, O my sisters, I beseech you that you will remember this people, lost and fallen under the snares of Satan; especially my mother, and brother, and all my friends. But more especially, I beseech you to remember me, a sinner, in your prayers, every time that you bow the knee before God, the Father of our Lord Jesus Christ, and the Father of all who fear him, and listen to his commandments."

Accompanying these was the following to Dr. Perkins, dated October 3d, 1851:—

"To you, O my spiritual father, Mr. Perkins, I presume to send two letters, for friends in Middlebury. If you please, you will translate them, and send them; but I fear that they will give you much trouble.

"Again, you wrote me in your letter, that I should teach children to read. Now, I am very needy myself of instruction. Yet I desire that that might be my employment. But that is a very difficult matter among such a people, of whom you have heard that although there may be here and there one who would walk in this way, yet there is a stone of stumbling and a rock of offence therein; so that every one that goeth in it, his foot stumbleth, and quickly he turns back.

"Again, O friend beloved, though I am unworthy to call you such, yet I beseech you that you remember me always in your prayers. I know that you do remember me, but I desire that you remember me more, for I greatly fear for my perishing soul. Greatly do I desire to see you once more in this world, if the Lord will."

He who is wonderful in counsel and excellent in working, commissioned these praying souls to prepare his way in the mountains, even as he chose those other three to show forth his grace in death; and they who live to mark the future course of the river of life in those rocky glens will find, we trust, that his strength was made perfect in their weakness.

CHAPTER XVIII.

LABORERS IN THE MOUNTAINS.

LETTER OF BADAL. — ACCOUNT OF HANNAH. — THE PIT. — LETTER OF GULY AND YOHANAN. — ACCOUNT OF SARAH. — LETTERS OF OSHANA. — LETTERS AND JOURNAL OF SARAH. — LETTER FROM AMADIA. — CONFERENCE OF NATIVE HELPERS.

BESIDES these, the Seminary has sent up other laborers into the same field. At the monthly concert in Oroomiah, June, 1858, there were present four graduates, with their husbands, either going there for the first time, or returning to resume their labors. Guly, the wife of Yohanan, who had already spent one year in little Jeloo, was now about to return there with her husband. Nargis, the wife of Khamis, who had spent the winter laboring alone in the vicinity of Amadia, on the Turkish side of the mountains, was now with him, going back to Gawar. Hannah, the wife of Badal, who had sent her husband, three days after marriage, to his winter's campaign in the same region, was now accompanying him to the chosen field of his labors; and Eneya, the wife of Shlemon, his associate, was also expecting to leave in a few days.

By the way of introducing the reader to one of these laborers, we subjoin a letter from Badal to Miss Fiske, dated December 12th, 1859. It is a good specimen of Oriental style.

"Writing to you brings to mind many sweet conversations with you. Dwelling on them, my mind is sad. My sighs rise like the swelling stream, and almost carry me away, especially when I look at your garden, where you labored with so much skill to graft in these wild olive plants, cutting off your sleep with watchings by night, that they should not be rooted up by the desert wind. Thus you watched them, till they became as noble forest trees that not even the avalanche can overturn. Your garden, now, not only gives a shade pleasant to the traveller, but it yields sweet fruits; clouds rise from it that give us the early and the latter rain; they empty themselves, — the plain rejoices, and the barren places become verdant. Yes, the vine that you planted has budded, and blossomed, and gives of its fruit to every passer by. Come to us, our beloved, open the door of your garden, that the traveller may enter in and be refreshed. You have left many pleasant remembrances in the work of your hands. On every side you have left a picture for our eyes, and the skilful work of your hands (his wife), lo, and behold! it is with me. I cannot be silent. My voice shall be heard as the turtle's: 'Behold, your feet are within my doors, and your counsels are ever in my family.' The Lord reward you for these pupils, that you have taught to be patient and persevering, so that they truly help us in the work of life.

"Beloved, give my love to your friends, and ask them, when they go up to Shiloh to offer sacrifice, to place me in the censer of their prayers.

"We are troubled that as yet we know not the Lord's thoughts concerning you, — whether he will allow you to meet your flock again, or says to you as to Daniel, 'Thou shalt rest, and stand in thy lot at the end of the days.' Like Moses, you are gathered to your fathers; but Miss Rice stands like Joshua, commanding the sun not to go down till the sword of the gospel shall triumph. We thank the Lord that she is still a judge in Israel, so that as yet the sceptre has not departed from Judah.

"Your affectionate friend, BADAL."

There are some things about Hannah, and the work of divine grace in her, that demand grateful record.

She was the daughter of one of the most intelligent and wealthy Nestorians, who placed her in the Seminary as early as 1845. She was then quite small, and the teacher objected very much to taking her; but paternal importunity prevailed. As soon as her father turned to go, she began to scream; but he left, saying she must remain, and "learn wisdom." The kind teacher took her in her lap to soothe her; but it was of no use; her bleeding hands bore the marks of the nails of her new protegée for weeks. She called for her father, but he was intentionally out of hearing.

The child remained, but learned wisdom very slowly. She had her fits of rage so often, that she was sent home sometimes for weeks, and again for months. She made little progress, either in study or other good, till the winter of 1850, when she seemed to begin to love the truth; yet, though her general deportment was correct, she often showed such a determined will, that her instructors feared she had never said from the heart, "Not my will, but thine," and often told her that, if she was a Christian, God would, in love, subdue that will. She could not feel her need of this, and thought that they required too much of her. So they were obliged to leave her with God, and he cared for her in an unusual way. The mission premises had formerly been occupied by an Oriental bath; and here and there were old pits, once used for carrying off the water, but now covered up, so that no one knew where they were. One evening Miss Fiske called the girls together, and told them some things she wished they would refrain from. They promised compliance, and went out; but hardly had they gone before their teacher heard the cry, "Hannah is in the well!" She ran there, but all was right. Then they led her to an opening just before the back door, saying, "The earth opened and swallowed her up." The covering of one of the pits had given way, and she had fallen perhaps twenty feet below the surface. Fortunately, as in the case of Joseph, there was no water in the pit, and in a few days she was able to resume her place in school, but much more gentle and subdued than ever before. The change was marked by all. Months after, in a private interview with her teacher, she gave an account of the whole matter. She said the girls went out, most of them saying, "We will obey our teachers;" but she, stamping her foot, said, "I did right before, and I shall do so again." With these words on her lips, she sunk into the earth. At first she did not know what had happened, but remembered all that had been said, and felt that God was dealing with her. Lying there helpless and bruised at the bottom of the pit, she made a solemn vow to God, "Never again my will." From that time she was a most lovely example of all that was gentle. She seemed to give up every thing, and "bear all things." Her father saw the change, and one day said to her teachers, "I am not a Christian; but Hannah knows nothing but God's will. If she should die now, I should know she was with Christ, she is so like him." Her Christian character developed beautifully; the school learned of her to be Christ-like. She longed to do good, and was ready to make any sacrifice for the good of souls. When Badal sought her hand from her father, the latter called her, and said, "Hannah, Badal the son of the herdsman, wants you to go to the mountains with him, and —— wants you to live here with him. It shall be as you say." She replied very meekly, "I wish to suffer with the people of God. I choose to go with Badal;" and June 8th, 1858, she left for her mountain home.

The parting prayer meeting with those four girls, going as missionaries to the mountains, was one of the pleasantest memories that Miss Fiske carried away from Oroomiah. She left soon after, but often heard from Hannah and her companions that she was happy in her life of privation for Jesus' sake, and did what she could. She suffered, however, from the change, and was advised to visit Oroomiah for her health. It was hoped she might soon recover; but she went only to leave her sweet testimony to the blessedness of knowing no will but God's, and then go home. She sent the following messages to Miss Fiske from her dying bed: "I love to have God do just as he pleases. I thank you for all your love, and especially for showing me my Saviour." She died in December, 1860.

Having given herself to Missionary work among the mountains, it is interesting to know that her little property also went to the same object. In the remarkable revival of benevolence, in Oroomiah, in the spring of 1861, her brother gave her inheritance, which had fallen to him, to sustain laborers in the mountains: thus, after her life had been laid down in the work, all her living went to carry it on.

Let Guly introduce herself to the reader by giving her own account of her conversion, in 1856: —

My dear Superintendent, Miss Fiske: I wish now, as far as I can, to describe to you my spiritual state. The first four weeks of the revival I did not realize that I was lost, but afterwards was more burdened; my sins were round about me like dark clouds. One night I went to Miss Rice to have her pray with me. I did not know how to find Christ. She told me; yet all that night I saw no light, but only darkness. I was almost in despair, yet felt that this was from Satan. In the morning the sun rose pleasantly, but it was as night to me; for I knew that I had no portion in God. So I continued all that day. I could not read in my class, but went to my room, and vowed not to leave it till I had some token that Christ was mine. I brought nothing in my hands save my sins, which were like mountains. I remembered that scripture, "Though your sins be as scarlet, they shall be as white as snow;" and I recalled the promises of God, and that no other could pardon me. With earnest longing, I laid my soul into the hands of Jesus. I heartily covenanted to serve him all my life, and sought help from him in prayer. Then suddenly I saw light, as if he were at my side; and I did not wish to rise from my knees, so blessed was that communion. From that time I had hope, but sometimes fear I may be deceived. Yet daily I find Christ more and more precious. Though old Adam is not dead, yet in the strength of God I will resist him.

Yes, my dear mother in Christ, my guide to the cross, my desire is to please God, and live for him, not for myself. I cannot say that I shall never sin, for I am weak, and my foe is strong; but I will seek help from Him who was tempted, and can succor me when tempted.

I am most thankful to you that you have been the means of my salvation, and can never forget your love till my tongue is silent in the grave.

Your affectionate Guly, of Seir.

She and her husband, Yohanan, have labored in the mountains ever since their marriage. He writes to Miss Fiske in February, 1861,—

"I have not forgotten your pleasant love, and trust I never shall until I die. I hope that, with all your friends here, I shall see you again. As our joy is not full in your absence, may you not rest till you return.

"We are now in Vizierawa of Gawar; for the people of Ishtazin, instigated by Mar Shimon, have cast us out. I had hoped to go to Amadia, but was robbed and wounded, in the autumn, by the Koords; and before I could recover my goods, it was too late to go so far. So I remain here; and, thanks to God, our labor in the gospel is more pleasant than ever. Some of the men wish to hear the whole will of God; and women and girls come to Guly to hear his words. A few children also are constant in learning to read. The work of God prospers this year in Gawar, and the laborers are more numerous and more faithful."

In estimating the zeal and self-denial of these Nestorian missionaries, it should be borne in mind that our missionaries there, think it requires as much self-denial for a native of Oroomiah to go to the mountains, as for an American to go to Oroomiah; and according to the testimony of a native observer, the married graduates of the Seminary, in the mountains, are centres of light in that great sea of darkness.

Besides those already mentioned, Oshana and Sarah, with Shlemon and Eneya, are laboring in Amadia. This Sarah is daughter of Priest Abraham, of Geog Tapa, and was one of the earliest pupils of the Seminary. When Deacon Isaac broke it up, in 1844, she was the only pupil who remained. She was hopefully converted in 1846, and while in the Seminary was supported by the Sabbath school in Owego, New York.

In 1849, it was proposed that her father labor in Ardishai, one of the darkest and most wicked villages of the plain, as one might expect the home of the notorious Mar Gabriel would be. Great opposition was made by the people to his coming among them; and his own wife—not then converted—did much to hinder his going; but Sarah did all in her power to encourage him; and a letter of hers on the subject decided him to go. She rejoiced to give up her friends, her pleasant home, and even her privileges, that he might labor in that unpromising field. Nor was she by any means idle. She spent all her vacations there, laboring with much acceptance and success; and after she graduated, in 1850, besides her day school through the week, she had a Bible class on the Sabbath, with the women; and on Friday, also, she sent out her pupils, in the afternoon, to invite their mothers and other women to a meeting she held with them in the evening. She thus acquired great influence, and led several to the Saviour. Her labors were very systematic. She had a plan for conversing personally with one pupil each day, and was noted for her tact and success in efforts with individuals. Others might act from impulse, and soon tire; but hers is an activity controlled by principle, and therefore uniform and enduring. Very faithful in admonition when admonition is required, she is at the same time noted for gentleness, and thus expresses to Miss Fiske her delight in laboring for Christ: "Separated from Christian friends, I am sometimes sad; but I am not greater than my Master, who left the holy society of heaven to come to earth, and I am glad for a corner where I may labor for such a Master. Come and spend a Sabbath here if you can; if not, pray much and often for these poor women." Again speaking of her school, she says, "It is the goodness of God that gives me these little girls. Pray for them. I see indications that they will be lovers of the Lord. Forty or fifty of the women come to meeting, and twenty-two are willing to receive the truth." She was accustomed to study the Bible with her father, and in that way also aided him in his labors.

But it is time to bring forward her husband, in letters which open up a new department of usefulness, and illustrate the meaning of Mar Yohanan, when he brought her first pupils to Miss Fiske, and said, "No man take them from you." The truth was, that the same parents, who at first could not trust their daughters in the Seminary for a single night, were now unwilling that they should be united to a husband who did not commend himself to its teachers as a suitable companion for their pupils. But let Oshana speak: —

Honored Lady, Miss Fiske: I have a petition to lay before your zeal, which is active in doing good to all poor insignificant ones like me. Dear lady, whose love is like the waters of the Nile, and spreads more than they; for it reaches the sons of the mountains of Kurdistan, as well as those of the plain. I am venturing to trouble you more than ever before. This summer, when I went to my country (Tehoma), my mother and uncles, who greatly love me, with a natural love, beset me to marry one of the daughters of my country, whomsoever I should please; but I made known to them that I wished, if possible, to take one of the pupils of your school, for I said to them, "If I take one of these who are so wicked, ignorant, immodest, and disorderly, they will embitter my life." I entreated of them not to put this yoke of iron on my neck. They listened a little to my petition, from the mercy of

God, but made me promise that if it should reach my hand, I would marry this winter. The girl on whom I have placed my eye, to take her, is Sarah; because she has the "fear of God, which is the beginning of wisdom," and she has been brought up in all the graces of Christianity, and has well learned the holy doctrines; and in the fear of God, and the knowledge she has acquired, she can help me, and strengthen me, in the work of God, on which I have placed my heart for life.

And now, to whom shall I look to help me in this matter? I will look to God, the Lord of heaven and earth. But he works by instruments. Then to whom shall I look, as the instrument to do this work? I am a stranger, poor, and without a name here. My relatives are far away. If I have friends in Oroomiah, they cannot do this kindness for me. If I remain silent, silence alone shall I see. Now, my lady, I look to you for help; and with confidence shall I do so more than I should to my parents; for you have guided me and my sister better than any Nestorians have guided their children. Yes, by your hand God will supply my need. Now do as you think proper. From your unworthy

Oshana.

P. S. The other letter (enclosed) is for Sarah, and on this subject.

Some time after he was engaged to her, she was very sick, when he wrote as follows; and the reader will notice that the "honored lady" gives place to

Dear Mother, and Nourisher of Sarah: I have no friend in whose pleasant, pure love I can delight as in Sarah, and she is now wasting away on a bed of sickness.

My heart is very heavy with sorrow on her account. Yes, I am so borne down with trouble, that for three days my tears have not been stayed. I do not say this to boast of my love. I *owe* her all this. I have a petition to make; which is, that you will do all you can for Sarah. But I need not ask this, for I am confident that your kindness will lead you to do, and cause to be done, all that can be done for her. But will you not let me know whether her sickness increases or diminishes?—if it increases, that my sighs and tears may increase in pleading before the Lord for mercy, and if it diminishes, that my thanksgivings may increase before our merciful Father in heaven.

Dear mother, if it is the will of our Father in heaven to take Sarah to the upper mansions,—though I shall be comforted on account of her being saved from all the bitter misery of this world, and her blessed rest with the Saviour, where she can praise his love with her pleasant voice, joined with the sweet songs of angels,—still it will be hard for me. If I live after she has gone, God forbid that I behold her dust, and not long to be her companion in heaven.

Your unworthy

OSHANA.

Our next letter is from Sarah to Miss Fiske, written at Seir, in 1859, more than two years after her marriage, and gives a good idea of her Christian spirit:—

BELOVED: The good news that you gave us of the revivals in your country, rouses our hearts to warmer zeal. Shall we not also prepare the way of the Lord? We know, by the gracious visits of God here this winter, that Christians there are ever praying for our poor people. For we hear from the preachers who come up to the concert every month, that the work of the Lord goes forward in the villages of the plain, and also in the mountains.

Here in Seir, the good work began among the women. I hear them say, "Though we have had revivals before, we have never seen a year like this, when the words of God had such deep effect." Mrs. Cochran and I have good meetings with these women. Our congregations make glad the Christian heart, and I am particularly happy in laboring for them, one by one. A portion of them, with tearful eyes, are covenanting to be the Lord's. We ask the Lord to strengthen them in their covenant, and we entreat of you and of your friends to pray for them.

Our Sabbath schools are very pleasant. Mr. Cochran will tell you how the work goes forward. Mrs. Cochran has a class of women, and so have I. Last Sabbath Mr. Cochran read one of your letters to the congregation, and we learned from it how the work of the Lord goes forward in your blessed churches. We praised the Lord, and then we entreated him to bless our churches, and make them more spiritual, for we are confident that his grace is sufficient for us all.

She visited Tehoma, in May, two months after the date of the preceding, with her husband, Oshana, and two little children, and gives the following account of their journey: —

"Through the favor of our heavenly Father, I have made a journey into these mountains, rejoicing in the opportunity to labor for my people. I am very happy that my father and friends brought me on my way in willingness of soul. From the day that I left my own country, in every place that I have entered, until now, my heart has been excited to praise my Guide and my Deliverer, and I have also been grateful to my teachers who brought me to labor in a desolate vineyard, joyfully, I, who am so weak, and such a great sinner. In all the various circumstances in which I have been, your counsels have been of great benefit to me.

"I think you will be glad to know that the gospel door is wide open here. You and your friends will pray that the Lord of the harvest would send forth laborers into his harvest.

"We left the city of Oroomiah, May 6th. We were ten souls — Hormezd, of Aliawa, Sagoo, of Geog Tapa, Matlub, the Tehomian, Guly, and little Gozel, Oshana and his brother, our two little girls, and myself. May 8th, we reached Memikan, and remained there three days.

"It was our first Sabbath in the mountains. I met that company of women for whom our departed Mrs. Rhea used to labor. May 12th, we left Memikan, and went up to the tops of the snowy mountains of Gawar. The cold was such that we were obliged to wrap our faces and our hands as we would in January. As we descended the mountain, we found it about as warm as February. That night we staid in the deep valley of Ishtazin, in the village of Boobawa, where Yohanan and Guly dwell. The people here are very wild and hard. Yohanan and Guly were not here, having gone to visit Khananis. Only a few came together for preaching. The people said, 'Yohanan preaches, and we revile.' May 13th, we left Boobawa, and soon crossed the river. Men had gone before us, and were lying in wait there. They stripped us, but afterwards, of themselves, became sorry, and returned our things. As we were going along this wonderful, fearful river, and beheld the mountains on either side covered with beautiful forests, we remembered Mr. Rhea, the composer of the hymn,

'Valley of Ishtazin.' And when filled with wonder at the works of the Great Creator, we all, with one voice, praised him in songs of joy fitting for the mountains. Here the brethren reminded me that our dear Miss Fiske had trodden these fearful precipices. This greatly encouraged me in my journey. This day we went into many villages, and over many ascents and descents. At evening we reached Jeloo, and remained over night in the pleasant village of Zeer, which lies in a valley made beautiful by forests, and a river passing through it. They showed great hospitality here, and were eager to receive the word of the Lord. May 14th, we left Zeer, and went to Bass. It was Saturday night, and we remained over the Sabbath in the village of Nerik. I shall always have a pleasant remembrance of the Sabbath we passed there. From the first moment that we went in till Monday morning, we were never alone, so many were assembling to hear the words of the Lord. With tearful eyes and burning hearts, they were inquiring for the way of salvation. They would say, 'What shall we do? We have no one to sit among us, to teach us, poor, wretched ones.' Truly, a man's heart burns within him as he sees this poor people scattered as sheep without a shepherd. May 16th, we mounted our mules, and went on our way. Half an hour from Nerik we came to the village of Urwintoos. An honorable, kind-hearted woman came out, and made us her guests. This was Oshana's aunt. As soon as we sat down, the house was filled with men and women. They brought a Testament themselves, and entreated us to read from that holy book. Did not my heart rejoice when I saw how eagerly they were listening to the account of the death of our Lord Jesus Christ! When the men went out, the women came very near to me, entreating for the word of the Lord, as those thirsting for water. Then I read to them from the book.

"There are many sad deeds of wickedness among these mountain Nestorians; and when Christians hear how anxious they are to receive the words of life, will they not feel for them? We reached Tehoma May 17th. Now, from the mercy of God, we are all well and in the village of Mazrayee. I am not able to labor for the women here, as I desired, because many of them have gone to the sheep-folds. It is so hot we cannot remain here, and we will go there also, soon. I trust, wherever I am, and as long as I am here, I shall labor for that Master who wearied himself for me, and who bought these souls with his blood.

"The Lord keep and bless you, our beloved, who have been a mother to the Nestorian girls, all of whom, with longing hearts are expecting your return. We continually pray Him who gave you to us, to restore you again in mercy to our people. If counted worthy, I should greatly rejoice to receive a little note from you."

She returned to Oroomiah in the spring of 1860, and left again in 1861 for Amadia. When she went away, her three children had the whooping cough; so she would not go into any of the mission families lest she should spread the disease among the children; but after she was all ready to go, and the heads of her own little flock were peeping out of the saddle-bag contrivance in which they rode, Mrs. Breath went out to bid her good by. Sarah told her how Miss Fiske had said, when she took her oldest child into her arms for the first time, "'Now, Sarah, you will not seek for this child a pleasant home upon the plain, as Lot did, but rather to do God's will, and then he will give you all things.' I have always remembered it," she added, "and am not willing now to be found seeking my pleasure here.

During the long winter of 1861–62, no messenger could cross the mountains from Oroomiah to Amadia; and she thus writes in March, 1862, to Miss Rice:—

"I did greatly long for the coming of the messenger. We were very sad in not hearing a single word from home. Now I offer thanksgivings to Him in whose hands are all things, that he has opened a door of mercy, and has delighted us by the arrival of letters. They came to-day. Many thanks to you and your dear pupils. The Lord bless them, and prepare their hearts for such a blessed work as ours.

"Give Eneya's salutations and mine to all the school. I think they will wish to hear about the work of the Lord here. Thanks to God, our health has been good ever since we came, and our hearts have been contented and happy in seeing some of our neighbors believing, and with joy receiving the words of life. Every Sabbath we have a congregation of thirty-five, and more men than women. For many weeks only the men came; but now, by the grace of God, the women come too, and their number is increasing. I have commenced to teach them the life of the Lord Jesus from the beginning. I have strong hopes that God is awakening one of them. His word is very dear to her. Her son is the priest of the village, and a sincere Christian. Four other young men and five women are, we trust, not far from the door of the kingdom. We entreat you, dear sisters, to pray in a special manner for these thoughtful ones, that they may enter the narrow door of life.

"From the villages about us we have a good report. They receive the gospel from Oshana and Shlemon, who visit them every Sabbath. In my journeys through these mountains, I have seen various assemblies of men and women listening to the gospel, poor ones, exclaiming 'What shall we do? Our priests have deceived us: we are lost, like sheep on the mountains. There is no one to teach us.' They sit in misery and ignorance. They need our prayers and our help. I verily believe that if we labor faithfully — God help us to labor thus — we shall soon see our church revived, built up on the foundation Christ Jesus, and adorned for him as a bride for her husband. With tears of joy we shall gaze on these ancient ruins becoming new temples of the Lord. Soon shall these mountains witness scenes that will rejoice angels and saints. Those will be blessed times. Let us pray for them, and labor with Christ for their coming."

Our latest news from Sarah is, that during the summer of 1862, her little son had died, and she herself was just recovering from a dangerous fever.

The joyful anticipations awakened by such a letter from a graduate of the Seminary, in ancient Amadia, are not diminished by accounts received of a conference of "Mountain helpers," held in Gawar, from May 30th to June 2d, 1862. They came from Gawar, Jeloo, Tehoma and Amadia. At the opening of each session, half an hour was spent in prayer; then carefully prepared essays were read on subjects previously assigned, and each topic was afterwards thoroughly discussed. The first subject was, "Hinderances to evangelization in the mountains, — such as their ruggedness, deep snows, superstition of the people, and persecution." Deacon Tamo, in speaking, admitted all these, but said, "For rough roads we have our feet and goats' hair sandals; for deep snows, snow shoes; for the darkness and superstition of the people, we have the light of the truth and the sword of the Spirit; and for persecution, we have God's promise of protection and the firman of the sultan." "The faithful pastor's duty to his flock," and "Means of securing laborers for the field," were among the topics discussed. Their discussions on the subject of benevolence showed that they regarded that duty as binding as any other. They engaged to observe the monthly concert, and take up monthly and also annual collections in their congregations, and apply the proceeds to the support of a laborer in the mountains. On Sabbath evening the monthly concert was observed, and after stirring addresses, the contribution amounted to what was for them the very large sum of fifty-two dollars. Among the offerings were a horse, an ox, a sheep, a goat, and different articles of jewelry. Arrangements were made at the conference for the formation of a Protestant community in Gawar, in accordance with the firman of the sultan. In all respects the meeting was a rich spiritual festival, and from the spirit its members manifested, and the progress already made, we may hope for extensive and important results before many years have passed away.

CHAPTER XIX.

EBENEZERS.

EXAMINATION IN 1850. — COLLATION AND ADDRESS. — VALEDICTORY BY SANUM. — SABBATH SCHOOL IN GEOG TAPA. — EXAMINATION THERE IN 1854. — PRAYER MEETING AND COMMUNION AT OROOMIAH, MAY, 1858. — SELBY, OF GAVALAN, AND LETTER. — LETTER FROM HATOON, OF GEOG TAPA.

THERE are occasions, interesting in themselves, that also serve to mark the progress which they promote. Such an occasion was the examination of the Seminary, June 6th, 1850. There have been examinations since, but none so marked in their influence for good; none where the teachers felt so much like calling the name of it "Ebenezer," and saying, "Hitherto hath the Lord helped us."

The pupils had improved, during the last weeks of the term, more than they had ever done in twice the same length of time, both spiritually and mentally. At the close of the term, their parents and friends, with some of the leading Nestorians, were invited to the examination. More than one hundred and sixty spectators, besides the pupils, were crowded into the large recitation room. This had been adorned with a profusion of roses, from the vineyard of Mar Yohanan, arranged in wreaths and bouquets, with festoons of sycamore leaves, and other devices. The people were delighted, — for, like other Persians, they are great admirers of flowers, — and many, on entering, involuntarily exclaimed, "Paradise! Paradise!" In their various studies, the attainments of the pupils would have reflected honor on a seminary in our own land; but their knowledge of Scripture exceeded all besides. Even on the details of the Tabernacle they rarely faltered; and their compositions showed an intimate acquaintance with Bible facts and doctrines.

Dr. Perkins delivered an address, comparing the early days of the mission with that scene, and felicitously answering various objections that had been raised against female education; and, at the close, diplomas were given to three of the oldest pupils.

The exercises were pleasantly diversified by a plentiful collation under the arbor in the court behind the Seminary, where lambs roasted whole, in the native style, lettuce, cherries, pilav (a preparation of rice), and some cake, prepared by the pupils, were duly discussed. Many of the women had never before sat at the same table with men, and it was amusing to witness their awkward embarrassment. Some snatched the food from the table by stealth, and ate it behind their large veils, as though it were a thing forbidden.

Hormezd, the father of John, now aged and blind, who had been led all the way from Geog Tapa, said, towards the close of the afternoon, "I wish Joshua were here." "And what do you want of Joshua?" "I want him to command the sun and moon to stand still, for the day is altogether too short." As the company dispersed, several old men took Miss Fiske and Miss Rice by the hand, saying, with moistened eyes, "Will you forgive us that we have done no more for your school?" But the best of all was, some sixty adult women, from different villages, begging for spelling books, that they might commence learning to read. Thirty of them did not rest till they could read their Bibles. The cause of female education never lost the impulse that it received that day.

Instead of the valedictory composed for this anniversary, is here subjoined the greater part of the one prepared by Sanum, for a like occasion, because it takes a wider range, and is richer in its historical allusions:—

"Now that another year is closed, and we are ready to leave each other in peace, it is fitting to review the past, that together we may praise the sweet Keeper of Israel for the blessings he has poured upon our heads. We fear to try to recount them all, lest we tempt the Lord; so we will speak of but a few.

"Let us renew the wings of our loving thoughts, send them to the years that are past, and see where rests the dust of some of the dear teachers of this school. Listen! There comes a voice, 'They are not to be found among the living.' Yes, the place of one is empty here, and of another there. Then, where are they? Thou, O country, art a witness that they have pressed thy soil; and you, ye blessed winds, answer us, 'They have gone!' and ye green leaves of time are true witnesses that they lie among the numbered dead. But where shall we find them? They lie far apart. We must visit one that first laid her hand on some of us to bless us [Mrs. Grant]; and though we remember her not, she often embraced us in the arms of love, and carried us before a throne of grace. She was one of the first that left all her friends, and ploughed the mighty waves of ocean, that she might come to Oroomiah's dark border. Though fierce tempests raged, and heavy waves raised themselves above the ship, her prayers, mingled with love for us, ascended higher still, and overcame all. At the foot of Mount Ararat she doubtless remembered the bow of promise; and her consolations were renewed, when she thought of it as a prophecy, that a company of the fallen daughters of Chaldea should become heirs of glory. She so labored, that her influence is widening from generation to generation.

"The Lord is rewarding her even to the third and fourth generation. But though she engaged in her work with such holy zeal, her journey was short. Some of us had not seen our eighth summer when those lips, on which were written wisdom, were still; and that tongue, on which dwelt the law of kindness, was silent in death. Now she rests in our churchyard. She sleeps with our dead, and her dust is mingled with the dust of our fathers, till that day when she shall rise to glory, and a company of ransomed Nestorians with her.

"But where is that other dear friend of our school [Dr. Grant], who was the beautiful staff of her support? He encouraged her to labor for us while many of us were yet unborn. His heart was large enough to love every son and daughter of our people. He sowed with many tears, and gave himself for the Nestorians. Shall we not believe that the fruits of his labors have sprung up among us? Then, where is he? Let us go silently, silently, and ask that ancient city, Nineveh. It will direct us, 'Lo, he rests on the banks of the noble Tigris.' Would that our whisper might reach the ear of the wild Arab and cruel Turk, that they walk gently by that stranger grave, and tread not on its dust. Then, shall we think no more of it? No; with a firm hope we expect that those mountains, on which his beautiful feet rested, shall answer his name in echoes, one to the other; and the persons who saw his faithful example there shall mingle in the flock of his Saviour.

"But the journey of our thoughts is not finished. We

must leave in peace this blessed grave, and go search for one with whom we were well acquainted [Mrs. Stoddard], and whose gentle, loving example is so graven on the tablet of memory, that it cannot be erased. Can we forget her prayers with some of us the week she left us? or how, when she took our hand for the last time, she said, 'The blessing of the Lord rest upon you'? We did not then expect that our eyes would no more rest on that lovely face, and our ears no more hear that sweet voice in our dwellings. When we heard of her departure to a world of light, it was hard to believe that she had gone and left us behind. Lo, on the shores of the Black Sea she has laid her down to rest. O ye angry waves, be still, and ye winds of God, fan gently that sacred spot. All our people are indebted to thee, thou blessed one. Thou, who didst first teach us to sing the songs of Zion, now removed from sin and sorrow, thou art singing with the myriads of the just. We would not call thee back, but rather praise the Lord that you and those other dear friends are entered into rest. No, ye are not lost, ye spirits made holy; but as it was necessary that some should come from a distant land to labor here, so ye were necessary to do a greater work in heaven. We believe that ye are doing there more than ye could have done here; yea, that ye form a part of that great cloud of witnesses that encompass us to-day. It is delightful to us to think that ye blessed ones guard us. It is a comfort to our teachers to think that you, who laid these foundations, are still round about us. Beloved ones, we would not call you back. Cling closely, and more closely, to your Saviour, till we, too, through free grace, shall share in your glory.

"And now, beloved friends, who with them flew on the wings of the gospel across the ocean to tell us of salvation, we rejoice to-day that the sharp arrows of death have not touched you. Ye have been more than fathers and mothers to us. Our hearts are full of love to every one of you, O blessed band! but we cannot express it, except with a heavenly tongue. When darkness reigned in the breast of every son of the Chaldeans, and no whisper of salvation had fallen on the ear of their daughters, you opened the beauties of the priceless pearl before our eyes, that it should enlighten us with heavenly brightness. We cannot make known all that you have done for us. Let it remain till that day of light when the Lord shall commend you before his chosen. When we look at our dear teachers, our hearts warm to you with no common love, because you led them to leave the sweet place of their nativity for our sakes. You have been parents to them, wiping away their tears with the soft hand of a mother, and sharing their trials with a father's heart. While you have helped them in every department of their school, the blessing has all been ours.

"If on the wings of an eagle we should fly to the extreme north, we should find no such school as this, crowned with blessings, but should see our sisters groaning in bitterness, saying, 'Not one ray from the divine sun rises on us in our misery.' If we turn to the south, there we see the daughters of Arabia lamenting, 'In all this desert, not one oasis yields the waters of life to quench our burning thirst.' Eternity alone will suffice to praise Him who sent you, the only heralds of his grace, to us sinners.

"But our southern journey is not finished. From one end of Africa to the other our sisters lie wrapped in the shadows of death; and if we turn to the east, all the way to China, the daughters cry, 'Wretched is our unhappy lot: no cloud of mercy, such as surrounds you, lights up the place of our abode. So on the west, as far as Constantinople, our companions in suffering have no school to sound in their ears the blessed name of Jesus.

"What are we, that the Lord should choose us from the midst of such darkness, and send you to us with the message of life? Let all nations, with wondering lips, praise the Almighty for his grace to us, so worthless.

"Now that we go from you, we leave with you this our handiwork as a token of gratitude. [A specimen of needlework now among the curiosities at the Missionary House in Boston.] Receive it, though a trifle. The figures on it show what you have taught us in our pleasant school. As we have first of all been taught to sit at the foot of the cross, and neither hope nor glory in any thing else, we have made that the foundation. Under the cross you have watered us with the showers of divine instruction and prayers, that, like this vine, we might entwine about it and bear pleasant fruit. From this cross we learned, while yet in the bloom of life, like newly-opened flowers, to join together in sweet friendship. Above this we have placed a circle around the Holy Bible, that bright lamp of the Lord, that will enlighten us like the sun if we follow its leading — that well of living waters, which will cause us to flourish like the palm tree. Thus will our leaf be ever green, and our fruit sweet till the day when the mystery of love shall be revealed, and we dwell in the mansions of the blest. There, joining with all the singers in heavenly places, we shall receive harps and sing glory to our heavenly King, who saved us from everlasting woe. There we shall inherit crowns of gold, and, with myriads of the saints, cast them down before the Lamb. If but one of us reach that place, will you deem your labor in vain? God, who rewards even the gift of a cup of cold water, will never forget what you have done to the least of his people, and if the least are on the earth, we are they. Now that you send us forth into the world, remember us, we beg you, whenever you bring your sacrifice before the Lord.

"Dear teachers, your acts of kindness have been more than the hairs of our heads; we cannot recount them. We can only ask Him, who alone is rich, to reward you from his good treasures, for none but He can meet our obligations to you. Each thought that reverts to the past demands a tear of gratitude. O blessed seasons, when God sent down his Holy Spirit, that through your labors these walls of Jerusalem, so long broken down, might be again rebuilt. It is sweet to think that in the hand of Christ, you have been the means of the salvation of our souls, which are to live forever. We believe that your prayers and tears are in the golden censer before the throne. Now that we go out from under your wings of love, which cannot reach to all your scattered flock, we entreat you to ask the Good Shepherd to lead us in green pastures and beside the still waters, and keep us under his wings of mercy in our weakness.

[Her address to the native teachers, bishops, &c., is omitted.]

"Dear parents, we rejoice exceedingly to see you here, looking on us with eyes of love. No words can express what you have done for us, especially in sending us here to learn of Jesus. We trust that it has been, or shall be, a blessing to you also. It is our hope that you will be willing to send your daughters to distant places, to make known eternal life. If you do, great will be your reward from the Lord.

"And now, sweet sisters, another year have we sat under

our own vine and fig tree unmolested. We have tasted the honey and milk of the blessed land, and drank of the waters from the Rock. But now the time has come to leave these bowers of knowledge, but not the lessons here learned, nor the counsels of our teachers, nor the sweet whispers of the Holy Spirit.

"Dear sisters, let us bear forth with us the light-giving countenance of the Saviour, which will scatter all the evil around us as the light dispels the darkness: without this we cannot go. Though separated in body, let us be united in fervent prayer. Let a conscience made sensitive by grace be our abiding companion. Let the tent of Abraham teach us that we have no abiding city here; and like him, let our first work be to offer those prayers to God which shall testify that he is ours. And now, before going forth, let us clothe ourselves with the meekness and gentleness of Christ. Yea, let us take with us all his virtues, being obedient, teaching our dying associates, and leading them one and all to Christ. Though we part, our love can never be sundered, and we will ask the Lord to send his ministering spirits to strengthen our faltering steps, and feed our souls with heavenly manna, so that if we never more see each other here, we may meet in heaven with our sisters who have gone before."

The teachers improved the interest awakened by the examination in 1850, to urge their older pupils to labor in the village Sabbath schools; and let us look in on their efforts in Geog Tapa. The children there were divided into ten classes, each with one of the pupils for a teacher. Others taught the women who could not read. Soon these were joined by both old and young men, who were taught by pupils from the Seminary at Seir, and as many as forty spelling books were in active use. The children, too, were taught to sing. Thus they labored till winter, when the school was put in charge of the village school teachers. In the spring the pupils resumed the work with undiminished zeal. Nor did they toil in vain, for the attendance increased from about seventy to four hundred; and some of the teachers testified that they spent there some of the most delightful Sabbaths they ever knew. Yonan, who superintended the school with Moses, had also a class of old women, that increased from six to thirty-seven, whom he taught from the book, well known to our Sabbath school children, "Line upon Line." His own account of it is very interesting. He says, "The women, especially the aged among them, have a habit, when they meet, of engaging in unprofitable conversation, and, both on the way to church and in it, we could not stop it. Awakening sermons produced no impression; and though they had heard preaching for fifteen years, they were still very ignorant. But now what I teach them on one Sabbath I require them to repeat the next; and so they are obliged to leave off their gossip, and talk over what they have heard, that they may not forget it. These women are so anxious to be taught, that if I am hindered a little longer than usual in arranging the classes, they cry out after me in the church, that all the other classes are being taught, but they forsaken."

A class of old men, taught by Deacon John, commenced with an attendance of ten, but soon numbered forty. Formerly they went to market on the Sabbath, or sat sunning themselves in the street, going to hear preaching about half the time; but they became so interested in the exercises, that they were unwilling they should close. They brought others with them, and if one of them was kept away one Sabbath, he mourned that the rest had got so far before him.

The women carried their books with them when they went out to the vineyards, and at resting time: while others slept, they read. Some, who could not afford oil at night, read by moonlight, and when they spun, they fastened the book open on a shelf, so that they could read at the same time. Once, when a woman was asked if she could repeat her lesson, she replied, "O, yes; I repeated it over just now while I was milking." The men also took their books out to the fields, that they might improve every spare moment, and one was so earnest that, when waked in the night to attend to the cattle, he read till morning; but his family, finding that he burned so much oil, took care after that to let him sleep. Good old Mar Elias rejoiced to see such a work among his flock; and it was most pleasant to see the large church so crowded by people, seated on the floor, that one could hardly walk about among them.

After the teachers had attended to their classes about an hour and a half, the younger scholars repeated the portion of Scripture they had learned during the week, and the parents were much pleased to hear their children recite.

The daily report of the Seminary was introduced into the Sabbath school in a way that only Orientals could do it. The older members of the school were required to report any cases of swearing, stealing, or quarrelling among the younger ones during the week, who were publicly reproved on the following Sabbath. This made the parents more careful to watch over their children, and the children more circumspect in their daily behavior. If any little trouble occurred among them during the week, they said to each other, "Let us be careful; Sabbath is near;" and though at first some of the people smiled when the children were reproved, it soon became more common for them to weep.

20 *

After taking an account of the attendance, the children sung, divided into two companies, on opposite sides of the church; and then Mar Elias, or some of the elders of the village, addressed the school. Yonan closes his account of it by saying, "We have learned in this work more than ever before the value of female education. Among our most energetic, faithful teachers are young women who love to sit down before little children, and the ignorant of their own sex, and teach them the way of life."

Thursday, June 1st, 1854, was a great day in Geog Tapa. The forenoon was devoted to the examination of a girls' school, taught by Hanee and Nargis, graduates of the preceding year, and both belonging in the village. As it was a feast day, a large number were present from the neighboring hamlets. At nine o'clock the examination commenced in the spacious church, which was crowded, the congregation numbering about six hundred in all. The fifty pupils occupied the middle of the church. The studies pursued were ancient and modern Syriac, geography, arithmetic, both Scripture and secular history, reading and spelling; and in all of them the pupils did credit both to themselves and their teachers. The singing, that day, especially pleased the parents, many of whom exclaimed with wonder, "Our daughters can learn as well as our sons." Miss Fiske rejoiced to see her children's children in the pupils of her first pupil, who gracefully managed her little flock with an easy control. The villages of Gavalan, Vizierawa, and Ardishai, had each a similar school, containing in all one hundred pupils; and each of these schools was as valued a centre of religious influence as of intellectual training. The teachers were in the habit of praying with one of their pupils alone every day, as well as of opening the school with prayer; and Friday afternoon was regularly devoted to a religious meeting with the mothers of the pupils. These schools fitted the teachers for usefulness, and the pupils for admission to the Seminary, as well as for teachers in the Sabbath school; and they furnish a delightful view of the present and prospective usefulness of the Seminary among the people.

Noon came, and the large assembly scattered, to enjoy the hospitality of the village. For the people opened their houses for those in attendance, just as they do with us at the annual meetings of the American Board. Geog Tapa could also boast of its committee of arrangements, in humble imitation of greater things.

After a recess of an hour and a half, the people reassembled for the examination of the Sabbath school, in a grove behind the church, as that building could not contain the multitude which now numbered more than a thousand. First came a class of men, from twenty to seventy years of age, headed by Malik Aga Bey, the village chief. They had been taught orally by Deacon John, and answered questions in Old Testament history very readily. Then followed a class of women, fifty or sixty in number, most of them over forty years of age. These had been taught by Yonan, and were quite familiar with the Old Testament, from the creation to the reign of David. One old blind woman wanted to point out the stopping places of Israel in the desert, on the map which hung on one of the tall trees: she had learned their names by heart, and was familiar with their location by touch.

Next came a class of twenty men, who had recently learned to read; for which they had each received a copy of the New Testament. A class of women then followed, numbering twenty-three, who had also been taught to read by the boys and girls in the village schools. Mr. Stoddard called for the teacher of each woman to step forward; and a copy of the Old Testament was presented to every one of them, as they stood in a row in front of their pupils. There was one woman who stood without a teacher. Mr. Stoddard called for hers also, and some one whispered to him that she had been taught by her husband. Mr. Stoddard thereupon led him out, and, placing his hand on his head, said, before the whole assembly, "All honor to the man who has taught his wife to read!" and presented him also with a Bible.

One who was frequently present often wept to see women giving a morsel to their infants to quiet them, that they might devote the longer time to their lessons; some of them so intent on the work of learning, that their faces were bathed in perspiration. She used to fill her pocket and reticule with cakes for the little ones, so that their mothers might be more free from interruption. The exercises of that day gave a great impulse to the cause of education in Geog Tapa. As many as seventy adults were soon poring over their spelling books; and the next summer one half of the adult women were either readers or engaged in the same employment; though previous to the examination of the Seminary in 1850, not one in thirty could read, or cared to learn.

Having given an account of these two interesting occasions, let us now look in on another equally interesting, though of a different kind, that took place in Oroomiah, three years later. During the interval, Mr. Stoddard had entered into rest; and his bereaved widow, Dr. Perkins and family, and Miss Fiske, were about to sit down together, perhaps for the last time, with the Nestorian converts, at the table of the Lord.

It was in May, and the day one of the finest of those charming May days in Oroomiah. The most of the Nestorians who had been admitted to the communion were present; and in distributing the guests among the mission families, it was understood that all who had been connected with the Seminary should go there. The object of this was, to gather all the scattered members of the family together once more in the place where prayer had been wont to be made, before they went to the Lord's table. As yet, no one knew that their teacher was about to leave them; for she did not wish any thing else to turn away their thoughts from Jesus. When they had assembled in the school room, she could not say much, but besought the Lord Jesus to be the Master of the assembly. After singing a hymn, the words "looking unto Jesus" were given as the key-note of the meeting. He came and whispered peace, and all felt that they sat together in heavenly places. The eyes of their hearts were opened, so that they realized the fulfilment of the promise, "There am I in the midst of you."

They were invited to speak freely of their joys and sorrows, in order that together they might carry them to Jesus. The first to speak was Hanee, one of the two whom Mar Yohanan brought to Miss Fiske at the commencement of the school.[1] She had, not long before, buried her only child; and holding her hands as though the little one still rested on her arms, she said, "Sisters, at the last communion you saw me here with my babe in these arms. It is not here now. I have laid it into the arms of Jesus, and come to-day to tell you there is a sweet as well as a bitter in affliction. When the rod is appointed to us, let us not only kiss it, but press it to our lips. When I stood

[1] See page 51.

by that little open grave, I said, 'All the time I have given to my babe, I will give to souls.' I try to do so. Pray for me." She told but the simple truth; for after the death of her child, she used to bring the women into the room where it died, and there talk and pray with them. Since then, she has received another little one, and in the same spirit given it back to Christ. When she ceased, the whole company were in tears. The leader could only ask, "Who will pray?" and Sanum, whose children had died by poison, and who could enter into the feelings of the bereaved mother, knelt down and prayed as very few could pray for mothers left desolate, and for those who still folded their little ones in their arms. There was perfect silence while she pleaded for them, save as the sweet voice of her own babe sometimes added to the tenderness of her petitions. A child in heaven! what a treasure! and what a blessing, if it draw the heart thither also!

There was a little pause after the prayer; and, to the surprise of all, the voice of Nazloo was heard in another part of the room; for they had supposed her near, if not already entering, the river of death. "Sisters," said she, "since seeing you, I have stood with one foot in the grave; and may I tell you that it is a very different thing to be a Christian then, from what it is in this pleasant school room. Let me ask you if you are sure that you are on the Rock Christ Jesus." A tender prayer followed, the burden of which was, "Search us, O Lord, and try us, and see if there be any wicked way in us, and lead us in the way everlasting."

The next to speak was one of the early pupils, who had come many miles that day to be present. She said, "I could think but one thought all the way as I came, and that was, 'Freely ye have received, freely give.' We have certainly received freely: have we given any thing? Can we not do something for souls? I fear the Lord Jesus is not pleased with us."

They were then asked if they were ready to engage in direct labors for souls, to search them out, and by conversation and prayer seek to lead them to Christ. Many pledged themselves to the work, and engaged to bring the names of those for whom they had labored to the next communion, that all together might intercede in their behalf to God. Before that time arrived, Miss Fiske left for America; but the first letter she opened, out of a large parcel that awaited her in Boston, was one containing the names of those with whom her pupils had labored and prayed in distant Persia. Is it strange that, as the slips of paper fell at her feet, her heart was moved?

But we cannot dwell longer on the prayer meeting. As many as twelve said a few words, and more than that number led in prayer, during the two hours they were together: from thence all repaired to the dining room, — the three upper windows on the right of the engraving belong to this, — where they did "eat their meat with gladness and singleness of heart." Then it was announced that arrangements had been made for class prayer meetings. It seemed to be just the thing that all longed for, though none had spoken of it; and at once each class went along the familiar passages to the room assigned it, and the voice of prayer arose from nearly every apartment in the building. The chapel bell rung, but it was unnoticed; and each little company had to be separately summoned to church. There, according to previous arrangement, Miss Fiske led each to a seat, that the communicants might be together, and then herself sat down behind them all. A glance revealed ninety-three sisters in Christ before her; and as the services had not yet commenced, her thoughts went back to the day when, asking concerning many of them, "Is this one a Christian?" "or that one?" "or that other?" the answer came, "You have no sister in Christ among them all!" No wonder she now inwardly exclaimed, "What hath God wrought? The Lord hath done great things for us, whereof we are glad." There was but one among the ninety-three with whom she had not bowed the knee in prayer, and that same evening, as she was devising methods to get her away from the rest to her room alone, the Lord sent her, unexpectedly, to the door; and with her also she enjoyed the privilege of personal religious intercourse and prayer.

At the communion, when all stood up to enter into covenant with thirty-nine new converts, six of them pupils of the Seminary, there seemed a deeper meaning than ever before in engaging to be the Lord's forever.

In Hanee we have seen the grace bestowed on one of the two whom Mar Yohanan brought to form the nucleus of the school. The other was Selby, of Gavalan, his own niece. She became hopefully pious in 1846, when hardly ten years of age. There were very few in whom her teachers took such uniform delight, though they felt some anxiety when she married Priest Kamo, of Marbeeshoo, a cousin of Mar Shimon — intelligent and influential, but unconverted. Yet she had strong faith that he would become a Christian, and soon gained a wonderful influence over him, without compromising in the least her own religious principles. She became his teacher in the Bible, — it was a new book to him, — and in her he saw the Christian life it described beautifully exemplified. She had just begun to hope that her prayers were answered in his conversion. He was much interested in aiding the evangelists in the mountains, and the mission was hoping great things from him, under the good influence of Selby, when he died. Her feelings, under this affliction, are thus described by her own pen, in a letter to her teacher, dated Marbeeshoo, June 4th, 1859: —

"It is not because I have forgotten you that I have not written you until now. How can I forget you? And were that possible, I could not forget your instructions. I remember them at all times, by day and by night. They comfort me in sorrow, and strengthen me in anguish. You have taught me the duties of this life, and you have pointed me to the world to come. I remember when you used to take me by the hand, and lead me into your closet, and there pray with me; and my heart fills with mingled joy and sorrow — with joy, that such precious seasons were given me; with sorrow, that they will be mine no more. Shall I never see your face again — that face, which bore to us more than a mother's love? You were a perfect mother, because in Christ.

"I grieve very much that I did not see you before you left; but I believe that the seed you have sown will continue to spring up to the end of the world. You asked me, in your letter, to tell you about my work. I have a greater work than any of my companions, but it is in a place covered with thick darkness, like that of Egypt. The people are stiff-necked, wise to do evil, but of God they have no knowledge. Temptations surround me as mountains; they rise up about me like the waves of the sea. While Kamo lived, I was comforted, for he loved the truth. Every day he used to read the Scriptures with me, and ask the meaning of each verse. I had hoped he would have Paul's zeal in the work of the Lord. I had expected that we should have schools in our village after a year or two, and that the places of concourse for idle conversation would become places for reading the Scriptures, and for prayer. But it has pleased the Lord to give me a great and heavy affliction. He has smitten me with his own rod, making this world a vale of tears. But it is the Lord; let him do what he pleaseth. It is all for my profit.

"I want to ask you and your friends to pray for me, that I may endure to the end."

The feelings of the pupils, after the departure of Miss Fiske, are graphically expressed in the following letter from Hatoon, of Geog Tapa:—

"My heart longs to tell you of the change in our dear school. Our return, after vacation, was much like that of the Jews from Babylon, when they found their city laid waste, and their temple in ruins. Every time they looked on the spot where it had stood, their hearts were crushed. So when we did not see you, and went not to take your hand and be kissed by you,—when we saw not your ready feet coming to the door, to bring in each one and make her happy,—our hearts were broken, and we could not restrain our tears; especially when I remembered the times that the daughters of the church used to meet in your room to mingle our prayers, our tears, and our joys together. These recollections leave an aching void which cannot be filled. It seems to me that the ways of your room mourn, because you come not to the solemn feasts. If Jeremiah were here, I think he would say, 'How doth Miss Fiske's room sit solitary that was full of people! How do the daughters of the Oroomiah schools mourn, and their eyes run down with water, because Miss Fiske is far from them!' These changes show us that this world is as down driven by the wind. Perhaps you will reply, in your cheerful way, 'Do you feel so? There is much that is pleasant in the world.' I know it; but our school was always such a pleasant place to me. I was so happy in it and its heavenly employments, that not even the death of friends could destroy that joy. But now I seem overshadowed by dark clouds, and sinking in deep mire. Yet I will try, in all this, to bow my will to the holy will of Him who doeth all things well."

CHAPTER XX.

COMPOSITIONS.

THE FIELD OF CLOVER. — THE LOST SOUL. — THE SAVED SOUL. — HANNAH.

It was very important that the pupils should be able to express their own thoughts, readily and correctly, with the pen, and unwearied effort was devoted to this end; but for a long time they seemed incapable of clothing an idea in words. The simplest sentence was copied over and over without the change of a single word; and even when it was expressed for them in other language, they only repeated over that variation of the first. Three years were spent in trying to teach them to write their own thoughts, with very little success; but in 1846, the Spirit of God secured the result that man had sought in vain. After that, both their ideas and their language were very beautiful. Nothing pleased them better than to be allowed to write; and it was matter of grateful remark that those compositions which were penned during a revival were always the best.

This was especially true in the awakening of 1850, which was noted for the prevalence of a spirit of meditation and holy communion with God. The pupils at that time came forth from private intercourse with their Saviour, to pen some of the sweetest writings in the Syriac language.

One day that winter, both the teachers wished to attend

an examination at Seir, and asked them if they would be diligent during their absence. "O, yes," was the reply, "if you will only let us write composition." The following was found on the slate of Nazloo, when they returned: —

"THE CLOVER FIELD.

"We walk out in the country, and the road leads us by a lovely field of clover. We see it in all its modest beauty. There are the green leaves, so regular in their form and outline; the beautiful flowers, so wonderful in their structure; and the sweet fragrance, that regales our senses as we pass. All these are there, but we see not whence they come. No showers descend to make it grow; the earth is parched on all sides. Do you inquire for the source of all this loveliness? A tiny rill of water flows gently underneath. No eye sees it. You cannot hear its quiet advance, for it does not murmur as it wears itself out in its work of love. Noiseless it hies to each little rootlet. It conveys nourishment to every leaf; not one is overlooked or forgotten. That unseen rill causes these fair blossoms to spring forth. It distils these odors for the enjoyment of all that pass this way. What that streamlet is to the field, prayer is to the Christian. We see it not; it is all hid from human eye; but O, the rich fruit that it yields every day in the soul thus made partaker of the life of Christ! That also makes the wilderness to rejoice and blossom as the rose."

At the annual examination in 1850, Sanum read her composition, a translation of which is here inserted: —

"THE LOST SOUL.

"I have dreamed a dream, dear friends — may I relate it?

"In my dream I was wandering about, seeking for earthly pleasures, though my life was crowned with blessings more plentiful than the dew of the morning. My father and mother did every thing they could to bring me to Christ. Their labors for me were enough to make me weep my last tear, but my hard heart remained unmoved. Four times did the Holy Spirit strive with me, and as often I grieved him away. I broke every promise that I made to serve the Lord.

"There came a beautiful day in spring. The sun lighted up every thing with gladness. The fields were dressed in green. The trees were in blossom. Loved by my friends, surrounded by every thing to make me happy, and rejoicing that so much enjoyment was still in store for me, I was saying to my soul, 'Take thine ease,' when suddenly a voice cried, 'This night thy soul shall be required of thee; then whose shall be all these?' Another voice added, 'These four years heaven and earth have pleaded with you to bring forth fruit to God, but you have refused. Your heart has said "I will fix my seat above the stars of heaven." Now you must go down to the abyss.' Like arrows these words pierced my heart; my strength departed, and others bore me to my home. There my parents were speechless with sorrow. The bed of down was made ready, but it afforded me no rest. I seemed to lie on thorns. Then I appeared to faint, though still able to hear their conversation. Sobbing aloud, they said, 'Sweet child, if you were only a Christian, gladly would we go with you to the gates of heaven, hoping soon to meet again; but this is more than we can bear. Alas, that one borne in the arms of our love, with whom and for whom we have prayed, must now say that our God is not her God, nor our Saviour hers! Is there no ray of light for her in the darkness? Can we never again point her to Jesus?' As I listened in anguish,

I cried aloud, 'Is there no hope for me?' They replied, 'We will implore mercy for you again and again, and possibly the physician may help you. Here he is.' As he came in the recollection of his past faithful warnings made me weep aloud. He said, 'Why weep? Do you not wish to see me?' 'Dear friend, it is not that; but the sight of you recalls your entreaties to come to Christ, and my neglect of them. If you can only give me one hour of quiet, I will try to come now.' He saw that the hand of death was on me, and replied, 'What you do you must do quickly.' 'What can I do in such distress?' 'Can you not cry, "Lord, remember me," like the dying malefactor?' 'Those words comforted me once, but now I cannot use them.' 'Can you not pray?' 'No. Once I would not hear God, and now he will not hear me. O father, mother, friends, pray for me. Send for my teacher to pray for me. Ask every servant of God to entreat for me while yet I live.' The request went forth. The weeping physician offered supplication at my side. My father and mother seemed to pour forth their last breath in intercession for me. As I turned, I saw my teachers, and conscience arrayed before me every word they had ever spoken to me of Christ and heaven. All my own actions were likewise spread out before my eyes. Then the whirlwind of my sins swept me away like a tiny leaf, to sink in a sea of anguish. My teacher now cried, 'We had hoped to see our dear pupil passing over to the new Jerusalem; but, instead of that, must she dwell among the lost?' A gentle voice then whispered, 'Go to Jesus; he will not cast you out.' 'To Jesus! nay, for knowingly my hands have pierced him. Willingly these feet have trampled on his precious blood. I have compelled his spirit to forsake me, and must perish.'

"Then I saw those whom I had led into sin and encouraged in unbelief, and said to them, 'Can you forgive me?' But a voice from heaven replied, 'You cannot be forgiven; for the name of Jesus you have set at nought, and there is none other.' Then my teacher pressed my hand; she could not speak. I said, 'You have ever shown great love; can you not help me now?' 'Dear child, have I not told you that though I love you, yet I have no power to help in this hour or hereafter.' 'O, dreadful thought! Must I leave you all, forever? parents, teachers, all! Can you do nothing for me?' 'We can only point you to Jesus.' 'I have no part in him. I am a Demas; and with such agony now, what will be the wrath to come?' I begged all present not to live as I had lived. 'Seize the moments that fly swifter than the lightning. There is no place for repentance now: my retribution begins. Forget not these words of your lost sister.' I turned to my mother: 'There is no love like a mother's; can that do nothing for me now?' What could she do? 'Can no one help me? Father, father, I am going; can you do nothing?'

"Now the light forsook my eyes. O for a few moments more! But even this was denied me; for, as I remembered, 'Cursed is the man that trusteth in man, and whose heart departeth from the living God.'

"I now heard a voice as of a rushing, mighty wind. Trembling seized me, as I discerned four fiends of darkness. I uttered a piercing shriek, and died. Then I found myself suspended between heaven and earth. Behind me, the world I loved so well had gone forever. Before me I saw the Ancient of Days seated on his throne, his raiment white as snow, his eyes as a flame of fire, his feet like brass glowing in the furnace, and a stream of fire issued from before him; thousand thousands ministered unto him, and ten thousand times ten thousand stood before him. Brightness radiated from him on all sides. He fixed his eyes on me, glowing with holy indignation, while a two-edged sword proceeded out of his mouth. My sins arose before me. Conscience condemned me. I could not look up. The pains of hell gat hold upon me. In a voice unlike all I ever heard before, he said, 'Slayer of my Son, despiser of my grace, what hast thou done? Thou hast set at nought all my counsels.' I longed to flee; but above me stood the Judge, below, the abyss. I could give no reply. Again he said, 'My covenant thou hast trodden under foot;' and he commanded his servants, 'Bind her hand and foot, and cast her into outer darkness, where is weeping and gnashing of teeth. There let her remain till that great day, when all mine enemies shall be trodden in the wine-press of my wrath.'

"Then a voice from out of the throne said, 'Praise our God, all ye his servants, and ye that fear him, both small and great;' and all cried, like the voice of many waters, 'Amen. Allelujah.' Heaven responded from all sides, 'Just and true are thy judgments, thou King of saints.' Then Satan and his angels clapped their hands; and mocking my misery, they thrust me into the inner prison.

"I now found myself associated with Cain, Judas, Jeroboam, and Jezebel. I understood what Christ meant when he said, 'Bind the tares in bundles to burn them,' for I was enclosed by them on all sides, and the flames from them kindled on me. Then a voice said, 'Judas sold his Lord once, but thou many times. Cain slew one brother; thou hast brought many to this place of torment.' Then all, especially those whom I had led there, cursed me. Fallen spirits gloried over me. The evil passions of all the lost were let loose on me. My own wicked feelings were kindled into a flame by the divine wrath. Now I understood that scripture, 'They have no rest day nor night.' My ears, that had taken pleasure in evil conversation, were filled with revilings. My tongue, which had set on fire the course of nature, now itself set on fire of hell, I gnawed for pain. I looked up to beg a drop of water; but instead of it came the word, 'Daughter, remember.' As I looked up, I got a glimpse of one of my companions in Abraham's bosom. Once we were together pointed to Jesus. Now the impassable gulf was between us. Hope now fled forever, and that word, 'Remember,' brought every moment of my life before me in characters of flaming fire. Gladly would I have exchanged this agony for the pangs of death endured a thousand times over, or for all the sufferings of earth till the final conflagration. I cursed my soul, weeping without a tear. Why were my associates, once, like me, children of wrath, now in heaven, while I was shut out? Ah, they listened to Jesus, while I rejected him, and to enjoy a momentary pleasure plunged into all this anguish. I had loved those who now tormented me, and cast aside the loving Saviour. No ray of mercy can ever reach me more. No friend will ever love me again. In my madness I sought to flee; but wrath held me rooted to the spot. Cloud on cloud rose above me, each inscribed, 'Eternity!' A voice cried aloud, 'Forever!' and another replied, 'Forever and ever!' The waves of fire now rolled over me, and the worm that dieth not seized hold of me. I begged for even the smallest mitigation of misery, and the vials of wrath were poured out upon me. In my anguish I cried, 'Roll on, ye eternal ages!' But why? They will be no nearer through. 'O Lord, how long?' With an earthquake, that seemed to shake the very throne, came back the reply, 'Forever! Forever!' I sank down in unutterable agony. Then I awoke, and lo, it was all a dream. The darkness of night was yet around me; a cold sweat covered me; and that word, 'Forever!' still rang in my ears. Friends, this was a dream, and only a drop in the ocean, compared with the terrible reality. Let us pray that we may be saved from it through Jesus Christ our Lord."

The large audience listened to these vivid delineations, part of the time, in breathless silence; and again the women beat on their breasts with half-suppressed cries for mercy. The reader, as well as they, will find relief from the companion picture by Moressa. Sanum's was an original conception of her own. The theme of this last was suggested by Miss Fiske, as a fitting counterpart to the preceding, but the treatment of it was left wholly with the writer.

"THE SAVED SOUL.

"While meditating on death, I fell into a sweet sleep, and dreamed a dream which rejoiced my spirit. I cannot refrain from relating it to you, dear Christian friends, who are looking forward to the glory that shall be revealed. I dreamed that my heavenly Father said to me, 'Dear child, heir of my kingdom, you have long enough borne the troubles of this vale of tears; now you shall be freed from them, and come to your heavenly home, to worship me in holiness.' As I listened, sickness came, and I laid me down on my bed of death with this thought: 'One more fruit of sin, and then — heaven.' My poor friends, not understanding this, inquired, with weeping, if I could not possibly recover; but when they saw that I was dying, they gathered round me, to go down with me to the banks of Jordan. My soul was exceeding joyful, for the light of the promised land shone on me, and the dread river was quiet, for Jesus had said to it, 'Peace, be still.'

"While in this joyful state, I remembered with sorrow how many years I had refused to acknowledge the Prince of life as my King, while he waited with open arms to receive me; and how often, after putting my hand to the plough, I had looked back. My backsliding, my evil example, my neglect of souls, all rose before me like a dark cloud, and I was in agony. But soon a voice said, 'Thy sins are forgiven!' and all was light. I said, 'Lord, I must praise thee for this forever; but I cannot forgive myself.' Yet, though the pains of death were on me, I was comforted to be nearer the land where they sin no more. Earthly pleasure now seemed emptiness. The pleasures of heaven filled my thoughts. I said, 'Is this death — that which we poor mortals fear?' My friends asked, 'Has he no terrors for you?' 'No; none. The king of terrors is to me the chief of joys.' One of my teachers said, 'So you have no fear of him — no sorrow that your body shall lie in the grave!' 'Why fear or sorrow, when Christ has overcome both death and sin?' My father then asked, 'Do you suffer much?' 'Yes; but if I suffered a thousand times more, what would that be to those bitter hours upon the cross. This veil must be rent asunder, though by suffering, before I can see Him, whom, even now, I long to behold.' My poor mother interposed, 'But are you willing to leave us?' 'You are all very dear to me; but there is only one who is altogether lovely. When shall I see him as he is, and be filled with his love?'

"It was now difficult to speak, but I could bid my friends farewell. I could thank my dear teachers for telling me of Christ, and ask their forgiveness for all I had ever done to grieve them. As my weeping mother wiped the cold sweat from my brow, she gently whispered, 'Where is my child going?' 'Mother,' I replied, 'your poor sinful child is going to that Saviour who has been willing to receive her.' His rod and staff then comforted me, till I had passed quite over into the blessed land. And, as I was borne on in my Saviour's arms, voices cried, 'Welcome, dear sister; you are now made whole — you shall sin no more — enter into rest.' Mortal tongue cannot tell what I now saw of the treasures which Christ has prepared for the redeemed. He gave me a mansion he had made ready for me, and I found myself gazing on the brightness of the Father's glory. What a change had come over me! I was among those without spot, for they had been made white in the blood of the Lamb. Their voices were one, for all praised the Lord. Now the glory of the Ancient of Days filled me with awe. He sat upon a throne of light, with seraphim on the right and cherubim on the left, and I could read the foundations of his throne. Legions of bright angels and happy saints were around him. I fell down with them to worship at his feet, when he touched me and raised me up, saying, 'Thou art blessed, for thou art redeemed with the blood of my Son.' Then he clothed me in a heavenly robe, and bade all heaven rejoice, saying, 'This my child was dead, and is alive again, and is saved from everlasting destruction.'

"He then revealed to me more fully that mystery of ages — the Redeemer standing on the right hand of the Father. He stood with open arms, saying, 'Come, daughter of my bitter grief, come in peace. I remembered thee on the cross. For thee I drank that cup of agony; thy curse has rested on me, that everlasting joy might dwell in thee.' As he thus spoke, I fell down to worship, and when I looked up, my eyes rested on his pierced hands and wounded side. Tears filled my eyes when I remembered that my sins had caused them; but they were tears that Jesus wiped away.

"When I saw the book of remembrance at his side, I thought, there is the record of my sins; but he opened it, saying, 'Fear not; from the day thou first camest to me, they have been blotted out.' He then held out to me the Book of Life, bidding me to read my name recorded there, and added, 'Ages hence, in the great day of account, the world shall know that I have saved thee; and as thou hast not denied me before men, I will confess thy name before my Father and before his angels; enter into the full joy of thy Lord; inherit the kingdom prepared for thee from the foundation of the world.' Then all the blessed ones cried, 'Amen.' Their harps were tuned to a new song, and they praised the living God that another soul was rescued from the great adversary. A crown was also placed upon my head, that, with the saints, I might cast it at the feet of the Redeemer.

"Afterwards I was led to our first parent, now for more than five thousand years in Paradise, but not walking amid forbidden fruit. Still, when he stretched out his hand to the tree of life, he seemed to remember that first sin, and to thank God more than others for the healing of the nations. His bright face glistened with a tear as he took my hand, saying, 'Heir of my fallen nature, welcome to this inheritance of the second Adam;' and I learned that tears are always wiped from that face when Christ brings home his fallen children.

"As I turned, I saw the great company of the patriarchs, perfect in holiness, and clothed in light. Faithful Abraham was there, his faith changed to perfect sight, and rejoicing in his spiritual children. The meek Moses was there, adoring the Prophet whom God raised up from the midst of Israel like unto him. And I beheld Isaiah, satisfied with the eternal sight of the glory of which he had a glimpse on earth. Jeremiah, too, was no more weeping for the slain of the daughter of his people, and all the holy prophets were clothed upon with immortality, and praising their Beloved with holy lips.

"While I stood gazing on them in wonder, my thoughts reverted to my former state. What a glorious change, from a world of sin to a world of holiness — from sinful friends to the Friend of sinners. How different these sweet sounds of praise from the rude sounds of earth! I am receiving my reward for every bitter tear of penitence I shed on earth; an age of joy is before me. Who am I, that I should be raised from companionship with sin to the society of heaven? My soul at length is at rest. But how? Not as rests my poor body in the grave, but in blessedness; for I rest from sin, but not from praise. I rest from suffering, but not from everlasting joy. How sweet to rest, while not ceasing to cry, Holy, holy, holy is the Lord God Almighty! I rest in the bosom of my Saviour. My prayers are turned to praise, and my love is perfect.

"While these thoughts filled my soul, I thanked the Lord with a new song on the golden harp that had been placed in my hands, singing with a loud voice, 'What is my worthiness, O eternal King, that thou hast made me to walk in thy presence, while millions are shut out from it?'

"Now a company of the holy ones led me through a street of pure gold, to where the river of water of life proceeded out of the throne of God. They showed me the hidden manna, and the tree of life yielding its twelve fruits, and leaves for the healing of the nations; and beyond, I saw a great company of martyrs who had been slain for the word and for the testimony of Jesus Christ. They stood beneath the altar, for they were living sacrifices. They were clothed in white, and wore crowns of glory on their heads, and they sang hallelujah to him who had been slain for them, and made them kings and priests forever in his kingdom.

"While thus wandering among those holy mansions, I met a spirit crowned with honor, — Mary, the mother of our Lord. She was specially delighted at seeing me, saying, 'How glad I am that you, from that erring people who trust in me, have found the right way to this blessed place! Are there other sisters of like faith, who believe in the only Mediator?' When I told her that there were, she embraced me, and led me where I could see the twelve apostles of the Lamb. They were all seated round their Master, just as they used to be on earth; but no more debating who should be greatest, for now they ascribed all greatness to their King, and dwelt in perfect love. Among them I saw Peter, zealous still, but with a holy zeal. I heard him ask, 'How long shall those precious souls, redeemed by thy blood, be led astray? May I not fly on the wings of love, and destroy that city of blasphemy on the seven hills, that the glory may be thine?' But Jesus looked on him with an eye of love, and said, 'Simon, son of Jonas, the time is not yet come.' Then Peter only replied, 'Lord, thou knowest. Thy will be done.'

"While in this joyful state, I walked in the green pastures of life. I went round about the holy city, and counted its towers. They were all of purest gold, and built with skill divine. I looked from the top of one of them, and beheld the sea of glass, and also caught a glimpse of the abyss, enough to see that the enemies of our God were all beneath his feet. I could see some, once my friends among them;

but I could say, 'Holy and just art thou, O Lord God; and O, wonderful grace, that has made such as I to differ.'

"But while thus filled with praise, and delighting myself in that ocean of love, I awoke, yet only to say, 'Blessed are the dead that die in the Lord.' Dear friends, let us cleave to Christ on earth, until he plants our feet on the Mount Zion above."

The next composition was written by Nargis, of Geog Tapa, in 1852. It is an account of Hannah, the mother of Samuel, and gives a very good idea of the Bible knowledge of the pupils, and their interest in Scripture themes. The allusions to the condition of Nestorian families, illustrate, and are illustrated by, the statements of Chapter I.

"About three thousand years ago, the family of Elkanah dwelt on the hill of Zophim, in Palestine. He was a just man, and one that feared God. According to the custom of those days, he had two wives, Peninnah and Hannah. Let us turn our thoughts to Hannah, for every memory of her is pleasant. She had no son, on whom she could look as a staff of joy for her old age. Yet Hannah had a worthy portion in the love of Elkanah, which flowed unceasingly like a crystal stream. Why was she thus loved? We believe because of the lovely spirit which she had received from that gentleness of the eternal Son which maketh great; and, like him, her voice was not heard in the streets. Instead of the contentious temper of the women of this age, we find in her a meek and quiet spirit; instead of pride, humility; and instead of anger, patience; she was kind, pleasant, and abounding in other graces. Shall not such a woman be praised?

"Now Elkanah took his family to Shiloh, to worship and

feast before the Lord. But the envious Peninnah so grieved Hannah that she could neither eat nor drink. Soon, however, she heard the sweet tones of her husband's voice. Was it not like an angel's? saying, 'Hannah, why weepest thou? and why eatest thou not? and why is thy heart grieved? Am I not better to thee than ten sons?' When she heard that she arose and ate. Love was rewarded by love. She would not grieve Elkanah. Unlike many in our day, she was obedient to her husband, yielding her will to his, and clothed with humility. They were not only one flesh, but one spirit; and they walked together in the valley of love to that world where love is made perfect. Now, after she had shown her love by partaking of the feast,* may we not suppose that she arose and whispered to Elkanah to know if he would approve of her intended vow; and did he not reply, 'Your vow is mine.' Then did she not seek a corner of the court where she might pray? Radiant spot, where Hannah communed with God! herself a bright light among the women of that age. There, in bitterness of soul, she wept before the Lord, and obtained his blessing. She believed that God would grant her request, as he saw best, and gave back her expected son to the Lord to be his forever. Here was true faith. She left all with God; and though, like her Saviour, she prayed the more earnestly: still her voice was not heard. But we hear the voice of Eli: 'How long wilt thou be drunken?' 'O Eli, Eli, why speak to her thus? She was of thy flock, and thou shouldst have distinguished her from other women round about her.'

"Bright star of that generation! Blessed art thou among the daughters of Levi. The moving of thy lips is like the

* In Oriental families, anger is shown by refusing to eat, sometimes for several days.

voice of the dove. There was a blessing in thy mouth, like the olive leaf of Noah's dove, that told of rest from the tossings of the flood; for thy request was about to give rest to the millions of Israel. Blessed art thou, daughter of Zion. Thou soughtest not a son for thy own glory, but for the glory of thy God.

"What a prayer was Hannah's! It brought a deliverer and a prophet to Israel, an intercessor and a preacher to the people of God. May the daughters of Hannah and the sons of Elkanah be multiplied among our people. She is a mirror into which we may look, to learn how to forsake our evil ways. Let us, like her, build up the kingdom of our Lord Jesus Christ.

"Her prayer finished, Hannah returned to her house. Her sorrow was now turned into joy, and her happy face was like the opening rose of the morning. No wonder she was joyful. The will of the Lord was her will, and what evil could befall her? Blessed Israel, that contains such a praying soul.

"Time passes on, and the answer to that prayer is a beloved son. The grateful mother calls him Samuel—'God heard.' Her full heart could give no other name to this child of prayer. She would remember ever, Not mine, but God's. And now the childless one folds in her arms a child of the covenant. New joy fills the heart of Elkanah. Their son was new to them every day; yet not alone as theirs, but His who answered prayer.

"The time now draws near for them to go again to Shiloh. The happy father does not forget God in his mercies. He appears before the Lord with his thank offering—a noble example to us. He asks Hannah to go with him: not in a voice of harsh command, but in love he said, 'Will you go?' and it was, doubtless, a gentle voice that answered, 'Not now, for then I must bring Samuel back with me. He is too small to leave; but when he is weaned, I will bring him, that he may appear before the Lord, and there abide forever.' The good Elkanah was satisfied, saying, 'Only the Lord establish his word;' for he had not forgotten the vow. So the happy Hannah remained at home another year, and taught the child as a mother only can.

"When the time came to go up again to Shiloh, Samuel was probably three years old. That praying mother did not say, 'He is small; let him stay with me one year longer.' No! With her whole heart she carried him to the house of the Lord, to abide there; and she went not up empty, saying, 'It is enough that I give my son;' but in the three bullocks we find the burnt offering, the sin offering, and the peace offering, and in her son the first fruits besides. She was ready to say, 'In all things I am a debtor to the Lord.'

"Nor did she come in pride of spirit, saying to Eli, 'You called me drunken, while offering a prayer that God hath heard;' but in all humility she accosts the aged priest, saying, 'I am the woman that stood by thee here, praying;' and then, leading forward the child, 'for this child I prayed, and the Lord hath given me my petition, and I have lent him to the Lord.' We seem to see little Samuel approaching Eli reverently; and then turning those speaking eyes to his mother, he says, 'Is this my father, of whom you told me, and with whom I am to live?' 'Yes, my child, he will be your father.' And now Eli places his hand upon the head of Samuel, saying, 'Blessed art thou, son of a true daughter of Levi. The Lord bless thee, and make thee a prophet of the Most High.'

"Hannah worships, and returns to her home. Her

little son asks not to go with her; for he has been taught that he is the Lord's, and is to abide in Shiloh. What a blessing are praying mothers, training their children for God!

"Still she does not forget the Lord's Samuel. Every year she goes up to Shiloh, with her husband, and as often does she carry for the little prophet a coat, made by a mother's loving hand. She did not say, like some of our mothers, 'If he is in the school of the prophets, let the prophets clothe him;' but she clothed him for the Lord's service, and he comforted Eli as he was never comforted by his own children. Will our mothers follow the example of Hannah? Should a voice come from the mountains to-day, calling for preachers, would they give their sons to go and save the lost? Blessed are those mothers who give their sons to be soldiers of the cross; who, like Hannah, lead the way to the throne of grace, and serve God in their households.

"The Lord helped Hannah to pray, and he helped her to write that beautiful song. Her words are golden and full of wisdom. It is fitting to call her a mother in Israel. Deborah sat as judge, but Hannah gave a judge and teacher to the people of God. Both were bright stars, but where is the people on whom they shone? The chosen people are scattered. Deborah, perchance, sleeps under the oak of judgment, and Hannah on the hill of Zophim. We love to think that her son stood by her dying bed to thank her for all her prayers and instructions, and see her reverently gathered to her people.

"We leave thee, mother of the holy prophet. Thou hast passed through this valley of humiliation. Thy works follow thee, and thy God hath crowned thee with glory and honor. Sweet singer of Israel, sing on in heaven, for with thy Saviour thou canst never sorrow more. Who will rise among us to carry forward the kingdom of our Christ? Such as honor the Master here, he will honor when mothers in Israel see their sons made kings and priests unto the Lord forever."

CHAPTER XXI.

KIND OFFICES.

HOSPITALITY OF NESTORIANS. — KINDNESS OF PUPILS. — BATHING FEET. — LETTERS OF GOZEL, HANEE, SANUM OF GAWAR, MUNNY, RAHEEL, AND MARTA. — HOSHEBO. — RAHEEL TO MRS. FISKE. — MOURNING FOR THE DEAD. — NAZLOO. — HOSHEBO'S BEREAVEMENT. — DEATH OF MISSIONARY CHILDREN. — LETTER FROM SARAH, DAUGHTER OF JOSEPH.

THE foregoing pages have told something of the change that grace has wrought among women in Persia. Let us now look at some points in that change more carefully.

The Nestorians are noted for their hospitality. Kindness to strangers is regarded as a part of their religion; and if, after bringing out the choicest of their stores, it is said, even in a strange language, "How can I eat this?" or, "Who could endure a dish like that?'" the words may be unintelligible, but not so the look and tone of the speaker. Yet even such treatment often only calls forth additional efforts to please. A stranger may not relish some of their dishes. Yet a spirit of kindness would be careful not to let this appear. In the Seminary, the pupils studied how to please, even in the folding of a table napkin; and the kind-hearted steward was perfectly delighted when reminded that the pains he took in the preparation of a meal was so much service to Christ, because it strengthened his servants to labor for him.

The girls were very kind to each other. When any one

was sick, her companions not only readily performed her share of domestic work, but nursed her tenderly besides. If their teachers were ill, they coveted the privilege of attending them by night and by day. It may comfort some timid one to know, that in Oroomiah Miss Fiske never had a missionary sister with her by night in sickness; not that they were backward to come, but the services of the pupils left nothing to be desired. It did good like a medicine to see those girls, once coarse and uncouth, showing even kindness in a way offensive to refined feelings, now move with noiseless step, anticipating every wish. They sought to conform every thing to the home tastes of their teachers; and yet there was nothing of that show of effort that says, "See how much we do for you." They seemed to feel that they could not do too much, or do it well enough. If Miss Fiske was exhausted and feeble during the day, they might say nothing at the time, and not trouble her even to answer a question; but when they supposed she was ready to retire, there would be a gentle knock on the door, sometimes on more than one door, and then, with a "Teacher, you looked tired to-day. Shall we come in and bathe your feet? The water is warm, and every thing ready," their loving service would not cease, till every thing was in its place, and they had put out the light after she retired.

Woman there, as in the days of our Saviour, still bathes the feet of the guest whom she wishes to honor. And sometimes, when stooping over them, she rubs them gently with her loosely-flowing hair—not as a substitute for a towel, but as a token of kindly welcome. This privilege belongs to the oldest daughter of the family; and the custom once liable to perversion, now shines with new beauty, as the expression of Christian love. He who once accepted the service in his own person, will hereafter say, to many a daughter of Chaldea, "Inasmuch as ye did it unto one of the least of these my brethren, ye did it unto me."

Their tender sympathy with the afflicted was not confined to their own household. In January, 1857, Miss Fiske was absent at Seir, assisting in taking care of Mr. Stoddard in his last illness; and from a number of letters written to her, at that time, by her pupils, we select the following:—

JANUARY 1st, 1857.

Many of your flock have observed this as a day of fasting and prayer; and all have looked on it as a blessed day. The pleasant voice of prayer has been heard during all its hours, and it seems as if the Saviour was about to come among us with great power. I trust that he will work in many hearts by the Holy Spirit. We greatly desire to have you here; but again, with all our hearts, we wish you to do for the sick one whom we love. Yes, if each pupil were to write to you, all would say, we wish you to remain, and do all you can for him; and may he be raised up again to labor for our poor people. Give our love to Mrs. Stoddard, and tell her we are glad to have the one we greatly love, with her at this time.

Your daughter, GOZEL.

JANUARY 2d, 1857.

My heart is drawn towards you all the time; but I thank God that he has given you strength to do for our beloved brother Mr. Stoddard. I am very much distressed when I think of him, and can only say, "The will of the Lord be done." I greatly desired to hear your voice yesterday. It was indeed a blessed day. Give my love to Mrs. Stoddard, and though it is hard for her to bear these bitter pains, tell her to try to trust the Lord of our beloved brother.

Peace be to you. HANEE.

The next is written by a graduate, who was then on a visit at the Seminary: —

JANUARY 3d, 1857.

I cannot tell you what great anxiety and anguish I have for Mr. Stoddard. He has won my whole heart by taking so much pains for my dear companions, and particularly for Elisha. I did not think he would be taken from us. This trial seems to me heavier than losing Elisha and Jonathan (her children, who died by poison), for it is not only a loss to his dear family, but also to this band of stranger missionaries, and a dreadful desolation to our poor people. May the Lord see how great is the harvest, and how few the laborers. I cannot write more; my eyes fail because of my tears. Give my tenderest love to dear Mrs. Stoddard. I know her sorrows in such trying days; would that I could help her.

From your truly afflicted pupil,

SANUM.

The following was written the day after the death of Mr. Stoddard, which took place the 22d of January, and refers to that sad occurrence: —

JANUARY 23d, 1857.

What bitter intelligence comes to us these days! — the taking away of those who carried us in the arms of love to the blood-stained cross of Christ. Truly, my mother, these afflictions fall very heavily on our heads. The guides of our souls are cut off from us. What shall we do?

Dearly loved sister Mrs. Stoddard, sorrow and mourning

are ours. There is hope that you will soon meet the ornament of your life. But in his school and in ours are those for whom there is no hope that they will ever see him. Wounded sister, blessed is the heavenly pilgrim who has spent his life in a strange land, and been a well of living water to many thirsty souls. I know this separation is bitter to you; but there is consolation for you, for it is not eternal. But what shall I say of our poor people?

O, how much more than any of you knew we loved that dear brother. It was a quarter past three o'clock this morning when your letter reached us (Miss Fiske's). I handed it to Miss Rice, and never saw such a bitter night except that in which my father died. I did not sleep till almost dawn; and when I slept, I saw the loved one standing in Miss Rice's room, his face shining like the morning star. Both his hands were raised to heaven, when suddenly he stooped and looked in my face. I said, "O, you are not dead!" He answered, "No!" and I cried aloud, "O, Mr. Stoddard is not dead!" and my own voice awoke me. How favored those of you are who see the face of our beloved friend!

MUNNY.

Still later, she writes to her teacher, who was again at Seir, during the sickness of Harriette Stoddard, whose death occurred March 16th, 1857.

Though it is a time of anguish, yet, blessed be God, he has given us One to whom we may look for comfort. A thousand thanks to the Saviour that he does not chastise us by taking away the Holy Spirit. Though the discipline is bitter, yet it is mingled with love, in that the Lord comes by death among his own, and by his Spirit to those who have not known him, that he may make them his own also. What grief would the lovers of the Lord have, if you now sat by the bedside of a sister of whom we had no evidence that her heart was purified by a Saviour's blood? If you are so distressed about one whom you trust your Father is taking to rest in the bosom of his Son, how would you feel if she were one of those who, as soon as the breath left her body, would dwell with everlasting burnings! How thankful we should be that it is not the bed of one of these!

I have never seen such a trying year; but I do not believe it is for the harm of those that fear the Lord. It only fulfils the promise, "Whom the Lord loveth he chasteneth." O that the gentle voice of Jesus might be heard, whispering, "Daughter, I say unto thee, arise!" Who knows but, if our faith were as Christ would have it, he would call this sister back to life, though now so near to death! But your Father knows what is for your good, and you know that here he often gives anguish to those who love him, that they may be exceedingly joyful with him hereafter. The Lord grant that these afflictions do not harden our hearts.

I have conversed and prayed with all the younger girls, save two. Eleven say that they are resolved to follow Christ; but I fear lest the vineyards and the cotton fields do not testify hereafter that they have walked with God. It is very pleasant to me to sit down by them and ask them of their state.

Yesterday (Sabbath) was a delightful day, but it seemed very short. The Lord help us in our weakness, and cause the dark clouds to rise from all your friends. The God of consolation heal the wounded spirit of your poor sister, Mrs. Stoddard. I have never seen the death of the righteous — only by hearing have I heard of it. The Lord be with you more and more.

MUNNY.

Others, written during the same period, are as follows: —

Sorrower for us, who hast also become as a stranger to us! Now we know your anxious love for us. We have no doubt that He who directs not according to man's thoughts has directed you to be away from us much this year. We had thought that it would be a very pleasant year; but the Lord has ordered it as he pleases, and let us say, "His will be done." We know that he does all for our profit. What a comfort this is to us who have given our all to the Saviour to do with us as he will!

It is very hard to look at your vacant place; but we thank God it is not made vacant by death. Though not with us in body, we believe that you are, in spirit, and we rejoice that you can do as few can, for the sick. The Lord be with you, who are the second in anguish, and strengthen your weak body. The prayer of your pupils is ever for your life. We have no words with which to comfort you; we can only say, "The Saviour, with whom you are better acquainted than we are, give you comfort."

What can we say to you, dear Mrs. Stoddard, who are shrouded in a cloud that is very dark? We know it is very hard for you to look on the great vacancy that is made in your dwelling. But do trust in the Lord; he will bring light out of darkness. We feel for you, plunged in a sea of sorrow, in the deep places of sighs. Our eyes are every hour upon the door, expecting what we shall hear from Harriette; and our prayer is, that if it can be the Lord's will, she may be brought back to you; but every letter increases our anxiety. We understand not the Lord's dealings this year, except this: we know that he does all things for the profit of our souls.

RAHEEL.
MARTA.

The writer of the following was at that time a teacher in the Seminary, and a striking illustration of the elevating power of a good education. Formerly a female who was either lame or deformed was so despised, that she could never hope to be the head of a family: she was doomed to drag through a miserable life, the object of universal neglect. But Hoshebo, though a fall in early youth had shattered her ankle, and the ignorance of native surgeons made her a cripple for life, yet because of her education was as much esteemed as before she would have been despised, and is now the wife of Meerza, our native helper at Saralon. Miss Fiske might have filled up her school with such, but, with a wise foresight, selected her pupils with an eye to their future usefulness among the people, as well as their own personal advantage.

When I understood from Miss Rice, that you would not meet your loved flock next Sabbath, I felt that I could not let all your absence pass without giving you an account of my charge. I have been sitting with them, as I do every Saturday evening, to search out their spiritual state; and I have good news to tell you of one for whom you, and also others, have been very anxious — Esli, of Takka. I noticed her changed all this week; but last night I saw a great breaking down under Mr. Cochran's preaching. She came out in anguish of soul. I then saw her alone, and found her contrition still increasing. I know this is not evidence that she has passed from death unto life; but I rejoice that she is visited by the Holy Spirit, and I trust she will become a Christian. I am anxious for her and for all the girls of my room. I look for the gentle shower that shall make the withered plants like the fresh springing grass. Though you are absent, we know well that you carry every one of your flock in the arms of love to Him who can do all things, whether you are far away or near to us. The girls send up many petitions for Harriette. We fear much when we recall your former going to Seir. How glad should we be to hear of indications that she will recover. Peace and love to Mrs. Stoddard.

Your affectionate HOSHEBO.

More than a year after this, Miss Fiske left Oroomiah, and at Salmas, on her way home, met her dear pupil Sanum, the wife of Joseph. Having no other place for devotion, they retired together to an orchard for the parting prayer. In a subsequent letter, Sanum thus beautifully alludes to it:—

"O, the remembrance of that bitter separation! and of those prayers, when the green grass was watered with our tears! How could I have borne it, but for the recollection of Him who prayed and wept in the garden of Gethsemane, and whose kneeling upon the tender grass was for the comfort of our souls!"

The gratitude of the pupils to their teacher extended also to her aged mother. Seldom have they written a letter to Miss Fiske, in America, without its message of kind remembrance to the parent who gave up her daughter, as Hannah gave up Samuel, to be the Lord's; and several wrote letters to her separately. From among these we select the following, written by Raheel (Rachel), of Geog Tapa, Sept. 10th, 1859:—

My dear Grandmother Hannah: Though I have never seen you, yet I must write to you, for I love all Miss Fiske's friends as I do my own, and especially yourself. I want to thank you for all your love to me. Blessings have thus reached me which were not given to my early sisters. When it was a great reproach for a girl to learn to read, God had mercy on us in that he poured such love into your heart as made you willing to send your daughter eight thousand miles, by sea and land, to show our people the great mystery that had been previously hidden from their eyes — that there is salvation for women. They used to dwell much on those words of Solomon, "One man among a thousand have I found, but a woman among all these have I not found;" but now they see their mistake, and that Christ died for women also. Many thanks for your patience all these years. I know something of it from the feelings of my own mother, for if she did not see me for five months during term time, she would mourn that she had not seen her daughter for so long.

It was certainly a sacrifice for Christ to come into this world, and deny himself; and it was also a sacrifice for the Father to send his Son, when he knew all the sorrows and wounds there were in the cup which he was to drink in this world of sin.

You will see your daughter much changed from what she was fifteen years ago; but I am confident that when that day comes, which will be longer than any day we have seen in this world, — when He whom the Jews could not bear to hear called king, shall sit upon his throne, judging the world, — then all troubles, sorrows, and separation from friends will appear to the Christian as the small dust of the balance; and I think that it will especially seem so to you, when you see a band of Nestorian girls on the right hand of the Redeemer, whom you, through your daughter, were the means of bringing there. Yes, justly might they have been left to dwell with Satan forever; but instead of that, they will have joyful life with Christ in his kingdom.

I can never repay your love; but there is one so rich that he can give you what man cannot, and I ask him to reward you in heaven.

Is there another Miss Fiske in your country? We can hardly believe it. I hope that I shall see her again, but it is difficult for me to expect it.

It is very pleasant for me to write to friends, and especially to my own dear mother, Miss Fiske. I should never be weary if I wrote to her every day; but I thought that this time she would like to have me write to you, and I trust that you will live to receive it.

Please give my love to Martha, and also to Mrs. Stoddard and Sarah, and tell them that our hearts are with them.

From your granddaughter, whom you have not seen,

RAHEEL.

No reader of the Bible needs any description of Oriental mourning for the dead. The rent garments and sackcloth (2 Sam. iii. 31), loud weeping and wailing (ver. 32), protracted lamentation as for Jacob (Gen. l. 10 and 11), and for Moses (Deut. xxxiv. 8), and the hired mourning women (Jer. ix. 17, and Matt. ix. 23), were to be found nowhere in greater perfection than among the Nestorians. It is very difficult for us, in this land, to realize the force of such habits; but it required much grace to break over them; and even now, when the Christian heart grows cold, it is apt to return to the old ways. One day, in 1845, the whole school were going to attend a funeral. When the time came, one of the pupils requested to be excused.

"Why? are you sick?" "No." "Why not go, then?" "I do not wish to tell. But another said, "May I tell you alone?" "It will be a great shame if we do not all weep. We all think we can do it but Sarah, and we are afraid her tears will not come; and so, lest she bring reproach upon us, we do not want her to go." The heart of the teacher sunk within her, as she found that she was about to lead a company of mourning women to the funeral. She asked them how they could make themselves weep. "O, when we go to such places, we call to mind all the sad things we ever knew, and so we weep; but if the tears do not come, we leave very quickly."

But grace has wrought a great change in this matter also. In the journal of Yonan, we find the following entry: "At the close of afternoon service, I had a Bible class with the women: this was followed by a prayer meeting. Then Munny came to see me: she has buried a little child recently. It is a matter of joy to me, that these women can lift up their eyes and see their children with the dear Saviour, and feel that they have treasures in heaven. I asked her, 'Did you ever do any thing for your little girl that you remember now with gratitude?' 'Many times I carried her with me to the stable, and knelt with her upon the straw in the manger, to ask blessings on her.' 'Christ was in the manger, and perhaps there your daughter was consecrated to him.'"

In another place, we find him asking Esli,—the wife of Joseph, of whom he had just said, "Her little daughter has died recently, and her heart is broken,"—"When your child died, did you weep and wail as your people do?" and she answered, "No."

Nazloo, of Vizierawa, a pupil who hoped she took Christ for her Saviour in 1849, and graduated in 1853, within less than a year after her conversion was summoned to the death-bed of her uncle; and scarcely had she returned to her studies before she was called to the bedside of her father. For three days she watched with him incessantly, by day and by night. Those who were present were greatly moved by her tender care of him. During the whole of his sickness, she never failed to improve every opportunity to point him to Christ. Even to the last, she begged him to look to the Lamb of God and live. And when he died, with his head resting on her hand, though she had no evidence that her efforts were successful, her wonderful calmness, under so severe a stroke, led many to feel that she possessed a source of consolation to which they were strangers. But her cup was not yet full. A few days passed, and she hastened once more to her afflicted home, to find her mother entering the dark valley. Others wept aloud, but she pointed the dying one to Jesus; and supporting her in her loving arms, she seemed to plant her feet in the cold waters of the river of death, and commit her departing mother into the hands of Him who could bear her safely to the other side. So sensible was her mother of the benefit she and hers had received from the school, that when the teacher came in, she beckoned her to her side, and said, with difficulty, "God is not willing I should be a mother to my daughters any longer. I commit them to you: they are yours." She soon fell asleep, as was hoped, in Jesus. After this, Nazloo was in the school most of the time till her marriage. As a teacher, no one could have been more faithful: her religious experience was very marked, and she labored wisely for souls. She still lives to show how God can make grievous afflictions yield the peaceable fruit of righteousness in his people.

In this connection, we cannot omit another letter, written by Hoshebo to her teacher, in 1860, on the death of her son Absalom. It is dated Saralon, where she and her husband Meerza reside.

Dear Mother: I received your letter just before I received a bitter stroke from the never-erring hand of my heavenly Father. Many thanks for your loving remembrances of me. I cannot reward you for one of a thousand of the good things that you have shown me, so unworthy. I have many thoughts of you, and of those pleasant days that we passed together in that blessed school. I am very sad when I think that perhaps I may never, in this house of my pilgrimage, see your face, which makes others to be exceeding glad.

Dear mother: like a daughter distressed, who would find a little rest by falling into the kind arms of her mother, I come to tell you what has pierced the heart of your poor child. It is true that you are so far from me that I cannot lean on your kind breast, and let you lead me in prayer to the Father who has afflicted me; but with a feeling like that I write you. Beloved, you used to write me that I must take good care of my dear and tender babe, Aweshalom. Perhaps I did not fully do as you told me. But one thing I know: the Lord, who loves little children, was not willing that I should keep him. And I believe that he will take better care of my dear child than I could. You must know that I am deeply wounded and crushed by the death of Aweshalom. My tears cease not. His first birth was October 14, 1858; his second and spiritual one, April 23, 1860. His life with us was a pleasant one, and he made our lives very sweet and delightful; but now he has gone to heaven, while we remain on the earth. He lives the new life, while we die daily. He is strong, while I am weak. He has grown beautiful, in the light and image of the Saviour, while I am pining away. If you have heard what a child he was, you will not wonder at my sickness since his death. My husband is greatly afflicted in the death of this, our first, our only child. We find no comfort except in casting our wounded souls at the feet of the Saviour, who was tempted that he might heal our wounds. It seems, sometimes, as if our comforters were far from us; but our Saviour is very near to help and comfort.

Our work has been as last year. My husband has taught in the Seminary at Seir, coming here to preach on the Sabbath. I have taught a school of eighteen boys and girls here. Before vacation, my babe sickened, and rested in Jesus. Since that time, I have had fever, and am still very weak.

Five in the village, besides ourselves, are communicants. My father and brother are among them. I trust that my mother and brother's wife will soon unite with us. The work of the Lord in the village goes forward better than formerly. I try to talk and pray with the women alone, and they are more ready to have me do it, which makes me to rejoice in the Lord.

Give my loving peace to my dear grandmother Hannah. Though with the eyes of this mortal body we have not seen each other, nor have I any hope that we shall, the Lord her God help me, that we may meet on the blessed hill of Zion above. I believe, my mother, that you will remember your weak, unworthy lamb, when you bow before the throne of mercy and grace. Perhaps this is the last letter you will receive from me, for death seems very near. Receive loving peace from the priest [her husband].

Your true daughter, HOSHEBO.

Jesus has seemed to be almost bodily present, taking up these lambs in his arms; and the mothers have not feared, for they felt sure that under such a Guardian it was well with their children.

Perhaps bereaved missionary mothers in Persia do not realize how much their patient suffering has done for their poor Nestorian sisters. The short lives of those twenty missionary children, who lie in Persian graves, were a precious offering to Christ. They were all missionaries, and did not go home till their work was done. Each one had a place to fill among the instrumentalities employed by the Master to promote his kingdom in Persia. There was no waste in the breaking of those alabaster boxes of precious ointment. Nestorian parents looked on, to learn how to lay their children into the arms of Jesus, and become more Christ-like themselves. No years of mature toil have been more blessed than the years of those thus early called home; and in this truth their bereaved parents may find abundant consolation. There are influences too deep and silent to be fully understood; but they are none the less real and powerful; and the mother who to-day misses the little feet, the loving eyes, and the pleasant voice, which God had lent to gladden her earthly home for a season, may rejoice in the assurance that her loving submission to a Father's hand is teaching a lesson to the people whom she loves, such as they could never learn from words.

During the revival of 1846, a little child of Dr. Perkins died; and as the missionaries laid it away, in the hope of a glorious resurrection, it helped them to point others to him who is the Resurrection and the Life. It was buried on a snowy Sabbath day, and the faces of the young converts, who stood in silence around the grave, showed that to them the associations of death were no longer fearful.

Turning away from the cemetery, Mr. Stoddard, feeling that he could not be separated from those young disciples even in death, said, "Do you not hope that you shall rest here to rise with these to everlasting life?" * Little did they who heard him know how soon that cemetery at Seir would become more sacred as his own resting place.

Before leaving this topic, we insert a letter from Sarah, daughter of Joseph, a former pupil in the Seminary, and the oldest of four sisters. The death of little Deborah seemed to draw her heart very closely to her Saviour, and she now sleeps by her side, doubtless understanding better the meaning of those arms of love that here she believed "folded her little sister in his own bosom."

"What word of fitting love can I write, and how tell you what God has done? We are afflicted, for he has taken from us our dear little Deborah. She was only two years and seven months old. We mourn, and yet are comforted; for we know that He who loves little children has taken her into his own arms, that we may love him more and better praise his glorious name. She did not leave us to go to a stranger. The dear Saviour, we think, has made her happier than we could; and now we dwell much on this scripture, 'Prepare to meet thy God.' Deborah was very sick, and suffered much; but when she died, there was a pleasant smile on her little face. Then she rested from sorrow, and Jesus folded the little lamb in his own bosom."

* See Nestorian Biography, page 242.

CHAPTER XXII.

PROGRESS AND PROMISE.

BENEVOLENCE, EARLY MANIFESTATION OF. — PROGRESS. — REVIVAL OF BENEVOLENCE IN APRIL, 1861. — INTEREST OF PARENTS FOR THE CONVERSION OF THEIR CHILDREN. — PEACE IN FAMILIES. — REFORMED MARRIAGES. — ORDINATIONS. — COMMUNION SEASONS. — MISS RICE AND MISS BEACH. — CONCLUSION.

THE pupils were early trained to form habits of self-denying benevolence. In 1844, the day scholars made as many as fifty garments for poor children. Early in 1845, when some mountaineers came to beg money for their ragged children, the question was put, "Who will give her own clothes and wear poorer ones till she can make others." Many responded at once, and she who gave her best dress was deemed the most happy. Some even wept because they could not do the same. In a letter written December, 1848, the pupils say, "The last day of the term was monthly concert. We had a good time of prayer, and then a collection, which went up to thirty-two sahib korans — (seven dollars.) We hope this will be increased, and used for sending the gospel to the poor people of the mountains."

They were accustomed to devote several hours a week to sewing for some benevolent object. At the close of one term the articles thus prepared were sold for sixteen dollars, and the proceeds sent to Aintab to pay for teaching women there to read.

The same virtue was assiduously cultivated in the people. Deacons John and Yonan had for some time been urged to take up a collection at the monthly concert at Geog Tapa, but they dared not try; not that they did not wish it, but they feared that the people, in their poverty, might take offence at the innovation. At length, on the first Sabbath of 1852, John preached on the subject, and a few korans (worth twenty cents each), were contributed. The first Sabbath of February it was Yonan's turn to preach there. So he prepared himself thoroughly on this subject, — Miss Fiske had read with him the prize essays on Benevolence, published by the American Tract Society, — and, carrying his map into a crowded church, he spoke at some length about missions in various parts of the world. His account was well received. Then Bibles were distributed through the church, and the readers were called on to read passages previously selected, showing, first, the antiquity of benevolent contributions; secondly, that the poor were to give as well as the rich; and thirdly, that the blessing of God was promised to the benevolent. The readers were scattered all over the church, and the people listened with great attention. Then several spoke on the subject, and the elders of the village gave the work their hearty approval. Afternoon came, and as the time for meeting drew near, old and young were eagerly engaged in getting ready their contributions (in Geog Tapa the monthly concert is held on Sabbath afternoon), and as many as two hundred came together. There were remarks and prayers, and while the missionary hymn was being sung at the close, the collection was taken up, amounting, in money and cotton yarn, to more than fifteen korans. One sick boy, who had heard what was going on, rose from his bed, and crept in to deposit his little coin. Instead of spending their saints' days in idleness, as had been the custom, many now wrought on those days to earn money for giving, saying to objectors that it was better to labor for the spread of the gospel than to be idle for Satan. Mr. Stoddard attended the March concert, with some idols from India, and so interested the people that the collection amounted to more than twenty-five korans, thus the good work went on.

After this the spirit of benevolence steadily increased, and instances of marked self-denial were not wanting. It shows at once their poverty and their disposition to do what they could, that at the monthly concert a basket was passed round along with the contribution box, to receive eggs from the little children and such as were too poor to give any thing else. Crosses of ivory or silver were often found among the contributions.

One day, a man was seen to take a silver coin out of his purse; and as the missionary went on to describe more of the condition of the heathen world, a second and a third was taken out, and held in readiness for the collection. At another time, a woman, whom she had not seen before, asked for a private interview with one of the ladies of the mission; and when alone, besides requesting prayer that she might become a Christian, she took out a gold ornament, the only one of any value that she possessed, which had been handed down as an heirloom in her family for several generations, and said she wanted to give that to send the gospel to others, only no one must know who gave it. The ornament was sold for four dollars and fifty cents, and the woman, in less than a year, became a useful Christian. Sometimes the amount of interest might be measured by the number of silver coins manufactured into buttons that were found in the contribution box; for when their feelings were aroused, the women cut off the fastenings of their outer garments, and cast them into the Lord's treasury.

But the most remarkable revival of benevolence occurred in April, 1861; and we condense the following account of it from a long letter of Yonan to Miss Fiske and Mrs. Stoddard: —

"The prayers and tears of our missionary friends have, this winter, received a joyful reward from our Father in heaven. We were told that the first week in January would be devoted by all Christians to prayer for great things, and my heart was never so enlarged before. It seemed as if Persia, nominal Christendom, and all the heathen were under the power of prayer; as if the Christian's measuring-line was stretched round the four corners of the earth. One day the missionaries met, as usual, for prayer in Dr. Wright's large room. It moved me much, and I said to my companions, 'They are praying for us while we are idle.' They said, 'It is good that we spend this half hour in prayer every day.' We did so. On the Sabbath, I went to my village, Geog Tapa, and mentioned these things to the people at the evening meeting. The Lord opened the mouth of Abraham, who said, 'Brethren, in these places we are always idle — let us meet for prayer half an hour before sunset.' They did so. The clouds over our heads seemed loaded with blessings: still they did not descend. Mr. Cobb and Mr. Ambrose had talked with me about commencing in our village to support preachers in the mountains. So did Mr. Labaree last week. I told him of our poverty. He said, 'I am grieved for that; but begin with some little thing.'

"We went to Geog Tapa the last Sabbath in March. John gave notice, as it was the gospel Sabbath, [monthly concert is so called], of the contributions for our brothers in

India. In his sermon he said that much of our poverty is from our indolence. Last year our collection was fifteen tomans. [A toman is about two dollars.] If we had more zeal, we might raise twenty, and that would support a preacher in the mountains. At once Guwergis cried out, 'I will give one.' I said, 'We will support one preacher and two schools among ourselves, and if any thing is over, we will send it far away.' Priest Abraham approved of this. Then all the brethren in the congregation began to speak. 'So is good.' 'Thus we will do.' John would have stilled them; but I said, 'Perhaps God is blessing your preaching; let them speak.' Praised be God's name forever; in a moment every obstacle was swept away. Had we known that God was so near, we would have bowed our heads before him. Now Aib Khan cried, 'I give one toman;' and 'I,' said Priest Moses, 'twelve korans;' and another, 'I two monats.' [A monat is seventy-five cents.] Moses now took out his pencil to write. The Malik said, 'I have often thought that I would put a gold imperial in the box [four dollars and fifty cents]; write that.' I then said, 'My family of eight souls hear preaching all the year, and three or four attend school. I am a debtor; write for me three tomans—it is not too much.' When God pleases, excuses flee away; high prices and oppression were not thought of; we were lords of wealth. Moses then said, 'I am troubled that I remain to the last; but we are three brothers in company, and I know not whether they will act through me, or each one for himself.' One brother cried out, 'Our agent and I, five korans more.' Another man then said, 'I also am at a loss on account of my brother;' and his brother replied, 'Four monats.' These things made brotherly love very firm. Guwergis now cried out, 'Women, where are you? In the wilderness women gave their brazen mirrors.' I said, 'Holy women, to-day ends fifteen years of the prayers of Christianity among us. Speak!' [It was fifteen years since the revival in 1846.] One replied, 'I half a monat;' and 'I a head-dress;' 'I a silver ornament;' 'I my ear-rings;' and so on. A widow said, 'I have kept my husband's coat till now; I will sell it, and give half the price.' And others made similar responses. Isaac, a poor old mountaineer, gave two korans; and another said, 'I have nothing but the mat I sit on: I give that.' It was a new one he had just finished. A mother said, 'I have nothing now, but I will give the work of my hands this winter — a tope [ten yards] of cotton cloth.' A pilgrim said, 'When I was in Jerusalem, an Armenian and a Russian bid against each other, and the Russian prevailed, giving five hundred tomans to the Greek convent. If they had such zeal for error, we ought to have more for the truth.' And one unaccustomed to come to church gave the fruit and prunings of fifteen rows in his vineyard. [The prunings of the vines are sold for fuel.] We were in the church about four hours. Time was given for all to contribute, and then we spent a season in joyful song and pleasant prayer.

"The report of what had been done spread quickly through the village, and my mother-in-law sent word that she would give a hundred and twenty-eight pounds of raisins. At evening meeting, the house was full. Benjamin said, 'Brethren, the teacher of our school was one day explaining the verse, "Thou shalt not muzzle the mouth of the ox that treadeth out the corn;" and Mr. Stoddard, who stood near, added, "But the Nestorian oxen eat from the straw of America." That word has worked in my heart ever since. I trust that, hereafter, we will eat our own straw.' That night we lay awake a long time for joy. In the morning, before I was up, my uncle and his wife came and promised a load of wheat [five bushels]; and when passing through the village, a woman put an ornament in my pocket to sell for the cause.

"Monday we came to the city for the gospel day [the concert is held there on Monday], and every one who met us remarked our glad faces. In the meeting, after Mr. Coan spoke, John opened a bundle of the gifts, and Moses described the scenes of the day before. I said, 'One toman led to sixty in our village yesterday: perhaps it will lead to hundreds more. Many times the good in the heart of the Christian comes up into his mouth, and then goes back; but when the power of God prevails, it not only comes into the mouth, but comes forth and abounds.' Priest Moses arose, and said, 'As long as a man is sick, it is no shame if he does not walk; but if the blood walks well in his veins, and he becomes fat, and still lies in bed, every one reproaches him. We have grown fat; and how long shall we lie under the quilts?' Priest Yakob added, 'For twenty-five years we have said, "Let the Lord go before;" and now that he has come, let us wait no longer, but give.' He gave two tomans, and others followed. Mar Yohanan's wife gave a toman of ornaments, and almost every girl in school from one koran to three or four. Isras, of Degala, gave fifteen tomans and a new vineyard that he had recently bought. Guwergis, who had already proposed to plough the field the second time, now rose, and opening his hand, said, 'If a man thrust his hand into a pile of gold, and give of it to God, is it a great thing when He has filled his hand with the blood of his Son, and given it to us?' Sagoo,[1] of Gulpashan, said, 'My father gave each of my two sisters thirty tomans. When Hannah died, hers became mine. I give it for the bride's

[1] See page 209.

veil; [The kingdom of Christ is here spoken of as the bride], also a silver watch.' One who had only two or three sheep promised one of them. My little girl, Sherin, had asked, a few days before, for a new dress. She now sent word to me that she would do without it for a year, if I would give the money for the gospel. I cannot fully describe the spirit of the meeting: we went out wondering and congratulating each other at having witnessed such a pleasant sight. At the evening meeting one said, 'I heard in the market what you were doing; I give a gun, the price of which was seven and-a half tomans.' Some gave for themselves, and others for their wives and children. Moses gave four monats for his brother's children. There were tithes and sixths, fifths and fourths, thirds and halves, of crops of hay and grapes. Priest Abraham said, 'We say a thief will never own a house. Did you ever see one that had wealth? We are thieves, and therefore are so poor. We have robbed God. I will give a tithe of my vineyard.' Another replied, 'And I of every thing.' And a man, who had before given one quarter of his vineyard, now gave the half. A widow, who had nothing but a cow, pledged a hepta [four pounds] of butter. A poor man, who has a few fruit trees in his yard, promised ten heptas of apricots. Guwergis spoke up, 'We have butter: what shall we cook in it for the bride?' A woman answered, 'I give four heptas of rice;' to which her husband added two.

"Mar Elias now kissed us much; he put nineteen korans into John's hand, saying, 'As yet I have not grown indifferent.' And Mar Yohanan said, with tears, 'The crown of the bride remains for me. I give thirty tomans.'

"In our village, besides the tithes, seventy tomans were collected, and in the city two hundred and fifty. I hope the whole will go up to five hundred or more. I stand amazed. I can think nothing but, 'I am a miserable sinner.' The glorious God has gone before us in mercy. For two or three years our village was going down; we were at variance and in trouble; but Immanuel has met us with a blessing, a hundred fold beyond our expectation. It is the beginning of a great work for future generations. I know that the joy of heaven is awakened in the joy of blessed Mr. Stocking and Mr. Stoddard. I want to fly to them and talk with them about it, but this veil does not allow it. You, too, will want to fly to the people that are so dear to you. I trust that this pouring out of such a spirit will be the door of many blessings. We have had a scarcity for seven years, so that wheat is six times its former price. Our people are poor and sorely oppressed. From the depths of their poverty they have given: I never knew them before. If all were Christians, what might we not see? Perhaps the poor widows and orphans, who have contributed for our good, have been discouraged; but truly their gifts have not been sown in vain among our people. I believe at the last day you will see fruit according to the word of Jesus — thirty, sixty, and a hundred fold. The time is not far off when every converted Nestorian will go to ten Mussulmen to teach them the word of God.

"Pray for us more than ever, for many are the enemies of Nehemiah and ruined Jerusalem. Our hope is in God. He has begun, and he will finish."

The pledges then made have since been fulfilled, with very few exceptions, and that not regretfully, but with a heartiness truly affecting to those who knew their poverty. In July, 1861, the mission resolved to furnish no teacher for a school — except in new villages — where a part of his support was not assumed by the people. The Barandooz congregation, in the spring of 1862, cheerfully assumed the burden of their schools; and some have also expressed a readiness to aid in the support of their pastors. A number of pupils, in both Seminaries, contribute liberally towards their support.

In bringing to a close these glimpses of the changes wrought by grace among the Nestorians, we must not pass by the number of pious parents who now aid the missionaries by their prayers. While, in the early days of the Seminary, its teacher was left to pray alone for her pupils, before she left, in 1858, she rejoiced to know that two thirds of them had either a pious parent, or other member of the family, who prayed for their salvation.

One cold morning, in 1856, a pious mother walked three miles through the snow, to inquire if there was any interest in the school. "Why do you ask?" replied the teacher. "I have thought of you continually for two or three days; and last night, after falling asleep, thinking about you, I dreamed that God was visiting you by his Holy Spirit. So, when I awoke, I arose and baked, and hurried here. I am so anxious about my daughter! Can I see her?" She was told that her daughter was among the inquirers the evening before, and sank down where she stood, weeping for joy. The heart of the teacher grew strong in the feeling that the mothers were wrestling with her. The mother passed into an adjoining room to see her daughter; and a missionary brother, who came in just then, could not restrain his tears as he listened to her earnest intercessions, saying, "This is more to me than any thing I have seen in Persia." After that year, some parents, when they came to the Seminary, were never willing to leave till they had prayed with their children. A father once wrote, "Yesterday I invited some Christian friends to my house, and had three prayers offered for the school; and while praying for you, we felt our own sins very much, and cried to God to save us from their power."

Nor were the pupils wanting in interest for their impenitent parents. During the long vacation in 1850, Hanee, who used to spend several hours a day in prayer for her mother, so pressed her with entreaties to come to the Saviour, that one day she roughly replied, "Enough! Enough! Stop your praying and weeping for me: you will weep yourself blind." "O mother," was the beautiful reply, "it seems as though I would gladly become blind, if thereby you might be brought to Jesus."

Perhaps the effects of grace were nowhere more conspicuous than in the effects it produced in those great households already described. Let us first look in on the hinderances they occasioned to a life of piety. Yonan writes, in his journal of March 7, 1858, "Widow Hatoon is a devout woman, and tries to erect the family altar in her house; but it is very difficult. She often collects the readers in the neighborhood on Sabbath morning, to read the Bible with her family. I asked her, 'Do you pray with your children? They have no father; they are left in your hands, and God will require them of you again.' 'I do; but I find it very hard in our house: we are all in one room, our beds very near each other, and there is no separate chamber: when about to retire, I gather them together behind a quilt, and talk and pray with them.'"

Again he writes, "Hatoon, the wife of Sarhoosh, is a member of a large family. Three of the women in the house, and one of their husbands, fear God; but the older members of the household are very wicked, and even violent in their opposition. She is much troubled about family prayer. While the devout ones engage in worship at one end of the room, the rest, at the other end, talk, laugh, and revile."

Yet, even in such households, grace reveals its divine power. We find Yonan putting this question to a communicant: "Do you and M. live pleasantly together?" M. was her sister-in-law, in a household of more than thirty souls. "She is a little quick tempered," was the reply; "but I try not to trouble her, and to have our love perfect that we may be a good example to the rest." Yonan prayed with her, and asked if he could do any thing for her relatives. "Dear brother in Christ," she replied, "in the name of the Lord Jesus, our precious Saviour, I beg you to pray with my husband: it may be God will bless him." "My sister, God will bless him: this your anguish shall be turned into joy." "My own heart was moved," adds the narrator. "I saw my own love very little, compared with hers, and felt my unworthiness very much."

The change in their social condition was beautifully illustrated by a little incident in the Seminary, in 1849. One of the older pupils had been betrothed; but when the ring of betrothal was brought, to be placed on her finger, she could not be found. After long search, her gentle voice was heard in the most retired part of the building, imploring the blessing of God to abide with her in that new relation. Only those who had seen the rioting and folly common on such occasions could appreciate the change.

The marriage of Mar Yohanan, in 1859, was a step in the work of lifting up woman to her true position. Formerly, marriage had been deemed something too unholy for a bishop; and the consequence was the general degradation of the sex. The entrance of the gospel corrected public sentiment on this point; and that act of the bishop only gave expression to the popular conviction that marriage is honorable in all, even the highest and holiest, nurturing some of the loveliest graces of the Christian character. The event for a time caused some stir among the enemies of the truth; but it soon died away, and the old ascetic views of piety are passing away with the social degradation in which they had their origin.

About the same time Yohanan, whom we have seen laboring in the mountains with his estimable wife, was ordained to the work of the ministry without any of the mummeries that had been added to the simple usage of the New Testament; the venerable Mar Elias uniting with the missionaries in the laying on of the hands of the presbytery. Two months later, six more of the most pious and best educated young men, who had long deferred ordination through aversion to the old forms, followed his example; among them our mountain friend Oshana, Deacon John, of Geog Tapa, and Deacon Yakob, of Supergan. Marriage ceremonies and entertainments have long been improved, and the revelling of former days on such occasions is going into deserved disuse among the more enlightened.

In the year 1858, the people of Memikan left off keeping their fasts, on the ground that they tended to nullify salvation by grace through Jesus Christ. Formerly this would have brought down on them the wrath of the patriarch, their village would have been devoted to plunder and the torch, and themselves to death or exile; but now it caused scarce a ripple on the current of events — not that men did not see the drift of things, but they allowed it to have free course.

There is another sign of the times that calls for more special mention. Other missions in Western Asia had been forced by persecution to the early formation of churches. They had to provide a fold for the lambs driven from their former shelter. Here there had been no such necessity; yet the converts longed for a more spiritual observance of gospel ordinances.

The mission had hitherto celebrated the Lord's supper by themselves, and with one or two exceptions, no Nestorian had witnessed its observance. There had been some thought of admitting them; but nothing had been done, till, in the spring of 1854, three of the converts, who had been reading an English treatise on the subject, asked one of the ladies of the mission to intercede with the gentlemen to allow them to be present. She informed Mr. Stoddard of their request, and he encouraged them to go forward. The matter was laid before the mission, and it was concluded that a few of those judged most fit for admission to the ordinance should be invited to partake.

The first communion to which the converts were admitted was celebrated in September, 1854, in the large room on the lower floor of the Female Seminary. Eleven Nestorians partook with the missionaries, and three of them were women, who had graduated there. After the service, some of the men went up stairs and sat down without speaking. Miss Fiske, not knowing the cause of their silence, and fearing lest they might have been disappointed by the simplicity of our forms, did not venture to allude to the subject, till one of them asked, "Is it always so when you commune, or was this an unusual occasion?" "Why, did you not enjoy it?" "Not enjoy it! Jesus Christ himself seemed almost visibly present; it was difficult to realize that it was not the Saviour in person who presided at the table. It must have been just such a scene when the ordinance was first instituted in Jerusalem; and I could not get rid of the inquiry, 'Shall one of us go out like Judas and betray him?'" It is a significant fact that those most accustomed to mediæval forms, when regenerated by the Spirit, relish them the least; and the more spiritual they become, the more they crave the simple forms of the New Testament, because they draw the least attention to themselves, and fix it most completely on the Saviour.

In January, 1855, as many as seventy of the converts, after careful examination, were allowed to partake; and once every four months the privilege was renewed, with an accession of from twelve to thirty communicants each time. These were occasions of unusual interest. Several days were devoted to religious meetings, and even in mid-winter pious people made long journeys, and crossed bleak mountains on the snow, to attend them. One woman, Hoimar, of Salmas,* travelled sixty miles, through deep snow and piercing cold, to be present at this ordinance in January, 1858.

In June of that year, the better to distinguish those entitled to this privilege, before the sacrament all entered together into solemn covenant with God. The whole number received up to that time was two hundred and forty-nine; at the close of 1861, it had swelled to five hundred. As the meetings became too unwieldy, and it was inconvenient for so many to come so far, the ordinance was administered at Seir also, in September, 1858; and here providentially another end was secured, for as Dr. Wright was then too sick to distribute the elements, some of the natives had to perform that service. In June following, a very interesting communion was observed at Memikan; Yohanan and his wife crossing a high mountain, even then covered with snow, to bring their little child for baptism.

* See page 171.

Next year, the ordinance was celebrated in every village where there was a sufficient number of hopeful converts to justify its observance. Thus has God led his people, step by step, in a way that they knew not, till now there are all the essentials of a church at every place where God has raised up members of the body of Christ. They enter into covenant with him and with each other. They keep his ordinances, and grow in grace, in knowledge, and in numbers. They may take one step farther. Since this last sentence was written, the converted Nestorians have proceeded even to the adoption of a creed and directory for worship.

Did the limits of this volume allow, it would be pleasant to dwell at length on the labors of Miss Mary Susan Rice, who joined Miss Fiske in November, 1847, and has ever since toiled diligently, and without interruption, at her post. Since the return of Miss Fiske she has entered into all her labors, both thoroughly and successfully. Her fifteen years of toil will never be forgotten by those who have been privileged to receive her instructions, both in and out of the Seminary. They form an important part of the instrumentalities God has employed to bring woman in Persia to the knowledge of her Saviour. A mass of her correspondence now lies before the writer, which he has read with much interest; but to quote from it would only be reproducing scenes already portrayed. It is not necessary to describe the laying of each course of brick in the walls of the spiritual temple.

One sentence, however, now arrests my eye, which I must quote, because it shows how the Saviour was preparing her for the sole care of the school, that has devolved on her ever since, owing to the protracted illness of Miss Aura J. Beach, who was sent out to her assistance in

February, 1860. Writing to her predecessor, three years ago, she says, "O, what a relief, to roll the burdens, which we cannot bear, upon the strong arm outstretched to help, and feel that, like sinking Peter, we shall be sustained amid raging billows!"

Labor among the Nestorians is becoming more assimilated to labor at home. Instead of the national peculiarities conspicuous at the outset, different from our own, and prominent because so different, things begin to move in familiar orbits, because they set out from similar conditions and tend to like results. In proportion as the gospel advances in its work, the distinguishing characteristics of a people fall into the background, to give place to those spiritual features common to the work of grace in every land. The river is most picturesque high up among the mountains, while its stream is yet small and many obstacles oppose its course; after it glides out from among the hills into the open plain, it moves with larger volume, but in a more monotonous current, to the sea.

May the work of God advance, till this unity of all nations in Jesus Christ shall every where replace the diversity and hostility under which to-day creation groans, till in the placid surface of such a river of life the Saviour shall see his own image reflected, as it is from the sea of glass above!

APPENDIX.

TABULAR VIEW OF SCHOOLS.

Year.	Seminary Pupils.		Schools.	Pupils in Schools.		Total.
	Male.	Female.		Boys.	Girls.	
1840	39	23	17	414	25	501
1841	28	18	29	430	40	516
1842	70	18	40	635	128	851
1843	55	22	44	948	117	1142
1844	30	26	Dismissed this year.			
1845	40	40	32	382 in all.		462
1846	40	36	30	441	21	538
1847	37	36	36	517	91	681
1848	40	30	33	463	45	578
1849	44	35	32	473	125	677
1850	44	30	35	487	166	727
1851	40	42	45	1023 in all.		1105
1852	40	50	60	777	261	1128
1853	42	48	79	990	365	1445
1854			73	1092	153	
1855	50	48	58	793	301	1195
1856	40	40	53	611	283	974
1857	54	39	63	1200 in all.		1293
1858	47	40	54	1135 in all.		1222
1859	50	30	68	936	494	1510
1860	54	30	48	678	367	1129

INDEX.

Valuable Works,

PUBLISHED BY

GOULD AND LINCOLN,

59 WASHINGTON STREET, BOSTON.

CHRISTIAN'S DAILY TREASURY: a Religious Exercise for every day in the year. By Rev. H. TEMPLE. 12mo, cloth.

WREATH AROUND THE CROSS; or, Scripture Truths Illustrated. By Rev. A. MORTON BROWN, D. D. 16mo, cloth.

SCHOOL OF CHRIST; or, Christianity Viewed in its Leading Aspects. By REV A. R. L. FOOTE. 16mo, cloth.

THE CHRISTIAN LIFE, Social and Individual. By PETER BAYNE, M. A 12mo, cloth.

THE PURITANS; or, The Church, Court, and Parliament of England. By Rev. SAMUEL HOPKINS. In 3 vols., octavo. Vol. I., cloth, *ready.*

MODERN ATHEISM; under its various forms. By JAMES BUCHANAN, D.D. 12mo, cloth.

THE MISSION OF THE COMFORTER; with copious Notes. By JULIUS CHARLES HARE. American edition; Notes translated. 12mo, cloth.

GOD REVEALED IN NATURE AND IN CHRIST. By Rev. JAMES B. WALKER. 12mo, cloth

PHILOSOPHY OF THE PLAN OF SALVATION. New, improved, and enlarged edition. 12mo, cloth.

YAHVEH CHRIST; or, The Memorial Name. By ALEX'R MACWHORTER. Introductory Letter by NATH'L W. TAYLOR, D.D. 12mo, cloth.

SALVATION BY CHRIST: Discourses on some of the most important Doctrines of the Gospel. By FRANCIS WAYLAND, D.D. 12mo, cloth.

THE SUFFERING SAVIOUR; or, Meditations on the Last Days of Christ. By FREDERICK W. KRUMMACHER, D. D. 12mo, cloth.

THE GREAT DAY OF ATONEMENT; or, Meditations and Prayers on the Sufferings and Death of our Lord.

EXTENT OF THE ATONEMENT IN ITS RELATION TO GOD AND THE UNIVERSE. By THOMAS W. JENKYN, D.D. 12mo, cloth.

THE IMITATION OF CHRIST. By THOMAS À KEMPIS. With a Life of à Kempis, by Dr C. ULLMANN. 12mo, cloth.

THE HARVEST AND THE REAPERS. Home Work for all, and how to do it. By Rev. HARVEY NEWCOMB. 16mo, cloth.

Gould and Lincoln's Publications.

(RELIGIOUS.)

LIMITS OF RELIGIOUS THOUGHT EXAMINED. By HENRY L. MANSEL, B. D. Notes translated for American ed. 12mo, cl.

THE CRUCIBLE; or, Tests of a Regenerate State. By Rev. J. A. GOODHUE. Introduction by Dr. KIRK. 12mo, cloth.

LEADERS OF THE REFORMATION. Luther — Calvin — Latimer — Knox. By JOHN TULLOCH, D. D. 12mo, cloth.

BARON STOW. *CHRISTIAN BROTHERHOOD.* 16mo, cloth.

——— *FIRST THINGS;* or, the Development of Church Life. 16mo, cloth.

JOHN ANGELL JAMES. *CHURCH MEMBER'S GUIDE.* Cloth.

——— *CHURCH IN EARNEST.* 18mo, cloth.

——— *CHRISTIAN PROGRESS.* Sequel to the Anxious Inquirer. 18mo, cloth.

THE GREAT CONCERN. By N. ADAMS, D. D. 12mo, cloth.

JOHN HARRIS'S WORKS. *THE GREAT TEACHER.* With an Introductory Essay by H. HUMPHREY, D. D. 12mo, cloth.

——— *THE GREAT COMMISSION.* With an Introductory Essay by WILLIAM R. WILLIAMS, D. D. 12mo, cloth.

——— *THE PRE-ADAMITE EARTH.* Contributions to Theological Science. 12mo, cloth.

——— *MAN PRIMEVAL:* Constitution and Primitive Condition of the Human Being. Portrait of Author. 12mo, cloth.

——— *PATRIARCHY;* or, The Family, its Constitution and Probation. 12mo, cloth.

——— *SERMONS, CHARGES, ADDRESSES, &c.* Two volumes, octavo, cloth.

WILLIAM R. WILLIAMS. *RELIGIOUS PROGRESS.* 12mo, cloth.

——— *LECTURES ON THE LORD'S PRAYER.* 12mo, cloth.

THE BETTER LAND. By Rev. A. C. THOMPSON. 12mo, cloth.

EVENING OF LIFE; or, Light and Comfort amid the Shadows of Declining Years. By JEREMIAH CHAPLIN, D. D. 12mo, cloth.

HEAVEN. By JAMES WILLIAM KIMBALL. 12mo, cloth.

THE SAINT'S EVERLASTING REST. BAXTER. 16mo, cl.

(BIOGRAPHICAL.)

LIFE OF JOHN MILTON, in connection with the Political, Ecclesiastical, and Literary History of his time. By DAVID MASSON, M. A. 3 vols., 8vo. Vol. I., cloth.

LIFE AND CORRESPONDENCE OF REV. DANIEL WILSON, D. D., late Bishop of Calcutta. By Rev. JOSIAH BATEMAN. With portraits, map, and illustrations. One volume, royal octavo.

LIFE AND CORRESPONDENCE OF THE LATE AMOS LAWRENCE. By W. R. LAWRENCE, M. D. 8vo, cloth. 12mo, cloth.

DR. GRANT AND THE MOUNTAIN NESTORIANS. By Rev. THOMAS LAURIE, his surviving associate. 12mo, cloth.

MEMOIR OF THE LIFE AND TIMES OF ISAAC BACKUS. By ALVAH HOVEY, D. D. 12mo, cloth.

LIFE OF JAMES MONTGOMERY. By Mrs. H. C. KNIGHT, Author of "Lady Huntington and her Friends." 12mo, cloth.

MY MOTHER; or, Recollections of Maternal Influence. By a New England Clergyman. 12mo, cloth.

MEMOIR OF ROGER WILLIAMS. By Professor WILLIAM GAMMELL. 16mo, cloth.

LIFE AND CORRESPONDENCE OF JOHN FOSTER. By JOHN E. RYLAND. 2 vols. in one, 12mo, cloth.

PHILIP DODDRIDGE. His Life and Labors. By JOHN STOUGHTON, D. D. 16mo, cloth.

MEMOIR OF ANN H. JUDSON. By Rev. J. D. KNOWLES. 18mo, cloth.

MEMOIR OF GEORGE D. BOARDMAN. By Rev. A. KING. Introduction by W. R. WILLIAMS, D. D. 12mo, cloth.

LIFE OF GODFREY WILLIAM VON LEIBNITZ. By JOHN. M. MACKIE. 16mo, cloth.

THE TEACHER'S LAST LESSON; A Memoir of MARTHA WHITING, of Charlestown Female Seminary. By C. N. BADGER. 12mo, cloth.

MEMOIR OF HENRIETTA SHUCK, the first Female Missionary to China. By Rev. J. B. JETER, D. D. 18mo, cloth.

MEMOIR OF REV. WILLIAM G. CROCKER, Missionary to West Africa. By R. B. MEDBURY. 18mo, cloth.

THE KAREN APOSTLE; or, Memoir of KO-THAH-BYU, the first Karen Convert. By Rev. F. MASON, D. D. 18mo, cloth.

MEMORIES OF A GRANDMOTHER. By a Lady of Massachusetts 16mo, cloth.

Gould and Lincoln's Publications.

(RELIGIOUS.)

GOTTHOLD'S EMBLEMS; or, Invisible Things Understood by Things that are Made. By CHRISTIAN SCRIVER. Tr. from the 28th German Ed. by Rev. ROBERT MENZIES. 8vo, cloth, Fine Edition, Tinted Paper, royal 8vo, cloth.

THE STILL HOUR; or, Communion with God. By Prof. AUSTIN PHELPS, D. D., of Andover Theological Seminary. 16mo, cloth.

LESSONS AT THE CROSS; or, Spiritual Truths Familiarly Exhibited in their Relations to Christ. By SAMUEL HOPKINS, author of "The Puritans," etc. Introduction by GEORGE W. BLAGDEN, D. D. 16mo, cloth.

NEW ENGLAND THEOCRACY. From the German of Uhden's History of the Congregationalists of New England. Introduction by NEANDER. By Mrs. H. C. CONANT. 12mo, cloth.

EVENINGS WITH THE DOCTRINES. By Rev. NEHEMIAH ADAMS, D. D. 12mo, cloth.

THE STATE OF THE IMPENITENT DEAD. By ALVAH HOVEY, D. D., Prof. of Christian Theology in Newton Theol. Inst. 16mo, cloth.

FOOTSTEPS OF OUR FOREFATHERS; what they Suffered and what they Sought. Describing Localities, Personages, and Events, in the Struggles for Religious Liberty. By JAMES G. MIALL. Illustrations. 12mo, cloth.

MEMORIALS OF EARLY CHRISTIANITY. Presenting, in a graphic form, Memorable Events of Early Ecclesiastical History, etc. By Rev. J. G. MIALL. With Illustrations. 12mo, cloth.

THE MISSIONARY ENTERPRISE. The most important Discourses in the language on Christian Missions, by distinguished American Authors. Edited by BARON STOW, D. D. 12mo, cloth.

THE RELIGIONS OF THE WORLD, and their Relations to Christianity. By FREDERICK DENISON MAURICE, Prof. of Divinity in King's Coll., London. 16mo, cloth.

THE CHRISTIAN WORLD UNMASKED. By JOHN BERRIDGE, A. M., Vicar of Everton, Bedfordshire. With a Life of the Author, by Rev. THOMAS GUTHRIE, D. D. 16mo, cloth.

THE EXCELLENT WOMAN, as described in the Book of Proverbs. With an Introduction by W. B. SPRAGUE, D. D. Twenty-four splendid Illustrations. 12mo, cloth.

MOTHERS OF THE WISE AND GOOD. By JABEZ BURNS, D. D. 16mo, cloth.

THE SIGNET-RING, and its Heavenly Motto. From the German. Illustrated. 16mo, cloth, gilt.

THE MARRIAGE-RING; or, How to Make Home Happy. From the writings of JOHN ANGELL JAMES. Beautifully Illustrated edition. 16mo, cloth, gilt.

Gould and Lincoln's Publications.

(SABBATH SCHOOL.)

POPULAR CYCLOPÆDIA OF BIBLICAL LITERATURE. Condensed, by John Kitto, D. D. Numerous Illustrations. 8vo.

THE HISTORY OF PALESTINE; with Chapters on its Geography and Natural History, its Customs and Institutions. By John Kitto, D. D. With Illustrations. 12mo.

ANALYTICAL CONCORDANCE TO THE HOLY SCRIPTURES; or, The Bible under Distinct and Classified Topics. By John Eadie, D. D. 8vo.

CRUDEN'S CONDENSED CONCORDANCE. By Alex. Cruden. 8vo. Half boards.

COMMENTARY ON THE ORIGINAL TEXT OF THE ACTS OF THE APOSTLES. By H. B. Hackett, D. D. 8vo.

ILLUSTRATIONS OF SCRIPTURE. Suggested by a tour through the Holy Land. With Illustrations. New, Enlarged Edition. By H. B. Hackett, D. D. 12mo, cloth.

PROF. H. J. RIPLEY'S NOTES.

——————— *On the Gospels.* For Teachers in Sabbath Schools, and as an Aid to Family Instruction. With Map of Canaan. Cloth, embossed.

——————— *On the Acts of the Apostles.* With Map of the Travels of the Apostle Paul. 12mo, cloth, embossed.

——————— *On the Epistle of Paul to the Romans.* 12mo, cloth, embossed.

COMMENTARY ON THE EPISTLE TO THE EPHESIANS. Explanatory, Doctrinal, and Practical. By R. E. Pattison, D. D. 12mo.

MALCOM'S NEW BIBLE DICTIONARY of Names, Objects, and Terms, found in the Holy Scriptures. By Howard Malcom, D. D. 16mo, cloth.

HARMONY QUESTIONS ON THE FOUR GOSPELS, for the use of Sabbath Schools. By Rev. S. B. Swaim, D. D. Vol. I. 18mo, cloth backs.

SABBATH-SCHOOL CLASS-BOOK. By E. Lincoln.

LINCOLN'S SCRIPTURE QUESTIONS; with Answers.

THE SABBATH-SCHOOL HARMONY; with appropriate Hymns and Music for Sabbath Schools. By N. D. Gould.

EVIDENCES OF CHRISTIANITY, as exhibited in the writings of its apologists, down to Augustine. By Prof. W. J. Bolton, Cambridge, England 12mo, cloth.

(*ELEGANT MINIATURES.* 32mo, *gilt*, 40 *cts. each.*)

THE BIBLE AND THE CLOSET. Edited by J. O. CHOULES, D. D.

THE FAMILY ALTAR; or, the Duty, Benefit, and mode of Conducting Family Worship.

THE FAMILY CIRCLE; its Affections and Pleasures. Rev. H. A. GRAVES.

THE MARRIAGE-RING; or, How to Make Home Happy. By Rev. J. ANGELL JAMES.

THE CASKET OF JEWELS, for Young Christians. By JAMES, EDWARDS, and HARRIS.

THE ACTIVE CHRISTIAN; from writings of JOHN HARRIS, D. D.

DAILY MANNA; for Christian Pilgrims. By Rev. B. STOW, D. D.

THE CYPRESS WREATH; Consolation for those who mourn. Edited by RUFUS W. GRISWOLD, D. D.

THE YOUNG COMMUNICANT; an Aid to the Right Understanding and Spiritual Improvement of the Lord's Supper.

LYRIC GEMS; a Collection of Original and Select Sacred Poetry. Edited by S. F. SMITH, D. D.

THE MOURNER'S CHAPLET; an Offering of Sympathy for Bereaved Friends. Selected from American Poets. Edited by JOHN KEESE.

THE ATTRACTIONS OF HEAVEN. Rev. H. A. GRAVES.

THE SILENT COMFORTER; a Companion for the Sick-Room. By LOUISA PAYSON HOPKINS.

GOLDEN GEMS, for the Christian. From the writings of JOHN FLAVEL, with Memoir of the Author. By Rev. JOSEPH BANVARD.

☞ Sets of the above *fourteen volumes,* forming a beautiful MINIATURE LIBRARY, put up in neat boxes, $5.60.

ELEGANT DOUBLE MINIATURES. 32mo, *gilt*, 75 *cts. each.*

THE WEDDING GIFT; or, the Duties and Pleasures of Domestic Life. Containing the "Marriage-Ring" and the "Family Circle."

THE YOUNG CHRISTIAN'S GUIDE to the Doctrines and Duties of a Religious Life. Containing "Casket of Jewels" and "Active Christian."

THE MOURNER COMFORTED; containing the "Cypress Wreath," and the "Mourner's Chaplet."

DAILY DUTIES; containing the "Bible and Closet," and "Family Altar."

THE CHRISTIAN'S DAILY COMPANION; containing the "Daily Manna" and the "Young Communicant."

CONSOLATION FOR THE AFFLICTED; containing the "Silent Comforter" and the "Attractions of Heaven."

☞ Sets of the above, in neat boxes, six volumes, $4.50.

Gould and Lincoln's Publications.

(SCIENTIFIC.)

ANNUAL OF SCIENTIFIC DISCOVERY. 11 vols., from 1850—1860. By D. A. WELLS, A. M. With Portraits of distinguished men. 12mo.

THE PLURALITY OF WORLDS; a new edition, with the author's reviews of his reviewers. 12mo.

COMPARATIVE ANATOMY OF THE ANIMAL KINGDOM. By Profs. SIEBOLD and STANNIUS. Translated by W. I. BURNETT, M. D. 8vo.

HUGH MILLER'S WORKS. *TESTIMONY OF THE ROCKS.* With Illustrations. 12mo, cloth.

———— *FOOTPRINTS OF THE CREATOR.* With Illustrations. Memoir by LOUIS AGASSIZ. 12mo, cloth.

———— *THE OLD RED SANDSTONE.* With Illustrations, etc. 12mo, cloth.

———— *MY SCHOOLS AND SCHOOLMASTERS.* An Autobiography. Full-length Portrait of Author. 12mo, cloth.

———— *FIRST IMPRESSIONS OF ENGLAND AND ITS PEOPLE.* With fine Portrait. 12mo, cloth.

———— *CRUISE OF THE BETSEY.* A Ramble among the Fossiliferous Deposits of the Hebrides. 12mo, cloth.

———— *POPULAR GEOLOGY.* 12mo, cloth.

HUGH MILLER'S WORKS, 7 vols., embossed cloth, with box.

UNITED STATES EXPLORING EXPEDITION, under CHARLES WILKES. Vol. XII., Mollusca and Shells. By A. A. GOULD, M. D. 4to.

LAKE SUPERIOR. Its Physical Character, Vegetation, and Animals. By L. AGASSIZ. 8vo.

THE NATURAL HISTORY OF THE HUMAN SPECIES. By C. HAMILTON SMITH. With Elegant Illustrations. With Introduction, containing an abstract of the views of eminent writers on the subject, by S. KNEELAND, M. D. 12mo.

THE CAMEL. His organization, habits, and uses, with reference to his introduction into the United States. By GEORGE P. MARSH. 12mo.

INFLUENCE OF THE HISTORY OF SCIENCE UPON INTELLECTUAL EDUCATION. By W. WHEWELL, D. D. 12mo.

SPIRITUALISM TESTED; or, the Facts of its History Classified, and their causes in Nature verified from Ancient and Modern Testimonies. By GEO. W. SAMSON, D. D. 16mo, cloth.

www.ingramcontent.com/pod-product-compliance
Lightning Source LLC
LaVergne TN
LVHW020237110826
845151LV00003B/946
9781425530747